# Ground Transportation for the 21st Century

By
Frank Kreith
Dena Sue Potestio
Chad Kimbell
Center for Technical Information

NATIONAL CONFERENCE *of* STATE LEGISLATURES

*The Forum for America's Ideas*

The American Society of
Mechanical Engineers

Three Park Avenue
New York, New York
10016

William T. Pound, Executive Director

1560 Broadway, Suite 700
Denver, Colorado 80202
(303) 830-2200

444 North Capitol Street, N.W., Suite 515
Washington, D.C. 20001
(202) 624-5400

August 1999

The National Conference of State Legislatures serves the legislators and staffs of the nation's 50 states, its commonwealths, and territories. NCSL is a bipartisan organization with three objectives:

- To improve the quality and effectiveness of state legislatures,
- To foster interstate communication and cooperation,
- To ensure states a strong cohesive voice in the federal system.

The Conference operates from offices in Denver, Colorado, and Washington, D.C.

Printed on recycled paper

# CONTENTS

Appendices

## LIST OF FIGURES AND TABLES

Figures

# About the Authors

Frank Kreith currently serves as the American Society of Mechanical Engineers' (ASME) legislative fellow at the National Conference of State Legislatures. Dr. Kreith has served as consultant and advisor on energy planning all over the world, including NATO, the U.S. Agency for International Development and the United Nations.

Before joining NCSL in 1988, Dr. Kreith was chief of thermal research and senior research fellow at the Solar Energy Research Institute (SERI), now the National Renewable Energy Laboratory (NREL). During his tenure at SERI, he participated in the Presidential Domestic Energy Review and served as an energy advisor to the governor of Colorado.

From 1951 to 1977, Dr. Kreith taught engineering at the University of California, Lehigh University and the University of Colorado. He is the author of books on heat transfer, nuclear power, solar energy and energy management. He is the recipient of many awards, including the Ralph Coats Roe Medal from ASME for " ... significant contributions to a better appreciation of the engineer's worth to society ... through provision of information to legislators about energy and conservation."

Dena Sue Potestio is the coordinator of the Center for Technical Information at the National Conference of State Legislatures (CTI at NCSL). CTI at NCSL serves the policy needs of the 50 state legislatures on issues that contain an engineering, technological or scientific component, including natural resources management, electric utility regulation, renewable energy, energy efficiency, and math and science education reform.

Before joining the National Conference of State Legislatures, Ms. Potestio was a senior consultant at Arthur Andersen in Chicago, Illinois, specializing in the oil and gas industry in the areas of environmental business consulting/cost accounting, ISO 14000+/ environmental auditing and environmental remediation/risk-assessment.

Before joining Arthur Andersen, Ms. Potestio was the American Society of Mechanical Engineers' (ASME) intern at NCSL, where she co-authored a *State Legislative Report* entitled, "Electric Vehicles: Promise and Reality," which also appeared in *Transportation Quarterly* and *Current Municipal Problems*.

Ms. Potestio holds a Bachelor of Science in Mechanical Engineering and an MBA from the University of Denver.

Chad Kimbell, through an opportunity provided by the Government Relations Program of the American Society of Mechanical Engineers, completed a one-year internship with NCSL, where he authored three *Legisbriefs* entitled, "Methane Landfill Gas Recovery and Utilization," "On the Road to Cleaner Cars," and "Recycling Markets."

Mr. Kimbell, a graduate of the University of Colorado at Boulder, holds a Bachelor of Science in Civil Engineering with a special emphasis in Environmental Engineering and Water Resources.

# ACKNOWLEDGMENTS

This book has been prepared with the support of the Engineering Foundation, the U.S. Department of Energy and the American Society of Mechanical Engineers as a part of the National Conference of State Legislatures' (NCSL) newly established Center for Technical Information (CTI at NCSL). The authors have received information from many sources, and particularly would like to express their appreciation to Dr. John D. Edwards, former Latin American exploration operations manager for Shell Oil Company, and currently an adjunct professor at the University of Colorado at Boulder, for providing valuable information on the expected peak of world oil production; Richard McLean, director of the Regional Transportation District (the public transit provider for Metro Denver, Colorado) for valuable input on public transportation issues; and Dr. Donald Stedman, professor of Chemistry at the University of Denver, for valuable information regarding remote sensing of automobile emissions, and authoring appendix D of this book, "Identification of Polluting Vehicles by Remote Sensing."

In addition, the authors would like to thank James Reed and Janet Goehring of the NCSL Transportation Program, for reviewing the entire book and providing information in the sections of the book entitled, "Federal and State Policy Background" and "Intelligent Transportation Systems."

The authors also would like to thank the following individuals for constructive review comments during the preparation of the book:

- Matthew Brown, program director, Energy, NCSL
- Jeff Dale, policy associate, Environment, NCSL
- Barbara Goodman, director, Center of Transportation Technologies and Systems, National Renewable Energy Laboratory (NREL)
- Paul Norton, NREL
- Dr. Ahmad Pesaran, NREL
- Kevin O'Connor, NREL
- Steve Burch, NREL
- Terry Penney, NREL
- Jim Ohi, NREL
- Keith Wipke, NREL
- Wendy Clark, NREL
- Joe Perkowski, NREL
- Dr. Stein Weissenberger, engineering scientist, Transportation Systems, Lawrence Livermore National Laboratory
- Dr. Peter Lehman, director, Schatz Energy Research Center, Humboldt State University
- Yazeed Kyayyat, Chicago Transit Authority
- Lu Ha, engineer and manager of technical support, Regional Transportation District
- M. Barbara Post, Transportation Research Board
- Dr. Michael Wang, Center for Transportation Research, Argonne National Laboratory
- Craig Sherman, Energy Services Department, Sacramento Municipal Utility District
- Dr. J.S. Szliowicz, director, Intermodal Transportation Institute
- Connie Steffen, Office of Legislative Research and General Council, State of Utah.
- Patty Stulp, Ethanol Management Company

The authors extend special thanks to Kathleen Gatliffe, ASME intern at NCSL; Leann Stelzer, book editor at NCSL, who aided in the development of the manuscript; Bruce Holdeman, who designed the cover; and Scott Liddell of NCSL, who formatted the publication.

# Abbreviations and Acronyms

| | |
|---|---|
| AFDC | Alternative Fuels Data Center |
| AFUP | Alternative Fuels Utilization Program |
| AFV | Alternative fuel vehicle |
| AMFA | Alternative Motor Fuels Act of 1988 |
| AMI | American Methanol Institute |
| APTA | American Public Transit Association |
| ATMA | Advanced traffic management systems |
| Btu | British Thermal Unit |
| CAA | Clean Air Act |
| CAAA | Clean Air Amendments Act |
| CAFE | Corporate average fuel economy |
| CARB | California Air Resource Board |
| CFC | Chlorofluorocarbon |
| CI | Compression ignition |
| CIDI | Compression ignition direct-injection |
| CNG | Compressed natural gas |
| CO | Carbon monoxide |
| $CO_2$ | Carbon dioxide |
| DC | Direct current |
| DOE | United States Department of Energy |
| EPA | United States Environmental Protection Agency |
| EPACT | Energy Policy Act |
| ETBE | Ethyl tertiary-butyl alcohol |
| EV | Electric vehicle |
| EVC | Electric Vehicle Company |
| FCEV | Fuel cell electric vehicle |
| FHWA | Federal Highway Administration |
| GNP | Gross national product |

| HC | Hydrocarbon |
|---|---|
| HEV | Hybrid electric vehicle |
| HOV | High occupancy vehicle |
| ICE | Internal combustion engine |
| ITAC | International Telework Association and Council |
| ITS | Intelligent transportation systems |
| ILEV | Inherently low emission vehicle |
| ISTEA | Intermodal Surface Transportation Act |
| KW | kilowatt |
| KWh | kilowatt-hour |
| LEV | Low emissions vehicle |
| LNG | Liquid natural gas |
| LPG | Liquid propane gas |
| MTBE | Methyl tertiary-butyl ether |
| NAAQS | National Ambient Air Quality Standards |
| NEV | Neighborhood electric vehicle |
| $NO_x$ | Nitrogen oxides |
| NLEV | National Low Emissions Vehicle Program |
| OECD | Organization for Economic Cooperation and Development |
| OPEC | Organization for Petroleum Exporting Countries |
| PEM | Proton exchange membranes |
| PGU | Power generation unit |
| PM | Particulate matter |
| PMT | Passenger miles traveled |
| PNGV | Partnership for a New Generation of Vehicles |
| SI | Spark ignition |
| $SO_2$ | Sulfur dioxide |
| SOV | Single-occupancy vehicle |
| SMUD | Sacramento Municipal Utility District |
| TCM | Transportation control measures |
| TPTS | National Transportation Study |
| TEV | Transitional low emissions vehicle |
| UHC | Unburned hydrocarbons |
| ULEV | Ultra low emissions vehicle |
| USABC | U.S. Advanced Battery Consortium |
| VOC | Volatile organic compound |
| ZEV | Zero emissions vehicle |

# Executive Summary

More than 97 percent of fuel consumed for transportation in the United States today is petroleum-based. Domestic oil production has been declining since 1970, and the Energy Information Administration expects that by the year 2000, imported petroleum will account for 56 percent of the total U.S. consumption, at a cost in excess of $50 billion. This represents an enormous transfer of wealth from the United States to oil producing countries. With gasoline prices relatively low, however, the general public is not seriously concerned about the future of automotive fuels. Experts from major oil companies worldwide predict that within the next 20 years, global crude oil production will reach a peak and then begin to decline (see appendix A, "World Oil Production Forecasts," for an explanation of the peak in oil production). Although peaking of oil production does not mean oil will no longer be available, it will mean the end of the availability of cheap oil and may create a sharp increase in the price of automotive fuel for the consumer. This could cause economic hardship for the average American and create havoc for the current U.S. transportation infrastructure.

Gasoline engines are the main contributors to smog and visibility problems in America's cities. Automobiles account for nearly 80 percent of carbon monoxide pollution, 40 percent of ozone-forming pollutants and half the total nitrous oxides emitted by human actions. Petroleum products are the leading source of carbon emissions—including carbon dioxide—in the United States. These pollutants can result in the formation of haze, brown clouds and acid rain, which create adverse health effects and may contribute to climate change.

Traffic congestion—or gridlock—is a growing problem in high-growth and metropolitan areas that adversely affects air quality, economic development and quality of life. Gridlock costs America $74 billion annually, according to a recent study by the Texas Transportation Institute (TTI). Researchers concluded that 88 percent of this amount is attributable to delays and the rest is due to wasted fuel. TTI reports that drivers stuck in traffic in 1996 wasted more than 6 billion gallons of fuel, enough to fill 670,000 gasoline tank trucks. The annual congestion cost per eligible driver ranged from $1,290 in Washington, D.C., to $125 in Boulder, Colorado. Furthermore, gridlock has more than quadrupled since 1982 in small and medium-size cities. Gridlock in these cities is increasing at a faster rate than in larger cities, indicating that the problem is spreading. Los Angeles remains the most congested city in America, while Washington, D.C., Miami, Chicago and San Francisco follow close behind. Researchers at TTI indicate that urban areas are not solving the problem simply by building roads. Many analysts believe that the construction of additional highways and road systems directly contributes to sprawl by encouraging commuters to live further from their workplaces and shopping areas.

Therefore, planners for the U.S. ground transportation system confront three main challenges:

- Economic and social effects of sharply increased gasoline and diesel prices when world oil production peaks and the demand for oil by a burgeoning global population continues to grow;

- Air pollution in urban areas resulting largely from the emission of pollutants by single-occupancy gasoline and diesel vehicles; and

- Traffic congestion and gridlock in high-growth and metropolitan areas, particularly during rush hours.

Any form of realistic transportation planning can benefit from reliable predictions of the traffic demand that has to be met in the future. Unfortunately, according to the Center for Transportation Technologies and Systems at NREL, the current state of traffic demand analysis in the United States is insufficient to validate any sophisticated traffic demand model. This inability to make reliable traffic demand predictions hinders the forecasting capabilities necessary to determine what new infrastructure investments are needed, irrespective what kind of model is used.

State, local and municipal governments can play an important role in softening the transition from the cheap oil era to one in which the average American cannot expect to use a single-occupancy vehicle (SOV) for all his or her transportation needs. Given the facts that world oil production is projected to peak within the next 20 years and that increased vehicle miles driven exacerbates air pollution and gridlock in high-growth areas, there is a need for state government officials to begin planning for a sustainable transportation system in their states. Such planning takes time and can be costly. Government officials and their staff must keep abreast of the current state of new transportation technology options and the prognosis for their future cost and availability. It is imperative that they be aware of the difference between technological feasibility as demonstrated in research programs and the realistic engineering assessment of the applicability of such new technologies in a transportation system. In particular, government officials must be aware that, except for the high-efficiency gasoline or diesel engine and the hybrid electric vehicle, all other alternatives to the conventional gasoline or diesel fuel engine will require a change in the fuel storage and dispersal infrastructure. Such a change takes time and the cost of deployment is high. Therefore, planning for any alternative fuel system must consider the time and the cost required to deploy it.

An important factor for transportation planners to keep in mind is the long lead-time needed to construct a new civil infrastructure system if a shift from gasoline and diesel to any kind of alternate fuel were to take place. The United States has undergone two major transitions in its energy infrastructure during its relatively short history. Before the Civil War, the country depended mainly on wood, wind and water power for energy. However, these sources gave way to coal, which was more economical and technically more convenient for transportation, power and heat. Coal supplied the major part of U.S. energy needs between 1885 and the beginning of World War II.

Engineering development after 1945 and increased availability of oil and gas paved the way for the second energy transition from coal to oil and natural gas. Both these transitions resulted from engineering developments, lower cost, availability and ease of supply. The time from the peak of supply of one source to the peak in supply of another was approximately 50 years. This suggests that, if a shift in the energy structure of the future were to occur, it would be gradual and take an appreciable time to implement, even if there were wide agreement on the type of energy source most suited for future transportation needs.

This book reviews the status of vehicles powered by electric batteries, fuel cells and alternative fuels. It also discusses the development of hybrid electric vehicles and high-efficiency gasoline and diesel engines. Finally, it provides an overview of public transportation technologies and assesses the potential of telecommuting and intelligent transportation.

The evidence in this transportation technology assessment in the short-term (2000 to 2005) and intermediate-term (2005 to 2020) suggests four key observations.

- The most realistic transportation option for the time frame between now and the predicted peak of world oil production is improved mileage vehicles, such as hybrid electric vehicles and high-efficiency gasoline and diesel engines.

- Except for hybrid electric vehicles, all alternative fueled vehicles—including electric batteries, fuel cells, ethanol, methanol and natural gas—require a new infrastructure that will take time, effort and money to construct if it is to serve the general public.

- To soften the effect of potentially sharp price increases in gasoline for the general public, as well as reduce air pollution and ameliorate gridlock, development of public transportation and intelligent transportation systems and the increased use of telecommuting will be important considerations.

- Based on evidence from other countries where gasoline costs as much as $4 per gallon, there is little reason to believe that an increase in the cost of fuel alone will dissuade people from using their automobiles. It is more likely that, when gridlock becomes so severe that it takes more time to commute by car than by public transport, people will be willing to give up the automobile and switch to public transportation. This change in behavior can be assisted by making public transportation affordable and convenient to the majority of people, particularly in metropolitan areas. Appropriate land use and public transportation planning and taxation also can assist this transition process.

A great deal of research on vehicle propulsion and transportation systems is in progress. This book represents a status report at the close of this century; its findings and conclusions should be reevaluated periodically to incorporate the results of research and development efforts that currently are under way.

# 1. INTRODUCTION

The United States faces major challenges in meeting the ever-increasing demand for the transportation of people and goods without creating adverse environmental, economic and health effects. Today, more than 97 percent of the fuel consumed by the U.S. transportation sector uses petroleum-based fuels, which accounts for two-thirds of the nation's oil consumption.[1] Although vehicle fuel efficiency has improved during the past decade, increases in population and per capita miles driven have offset these gains. With gasoline consumption growing at a rate of more than 1 percent per year and domestic production declining by about 1.4 percent per year, the Energy Information Administration predicts that imported petroleum will account for 56 percent of total U.S. consumption by the year 2000 and will exceed 60 percent by 2010.[2]

> *"We've embarked on the beginning of the last days of the age of oil."*
> —Mike R. Bowlin, chairman and chief executive officer of ARCO

The growing level of imported petroleum represents a massive transfer of wealth from the United States to oil exporting countries. In 1995, the United States paid $49 billion for imported petroleum, which represents about 50 percent of the nation's total oil consumption.[3] The growing reliance on imported petroleum is a national concern, especially since the most significant oil reserves are in parts of the world that are subject to social and political instability.

With gasoline prices hovering around $1 per gallon in 1999, the general public is not seriously concerned about the future cost of automotive fuel. A number of recent studies by industrial experts, however, suggest that there is reason for concern. Cumulative world oil consumption to date has totaled about 825 billion barrels. Total known world reserves are currently estimated to be about 1,000 billion barrels. Future discoveries, although uncertain, are estimated to range from 200 billion to no more than 1,000 billion barrels. Thus, estimates of ultimate world oil recovery range from 2,000 billion to 2,800 billion barrels. With this range of total crude oil in the world and a 1.5 percent annual demand growth, peak world oil production is likely to occur between the years 2000 and 2020, according to the best estimates of oil industry experts (Appendix A contains additional information about this topic). Although the peak in oil production does not mean the end of the availability of oil, most economists expect that it eventually will create a sharp increase in the price of crude oil. With the reliance of the average American commuter on cheap gasoline, a sharp increase in price could cause economic hardship and potentially create havoc for the current transportation infrastructure.

Apart from the problems of price and availability, fossil fuel emissions from automobiles contribute to air pollution, cause adverse health effects, and may contribute to global warming. Changes in the U.S. transportation system will be necessary to reduce emissions from the combustion of fossil fuels and facilitate the movement of people and goods. Additionally, the gridlock caused by single-occupancy vehicles in our big cities is estimated to cost Americans approximately $74 billion per year in lost time and wasted fuel on top of increased driver aggravation and tension.[4] Many environmentalists express concern about population explosion because world population has doubled from 3 billion to 6 billion since 1950. But in the same period, the number of automobiles has increased tenfold, from 50 million to 500 million vehicles.[5] To understand the effects of these issues on the U.S. transportation system—and to plan new infrastructure investments accordingly—a better understanding of traffic demand modeling is necessary.[6]

In planning to meet the energy needs of the future, there are a variety of fossil and renewable sources available that can produce heat and electric power including coal, natural gas, nuclear, solar and wind. For each of these options, the conversion technology is ready and the difference in cost is relatively small. On the other hand, the transportation system in the United States is almost totally dependent on gasoline and diesel fuel, which are produced from oil, a nonrenewable fossil fuel. And, most importantly, no convenient and reasonably priced fuel substitute is available in the near future.

Transportation planning for the next century confronts three main issues:

- A predicted peak in crude world oil production between the years 2000 to 2020, with an anticipated steep rise in oil prices as the peak nears.
- Pollution and associated health problems resulting from the dependence on internal combustion engines for transportation. This is exacerbated by the rush-hour stop-and-go movement of automobiles that increases the emission of pollutants per miles traveled, causes traffic delays and creates emotional tension in drivers.
- Gridlock due to the preponderance of single-occupancy vehicles used for commuting in and out of high-growth and metropolitan areas.

As state legislators and those involved in local government consider transportation-related laws and regulations, they clearly can benefit from an understanding of the advantages and disadvantages of transportation alternatives based on objective technological and economic evidence. Solutions to many of America's transportation dilemmas—including dependence on foreign oil, urban air pollution and gridlock—are based on a single (sometimes emotional) set of decision criteria offered by the various groups involved in the transportation debate, all of whom have a stake in the data presented and the legislative outcome. For example, automakers have a different perspective on how best to curb air pollution than do environmentalists. This debate often creates a legislative dilemma because legislators are unsure of whom to believe, or what elements should be included in legislation to effectively address the problem at hand.

*Ground Transportation in the 21*st *Century* does not attempt to provide an agenda for the research and development that are necessary to develop a future ground transportation system. A science and technology strategy designed to develop an advanced U.S. transportation system for the 21st century was prepared in 1997 by a cabinet-level committee representing the departments of Transportation, Defense, Energy and Commerce, the U.S. Environmental Protection Agency, the National Aeronautics and Space Administration, the National Science Foundation and the White House. The report, *Transportation Science and Technology Strategy*, was released in November 1997 by Dr. John H. Gibbons, assistant to the president for science and technology. The report presents a long-term strategy for guiding federal partnership initiatives for long-term strategic research that will make the U.S. transportation system safe, productive and efficient in the next century. (Copies of the report are available from the National Science and Technology Council [NSTC] at [202] 456-6100. Additional information can be found at the NSTC homepage, http://scitech.dot.gov.)

This book does not deal with research and development goals, but provides an overview of the current state of the following transportation technologies.

- Electric Vehicles (EVs)
- Hybrid Electric Vehicles (HEVs)
- Fuel Cell Vehicles
- High-Efficiency Gasoline and Diesel Vehicles
- Alternative Fuel Vehicles (AFVs)
- Public Transportation
- Telecommuting
- Intelligent Transportation Systems (ITS)

The goal of this book is to provide legislators and their staff with information to draft legislation that can help to reduce air pollution, facilitate the movement of people and goods, and soften the social and economic effects of the inevitable transition to a world in which oil is more expensive. There are many options available that include more efficient cars and trucks, land use planning, alternative fuels and mass transport systems. To retool our transportation system, however, legislators first must recognize that a serious energy supply problem looms, know which questions to ask, receive objective and realistic information, and then craft legislation that can help solve their state's or region's transportation dilemmas.

# Approach to Analysis

The mission of the Center for Technical Information at the National Conference of State Legislatures (CTI at NCSL) is to provide objective, timely and unbiased analysis and information to state governments. In this book, CTI at NCSL evaluates the current state of technology of several alternative transportation options compared to the conventional gasoline or diesel vehicle, which at present is the choice of most Americans for their transportation requirements. Gasoline and diesel vehicles serve as the baseline technology to which electric vehicles, hybrid electric vehicles, alternative fueled vehicles and fuel cell vehicles are compared in terms of cost, performance, range and emissions. The book also discusses intelligent transportation systems, telecommuting and public transportation as additional options to the single-occupancy vehicle for the nation's transportation requirements.

The time period that serves as the framework for analysis in this book is between 2000 and 2020. These dates were chosen because most world oil experts predict that world oil production will reach its peak within this period. When oil production peaks, gasoline and diesel fuel prices will rise. Appendix A presents an explanation of peak oil production and the dates experts predict that world oil production will begin to decline. In this book, the short-term is between 2000 and 2005, the intermediate-term is between 2005 and 2020, and the long-term is beyond 2020.

In addition to analyzing alternative single-occupancy vehicles to the baseline conventional gasoline or diesel vehicle, SOVs also are evaluated against two other analysis criteria. First, future single-occupancy vehicle alternatives must have the acceleration, range and other performance criteria similar to the conventional gasoline or diesel powered vehicle to compete in the marketplace and be attractive to the average consumer. Second, single-occupancy vehicle alternatives must be mass-market vehicles produced in large volumes, usually in the range of hundreds of thousands. Single-occupancy vehicle alternatives will have to compete on an equal basis with the conventional gasoline or diesel vehicle in the marketplace, and will not make significant inroads in solving national goals such as reductions in air pollution or dependence on foreign oil unless they exist in large quantities on America's roadways or are replaced by other means of transport.

Additionally, it must be recognized that the preponderance of single-occupancy vehicles on American roadways, alternatively fueled or not, will create gridlock. It is generally understood among transportation analysts that building additional road lanes is only a short-term solution to ameliorating gridlock, and in the long-term may encourage the use of single-occupancy vehicles and vehicle miles driven; public transportation, land-use planning, telecommuting and intelligent transportation systems are sustainable options that can help ameliorate gridlock and its associated effects on air quality.

## Dealing with Uncertainty

Forecasting the long-term future cost and performance of emerging technologies is a difficult and unreliable undertaking. This is especially true when a technology assessment attempts to make quantitative projections. Predicting when a technology is ready for commercialization is difficult because the process of commercialization is a combination of technical, marketing and political decisions that depends largely on a company's willingness to accept risk and its assessment of the marketplace and regulatory environment. Therefore, this book offers no quantitative predictions on future technology development or market readiness in the long-term, but emphasizes the current state of the technology and its short-term market viability.

Obtaining objective information is difficult. The abundance of information available today—much of it accessible on the internet, which is not peer reviewed—provides confusing and conflicting information to policy makers, as well as to the media. Many sources promote self-serving agendas that are detrimental to the broad constituency that legislators attempt to serve. Hence, policymakers at all levels of government are increasingly in need of access to professional and objective technical information—such as that contained in this book—to aid them in reaching appropriate policy decisions.

When considering the commercialization of a transportation technology, one should keep in mind that its prospects for success depend ultimately on manufacturing cost and retail price, operating and maintenance costs, and consumer attributes such as performance and range. It should be understood that predicting the future success of a transportation technology is particularly difficult because most of the technologies discussed in this book are far from commercialization and their costs and performance in the mass-market are unknown. Therefore, this book presents a series of questions at the beginning of each section that should be asked before considering an advanced vehicle technology as a policy option. Answers to some of the questions are not known at this time, and some answers will change as research and development continue in the intermediate-term (2005 to 2020). Nevertheless, the questions should be asked and answers sought before preference is given to any specific technology.

# 2. FEDERAL AND STATE PUBLIC POLICY BACKGROUND

Multiple congressional acts and administrative policies set the backdrop for the states' consideration of transportation policy involving alternative transportation options to the gasoline or diesel powered vehicle, including the Clean Air Act Amendments of 1990 (CAAA). The CAAA focus on attaining national ambient air quality standards through reductions of air pollution. The amendments require, among other provisions, that certain fleet vehicles in some of the nation's most polluted areas begin operating on alternative fuels. They also require automakers to reduce the exhaust emissions from conventional vehicles. To comply with many of the conditions of the Clean Air Act, each state must develop a state implementation plan (SIP) for achieving its goals.

In 1991, Congress passed the Intermodal Surface Transportation Efficiency Act (ISTEA), which encourages economically efficient and environmentally sound transportation policy. The act provides for the reduction of energy consumption, air pollution and traffic congestion as considerations in transportation policy planning programs.

ISTEA also contains a section that provides funding for the research and development of super high-speed (250 mph to 300 mph) magnetically levitated (maglev) trains. These trains travel along a fixed guideway propelled by powerful electromagnetic fields. The Japanese and Germans have tested and developed prototype maglev trains, but none are in commercial service. Congress appropriated $19.2 million for this program in FY 1996.

A related act is the Swift High-Speed Rail Act of 1994. This act provides funding for research, development and demonstrations of high-speed rail technology. These activities are to be carried out by the Federal Railroad Administration in cooperation with the states. In 1995, approximately $20 million was spent on this program; in 1996, Congress reduced the appropriation to the program to $5.4 million.

In 1992, Congress addressed the United States' dependence on foreign oil through the Energy Policy Act (EPACT). The legislation seeks to curb the nation's dependence on imported oil by encouraging conservation, energy efficiency and increased use of domestic fuels. It specifically promotes vehicles that run on non-petroleum based fuels (alternatively fueled vehicles or AFVs) by requiring federal, state and local governments and private fleets to buy AFVs in increasing percentages over time. The goal is to achieve acceptance of non-petroleum fuels in the light-duty vehicle market.

Finally, President Clinton reinforced the commitment to cleaner vehicles through Executive Order 12844, signed in April 1993. The order calls for the federal government to exceed the AFV purchase requirements in EPACT and for action to provide market impetus for development and manufacturing of AFVs.

In 1998, the Transportation Equity Act for the 21st Century (TEA-21) authorized highway, highway safety, transit and other surface transportation programs for six years. TEA-21 builds on the initiatives established in ISTEA, which was the last major authorizing legislation for surface transportation. This new act combines the continuation and improvement of current programs with new initiatives to meet the challenges of improving safety as traffic continues to increase at record levels; it also aims to protect and enhance communities and the natural environment.

As a part of TEA-21, a total of $1.282 billion in contract authority is provided for fiscal years 1998-2003 to fund the Intelligent Transportation Systems (ITS) program. Of this total, $603 million is targeted to research, training and standards development. Programs to accelerate integration and interoperability in the metropolitan and rural areas and to deploy commercial vehicle ITS infrastructure are established and funded at $482 million and $184 million, respectively. Funding for metropolitan areas is limited primarily to integration of infrastructure.

Before these federal actions, California was addressing its severe air pollution problems through the California Air Resource Board (CARB), created by the state Legislature in 1968. The Clean Air Act Amendments specifically allow California to initiate and establish stricter emissions standards and other states to adopt, or choose to use the California program. In 1990, CARB established the Low-Emission Vehicle (LEV) Program, which seeks to reduce emissions in light- and medium-duty vehicles by more than the federal standards required for model years 1994-2003. It requires each manufacturer's vehicle sales to be a combination of conventional and low-emission vehicles. Each vehicle may be certified to a set of increasingly stringent emission standards, including transitional-low emission vehicles (TLEV), low-emission vehicles (LEV), ultra-low emission vehicles (ULEV) and zero-emission vehicles (ZEV).

As part of the original California LEV Program, CARB set out a ZEV mandate that required 2 percent of the biggest selling manufacturers' fleets (General Motors, Ford, Chrysler, Toyota, Nissan, Honda and Mazda) to consist of ZEVs by 1998, with the percentage increasing gradually to 10 percent in 2003. In July 1994, NCSL published a *State Legislative Report*, "Electric Vehicles: Promise and Reality," which described the current state of electric vehicle technology expected to be used in the vehicle that would meet the California ZEV requirement. The report, reprinted in *Current Municipal Problems and Transportation Quarterly*,[1] concluded that, although available, EVs cost twice the amount of a comparable gasoline vehicle and have limited range and performance due to the technical limitations of EV battery technology.

In 1995, CARB began to reconsider its mandate due in part to the automakers' claims that current battery and vehicle technology fall short of that necessary to produce a car that meets consumer expectation and acceptance. An extensive study of battery technology completed at the request of CARB expressed the same concerns. Although CARB remains committed to its clean air goals, it recognized that giving car manufacturers more time to develop ZEVs may help the program's future success. In response to the concerns about technology and consumer acceptance, the CARB staff developed a new proposal that retreated from the 1998 2-percent mandate.

The new proposal suspends the ZEV requirements until 2003 and applies a market-based approach in the interim, meaning the market will determine how many ZEVs will be produced each year. The mandate remains that 10 percent of vehicles manufactured in 2003 be ZEVs. As a part of the proposal, CARB entered into binding memorandums of agreement with the seven manufacturers subject to the mandate. The agreements require that the car companies develop a technology partnership and continue developing advanced battery technology. In addition, the automakers agreed to build a cleaner car nationally, meeting low-emission standards in 2001 rather than the federally mandated deadline of 2004. The agreements contain penalties for failure to comply, including CARB's authority to reinstate the mandate. After a period of public comment, CARB unanimously approved the new proposal on March 29, 1996.

New York and Massachusetts have adopted the original California ZEV mandate and numerous other northeastern states have considered it. The courts are in the process of deciding whether these and other states can adopt or uphold the regulation in light of California's decision to delete the first part of the mandate.

Furthermore, a northeastern and mid-Atlantic state consortium—created by the CAAA and called the Ozone Transport Commission (OTC)—has evaluated various options for a regional emissions reduction program. In order to achieve better air quality nationwide in a cost effective manner, the OTC, auto manufacturers, environmental groups, fuel providers and the U.S. Environmental Protection Agency (EPA) negotiated a 45-state agreement, launched in February

1998, known as the National Low Emission Vehicle Program (NLEV). The 45-state agreement—accepted by all states except California, Maine, Massachusetts, New York and Vermont—seeks tailpipe emission standards that are less stringent than those imposed in California. However, the standards are stricter than current federal emissions levels.

Under this program, vehicles that meet NLEV standards would eliminate 99 percent of the pollution emitted by pre-regulation cars of the 1970s. It should be noted that 1999 vehicles already eliminate about 97 percent of those pollutants, but do not reduce emissions of carbon dioxide, which are believed to contribute to global warming. Carbon dioxide reductions would be achieved only by developing more fuel-efficient engines or driving fewer miles.

As a whole, the federal legislation and policies mentioned previously seek to reduce liquid fuel consumption and improve air quality. The bulk of the responsibility for implementation falls to the states, however. As is often the case, California was the first state to issue regulations, legislation and mandates to achieve the goals of the federal government. Other states tend to follow and learn from the experience in California.

The federal and state legislation discussed in this chapter was introduced to ameliorate air pollution and reduce U.S. dependence on imported oil. Although the intent of these laws and regulations is praiseworthy, some were introduced without a complete appreciation of the cost and technical limitations of the propulsion technologies addressed. Although the need to reduce dependence on imported oil continues to be an important national goal, the economic implication of mandating certain fuels to replace gasoline is subject to uncertainty. For example, developments in producing liquid fuels from more plentiful resources such as coal or Canadian tar sands may offer greater economic benefits and still meet the national security goals. There is a need for legislators at all levels of government to understand the advantages and disadvantages of alternative policy options, and to choose one that is economically and technically viable. There also should be a continuing dialog between experts in the industrial transportation sector and legislators and their staff to devise laws and regulations that take into account the technical status and advances in transportation engineering. The following eight chapters attempt to provide an objective overview of the transportation options that currently are the subject of discussion and legislation at all levels of government.

# 3. ELECTRIC VEHICLES

State government mandates require that thousands of electric vehicles (EVs) be put on American roads in just a few years in an effort to curb air pollution. The California Air Resources Board (CARB) adopted a plan in 1990 requiring 2 percent of all 1998 cars sold in California be zero emission vehicles (ZEVs). When it became apparent that the only available technology that could meet this zero emission criteria—the electric vehicle—would not be ready at a reasonable cost and performance level to satisfy the consumer, CARB deleted the first part of the mandate. CARB maintained the back-end of the mandate, however, requiring 10 percent of all cars sold in California in 2003 be ZEVs.

New York and Massachusetts have adopted the original California ZEV mandate and numerous other northeastern states have considered it. The courts are in the process of deciding whether these and other states can adopt or uphold the regulation in light of California's decision to drop the 1998 mandate.

Most recently, Honda Motor Company announced that it will stop production of its EV Plus, becoming the first major automaker to acknowledge that, " ... it sees no future in marketing costly battery-powered electric cars."[1] Although the concept of a zero emission vehicle is engaging in light of the health hazards from urban air pollution, state legislators should consider the economic consequences of mandating a new technology even if it is technically feasible. Questions that legislators and potential buyers should ask before considering EVs are:

- What types of EVs are available, and how does their performance and cost compare to gasoline powered vehicles?

- Will fleet operators and private consumers purchase EVs to meet the sales mandates, or will the state government have to buy them?

- What types of incentives are necessary to increase the sales of electric vehicles?

- What environmental benefits does an EV provide? Do they truly emit zero emissions?

- Are there any safety and health hazards associated with producing and disposing of EV batteries?

- What is the cost of the new infrastructure necessary to charge the EV batteries?

- What is the cost of operating and maintaining EVs?

## History of Electric Vehicles

Electric vehicles captured a greater part of the U.S. automotive market in the early 1900s than internal combustion engine (ICE) vehicles, but the ICE gained the upper edge due to a combination of unusual technological and business foresight among industrialists, their ability to control basic processes by patent or otherwise, and a substantial dose of good luck.[2] A number of historians have speculated why the internal combustion, gasoline-powered engine advanced in the marketplace. This information can be useful to policymakers 100 years later, as EVs again attempt to make inroads into the marketplace to compete with the internal combustion engine.

Dr. John B. Rae, one of the leading automotive historians of the 20th century, published an early article on electric vehicles in *Business History Review*. His academic treatment of the EV emphasized the technological liabilities of electric vehicles as the source of their early failure to capture the American automotive market. Rae has concluded that, " ... attempts to monopolize the automobile industry began early in its history but were never successful because the industry possessed characteristics which made monopolization exceptionally difficult. It would be difficult to envisage a less promising situation for the would-be monopolist. The Electric Vehicle Company (EVC) proved to be singularly deficient in all these attributes. The Electric Vehicle Company began its operations on the assumption that the electric automobile was going to be the dominant type; when this became demonstrably a bad guess, the company tried to compensate by using the Selden patent to collect royalties from the manufacturers of gasoline automobiles. This scheme likewise misfired, and the company collapsed into bankruptcy. The scheme also brought disaster to the Pope Manufacturing Company of Hartford, Connecticut, which abandoned a very promising position of leadership in the automobile field in order to participate in a highly speculative enterprise."[3]

David A. Kirsch, in his article entitled, "Studies in Automotive Systems Rivalry in America, 1890-1996," has explored the path-dependent process by which internal combustion vehicles emerged at the turn of the century as the automotive technological standard. Kirsch concluded that, " ... had the Electric Vehicle Company succeeded in establishing dependable, for-hire transport service at the turn of the century, central stations might have recognized the potential of electric vehicles sooner than they did. Battery service might have been introduced ten years earlier, and with an expanding market for electric vehicle service, progressive central stations might even have established remote battery exchange depots to extend the overall service area. Although by 1900 electric vehicles were already at a disadvantage for touring and an all-electric system might have been out of the question, a hybrid system in which gasoline and electric vehicles served separate markets might have persisted for years, if not decades. Both the timing and the scope of the failure of the EVC were crucial; only a massive venture that provided transportation service as a system stood a chance of fending off the dominance of internal combustion. Yet it was the very scope of the EVC's failure that soured public opinion against electric vehicles and undermined other efforts to introduce the technology."[4]

# How Does an EV Work?

The chassis of electric vehicles are essentially the same as gasoline vehicles. The difference is how the EV is powered. Three main components power an EV: 1) the battery pack, 2) the inverter and rotor, and the 3) charging/regenerative breaking system. These three operational components differ substantially from the internal combustion engine, which contains hundreds of moving parts. The simplicity of the EV provides much quieter travel, and because an EV has no catalytic converter, no muffler, no tailpipe, no radiator, and no carburetor, an EV requires no oil changes or tune-ups. The only routine maintenance for an EV involves replacing the brakes and the battery pack.

The key to the EV is its batteries. As many as 30 12-volt batteries similar to those used in conventional cars may be needed to power a light-duty EV. Such a battery pack weighs nearly a ton, has a high initial cost and takes up a lot of space in the car.

Figure 1 shows a typical lead-acid battery with several cells that store electric energy. Each cell contains a positive plate, a negative plate and an electrolyte. Using the common lead-acid battery as an example, the positive plate is made of lead dioxide ($PbO_2$) and is called a cathode. The negative plate, or anode, is pure lead ($Pb$), while the electrolyte is sulfuric acid ($H_2SO_4$) diluted with water. When the battery is connected to a circuit (e.g., pushing the drive pedal down in an EV), an electrochemical discharge takes place between the positive and negative plates, which completes an electrical circuit and supplies power to the drive train.

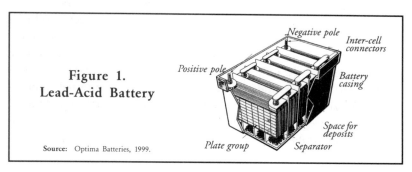

**Figure 1.
Lead-Acid Battery**

Negative pole

Inter-cell connectors

Positive pole

Battery casing

**Source:** Optima Batteries, 1999.

Plate group

Separator

Space for deposits

## Performance

The performance of electric vehicles depends largely on their battery pack. In 1991, the Big Three domestic automakers—General Motors, Ford and Chrysler—the U.S. Department of Energy, the Electric Power Research Institute (EPRI) and a variety of battery manufacturers formed the United States Advanced Battery Consortium (USABC). Through the formation of USABC, the preceding organizations hope to advance battery technologies and thereby increase the market potential of electric vehicles by pooling technical knowledge and funding. The goals of USABC include establishing the technical capability for advanced battery manufacturing in the United States, developing electrical energy systems capable of providing electric vehicles with range and performance competitive to gasoline powered vehicles, and leveraging funding for high-risk, high-cost advanced battery research and development.

Except for cost targets, the USABC is close to meeting its midterm performance goals using nickel-metal hydride (Ni-MH) batteries. Energy and power performance targets, which determine range and acceleration, appear to be within reach. Although testing of battery lifecycle is incomplete, it indicates the technology is developing as scheduled.

Table 1 presents USABC's midterm and long-term goals; table 2 lists the current status of battery development.

Factors that adversely affect the performance and viability of EV batteries are difficult to show quantitatively. Temperature has the greatest effect on the EV battery pack. The performance of lead-acid batteries is greatly reduced in cold weather, while nickel-metal (Ni-MH) hydride batteries do not perform as well in hot weather.[5] The reliability of operating nickel-zinc, nickel-cadmium and lithium-ion batteries in temperature extremes also is questionable. Presently, there is no battery that is unaffected by temperature. Battery thermal management systems therefore may need to be developed.

Manufacturers began to use lithium-ion and nickel-metal hydride batteries to power some EVs in 1998. Despite their high production

## Table 1. United States Advanced Battery Consortium (USABC) Battery Goals

| | Market Availability | Range per Charge (miles) | Life (years) | Cycle Life** | Cost ($ per kWh) | Specific Energy (Watt-hours per kg) | Energy Density (Watt-hours per liter) |
|---|---|---|---|---|---|---|---|
| **Battery Goals** | | | | | | | |
| Mid-term Goal*** | — | — | 5 | 600 | less than $150 | 80 to 100 | 135 |
| Long-term Goal**** | — | — | 10 | 1,000 | less than $100 | 200 | 300 |
| **Current Status** | | | | | | | |
| Nickel-Cadmium | Available | 65 to 140 | 8 | 700 to 1,200 | $300 to $500 | 45 to 55 | 100 to 150 |
| Lead-Acid | Available | 50 to 70 | 2 to 3 | 300 to 400 | $150 to $200 | 35 to 40 | 100 to 130 |
| Nickel-Metal Hydride | Available | 100 to 120 | 8 | 700 to 1,200 | $300 to $700 | 60 to 70 | 150 to 200 |
| Lithium-ion or Lithium Polymer | 1 to 4 | 150 to 300 | 5 to 10 | 400 to 1,200 | $150 to $220 | 100 to 150 | 100 to 200 |

*USABC did not set range goals. Range depends on vehicle and battery size.
** Number of discharges in battery lifetime.
*** Goals approximately for 1998.
**** Goals for beyond 2000.

**Source:** USABC, 1999.

Table 2.  Status of United States Advanced Battery Consortium (USABC) Funded Battery Technologies

| | Battery Type | Status | Driving Range per Charge (in miles*) | Life in Years | Cycle Life (Total No. of discharges) | Cost ($ per kWh) | Specific Energy (Watt-hours per kg) | Energy Density (Watt-hours per liter) |
|---|---|---|---|---|---|---|---|---|
| Short Term (1999) Technologies | Nickel-Cadmium | Available | 65 - 140 | 8 | 700 - 1,200 | $300 -$500 | 45 - 55 | 100 - 150 |
| | Lead-Acid | Available | 50 - 70 | 2-3 | 600-900 | $150 -$200 | 35 - 40 | 100 - 130 |
| | Nickel-Metal Hydride | Available | 100 - 120 | 8 | 700 - 1,200 | $300 -$700 | 60s-70s | 150 - 200 |
| Long-Term (2004) Technologies | Lithium-ion or Lithium Polymer | 1 - 4 years | 150 - 300 | 5-10 | 400 - 1,200 | $150 -$220 | 100 - 150 | 100 - 200 |

*USABC did not set range goals.  Range depends on vehicle and battery size.

costs, the cycle life and range benefits over lead-acid have convinced Japanese auto manufacturers to use these alternative chemical components. General Motors, DaimlerChrysler and Ford began offering nickel-metal hydride EVs in 1999.

## Cost

The cost of an EV consists of two components: the purchase price and the operating expenses, which include battery replacement costs.

The United States Advanced Battery Consortium reports that serious challenges remain in battery cost and manufacturing. To cut costs, USABC is focusing on three key areas: raw materials, battery design and volume manufacturing. USABC partners and their suppliers are investigating ways to lower material costs or use materials more effectively. Battery developers are working to design batteries that are small and lighter, which automatically leads to an increase in vehicle performance.

USABC believes that the most difficult challenge may be addressing the issues of volume manufacturing, assuming that if the volume goes up, the cost will come down. However, increasing volume on a product that most consumers cannot afford is a challenge. Additionally, except for the lead-acid battery, most EV batteries have never been produced in large quantities. New production techniques for efficiency must be developed and adopted to help reduce costs.

### Purchase Price

The initial purchase price of an electric vehicle is roughly twice that of a comparable gasoline powered vehicle. EVs are compared to their gasoline counterparts on the basis of size, range and vehicle performance. For example, General Motors offers a compact EV called the EV-1, with a manufacturer's retail sale price (MSRP) of $33,395. The EV-1 is comparable to the Saturn SC1, which has an MSRP of $15,000. Ford offers a Ranger EV Pickup at an MSRP of $32,795, illustrated in figure 2, which is targeted to fleet customers. The gasoline powered Ranger Pickup sells for $14,500. Both the EV-1 and the Ranger EV Pickup use lead-acid batteries in their power packs.

**Figure 2. Ford Ranger EV**

Source: Electric Vehicle Association of the Americas, 1997.

EVs that use nickel metal-hydride battery packs are priced higher than those using lead-acid batteries. Honda's EV Plus, which was discontinued in early 1999, had an MSRP of $53,999; Toyota's RAV4 EV has a 1999 MSRP of $42,000.

It should be noted that the purchase price of an EV has not declined in the previous 10 years. In 1988, an alternative fuel investigation by the Urban Consortium for Technology Initiatives concluded that the price tag for electric vehicles would be approximately double that of a comparable gasoline powered vehicle.[6] This economic estimate appeared correct in 1991, when the Arizona state procurement office received bids for new model year vehicles that included several types of light-duty electric vehicles, including sedans, pickups and vans of various sizes. The lowest bid was about $20,000 for a compact sedan, which the state usually purchased for $8,000.[7] The price tag of 1999 EVs remains more than twice that of their comparable gasoline powered models, although the performance and range offered by 1999 EVs is greater than that offered by 1991 models.

## Operating Expenses

The operating expenses for an EV include battery-pack replacement, preventive maintenance, repairs, tire replacement and electric power for battery charging.

The life of the batteries depends on a number of factors, including climate, frequency of use and charging habits. Battery pack and individual battery units in the pack will require regular replacement. Estimates for lead-acid batteries range from individual units every 10,000 miles to full battery pack replacement every 25,000 miles. The cost of a typical battery pack for an electric vehicle is between $2,000 and $8,000.[8] As new battery technology enters the market, battery replacement frequency will change. Several years of experience with each new vehicle and battery type will be required to provide reliable estimates of battery replacement frequency.[9]

Maintenance will be specific to each electric vehicle, but, in general, maintenance inspections will include checking the condition of the motor(s), brakes, batteries, electrical connections, battery pack mounting brackets and battery pack integrity. The batteries will generally require watering every three weeks or 500 miles, varying with climate.[10]

## Cost of Infrastructure Development

The cost of an infrastructure to charge an EV's batteries and support its operation also must be considered by policymakers when considering EV mandates. Developing an infrastructure to fuel EVs is complicated and will be expensive. The Sacramento Municipal Utility District (SMUD) prices a conductive charging device at $1,800 and an inductive charger at $2,184. Pedestals or wall mounts for the chargers cost an additional $300 to $450 per device.[11] Figures 3 and 4 show the SMUD chargers installed at the Arden Fair Mall in Sacramento, California.

**Figure 3.**
A Saturn $EV_1$ is refueling at the Sacramento Municipal Utility District's public charging station located at the Arden Fair Mall in Sacramento, California.

Source: Sacramento Municipal Utility District (SMUD), 1999.

**Figure 4.**
The Sacramento Municipal Utility District's public charging station, located at the Arden Fair Mall in Sacramento, California, features EVI ICS200 charging units. These devices also recharge electric vehicles from Ford and Honda.

Source: Sacramento Municipal Utility District (SMUD), 1999.

Issues such as safety, technical hardware conformity at all refueling stations and the price tag of such an effort all must be considered. Certain states already have installed public charging sites at shopping malls, airports and parking structures, but this infrastructure is minimal and localized. For example, as of January 1999, Arizona had eight public sites (10 total) and California had 41 public charging sites (103 total).[17] These chargers are usually of the 220-volt variety, although some 440-volt chargers can be found. Compatible EVs can be charged in an hour with 440-volt chargers for a larger energy fee. Testing on quick charges is an ongoing priority. DaimlerChrysler and Norvik Technologies have developed a system to charge advanced batteries to full capacity in 25 minutes. The feasibility of this system is not yet proven.

## Availability

Appendix B contains information about the 1999 EV models, including their manufacturer, purchase price, leasing details, special features, battery and charging information, and vehicle performance.

## Environmental Impact

### Emissions

An electric vehicle is called a zero emission vehicle (ZEV) because it emits no tailpipe emissions. However, this classification can be misleading because the power source used to charge the EV's battery pack also must be considered. If fuels like nuclear, hydroelectric or renewable energy are used to charge the battery pack, an EV is close to "zero emission" because these fuels emit very little or no pollutants at the electricity generation plant.

However, when coal or natural gas is the fuel used to create the electricity for charging, there can be significant emissions associated with operating EVs. Coal-burning and gas power plants emit pollutants like sulfur dioxide ($SO_2$), nitrous oxides ($NO_x$) and carbon dioxide ($CO_2$). Natural gas power plants emit about half as much $CO_2$ and $NO_x$ as coal-burning facilities per kilowatt-hour (kWh) and virtually no $SO_2$. Carbon monoxide (CO) emissions are negligible in both.

Appendix C, "Regional Vehicle Emissions Produced by Electric Vehicles," presents regional emissions data associated with charging the battery packs of an electric vehicle and compares these emissions data to that generated from operating gasoline powered vehicles. Gasoline vehicle emissions include tailpipe, production and refining emissions, and are otherwise known as the total fuel-cycle emissions. Because the electricity fuel mixture varies greatly across the country, EV emission values are presented by region.

In the west, EV emission values are much lower than those in any other region. Electricity in this region is generated primarily by hydroelectric, nuclear and natural gas plants. For every mile driven by an EV (as opposed to a gasoline vehicle) in the west, $CO_2$ and $NO_x$ emissions are reduced by 80 percent to 90 percent. $SO_2$ emissions remain about the same.

On the other hand, EV usage in the Midwest and the South result in a much different outcome. Carbon dioxide emissions can be reduced by 30 percent to 50 percent and, in most cases, $NO_x$ can be reduced by 15 percent to 45 percent. However, driving an EV in the midwest or south may actually increase $SO_2$ emissions by 1 gram to 3 grams per mile—a 2,500 percent to 3,500 percent increase over conventional gasoline powered vehicles. This dramatic increase in $SO_2$ emissions can be attributed to the type of coal used as the primary fuel for power generation in the midwest and south. In most areas of this region, the coal contains high concentrations of sulfur. This dramatic increase in $SO_2$ emissions may substantially increase acid rain in the midwest and south.

The mountain region also uses coal as the primary power fuel source, although the coal used in this region is low-sulfur. Even so, EVs will increase $SO_2$ emissions by 0.4 gram to 0.8 gram per mile, or 600 percent to 900 percent over gasoline engines. $CO_2$ and $NO_x$ emissions are similar to those in the midwest and the south. Despite a more diverse fuel mix, the northeast has higher $NO_x$ and $SO_2$ emission values than the mountain region, but lower carbon emission values. High sulfur coal is the culprit.

It is important to note that these figures represent only what is emitted inside each region's borders. Imported electricity is not included. For example, if the mountain region burns coal to make electricity and exports it to the western region, the mountain region, not the west, will experience increased emissions.

Further explanation about the calculation procedure and the assumptions made in this analysis can be found in appendix C.

## Safety and Battery Disposal

Most EV batteries require special handling for disposal. Lead-acid batteries are banned from landfill disposal in most states, while nickel-cadmium batteries are banned from disposal under federal regulation (the Mercury-Containing and Rechargeable Battery Management Act of 1996). In response to landfill bans, recycling battery material has become common practice.

Current batteries and current designs for future batteries contain materials that are harmful to humans. Additionally, temporary storage of batteries for salvage should not be permitted in areas with freezing temperatures (battery electrolyte expands as it freezes, which cracks the battery case and allows the battery acid to leak into the surrounding area).

## Conclusion

Large-scale deployment of electric vehicles depends on the development of a new type of battery that can extend the range of the vehicle and decrease the time required for charging. Despite research during the past 100 years by private industry to develop a new and better battery, none of the candidates under development are able to compete economically with a lead-acid battery, which is almost universally used today. Although there may be niche markets for electric vehicles, the expectation that electric vehicles (with currently available technology) could replace internal combustion vehicles in the short-term does not appear to be realistic. The United States Advanced Battery Consortium continues to work on developing a cost-effective battery technology that will make EVs competitive with gasoline powered vehicles in regard to vehicle performance.

Environmental benefits from the use of EVs can be obtained only in those areas of the country where electricity is generated from hydroelectric, solar, nuclear or natural gas plants. In areas where coal is used to generate electricity, the additional emissions caused by increased electrical production will often negate the anticipated benefits of driving an EV.

Although the fundamental concept of the electric vehicle is engaging—especially in light of the ever-increasing health hazards of urban air pollution—when compared to the internal combustion gasoline powered vehicle in terms of range, cost and performance, electric vehicle technology cannot compete. Moreover, the initial cost of an EV is at least twice that of a comparable conventional internal combustion engine vehicle, and operation and maintenance costs also are higher. Until such time that developers have solved the environmental and fiscal problems associated with EVs, any policy regarding electric vehicles should be carefully researched before a state or local government decides to mandate their use on a large scale.

# 4. Hybrid Electric Vehicles

Hybrid electric vehicles (HEVs) represent another alternative to vehicles powered only by a liquid fuel. HEVs have the potential to offer the travel range and flexibility of internal combustion engine vehicles, but can appreciably increase fuel-efficiency and reduce emissions.

Unlike electric vehicles—that are commercially available and have an array of technical data describing their cost, performance and range capabilities—the HEV information to demonstrate and prove HEV technology is mostly proprietary. This makes a technical analysis of the HEV difficult.

It is widely known, however, that Toyota introduced an HEV to its Japanese market at a competitive price. The only commercially available HEV on the market at this time is the Toyota *Prius*. It sells for between $15,000 and $16,000, and has surpassed sales estimates in Japan. The *Prius* is not yet available to the U.S. market. Ford and Dodge also revealed HEV technology at auto shows in 1998, although they are not yet commercially available.

HEVs offer a policy option for alternative fuel fleet requirements and emissions reduction standards. Although the HEV does not satisfy the California ZEV mandate, an HEV can reduce emissions considerably. For example, Toyota claims that emissions of carbon monoxide, hydrocarbons and nitrogen oxide from the *Prius* are reduced from

50 percent to 90 percent.[1] Questions that should be asked before considering HEVs as a required alternative are:

- Are the benefits of hybrid electric vehicles proven with sufficient data?

- When will reliable hybrid electric vehicles be commercially available?

- What kinds of emissions standards are appropriate for hybrid electric vehicles?

- What types of incentives can be used to increase the sales of hybrid electric vehicles?

- Should EV mandates be adjusted to include hybrid electric vehicles?

- What are the operating costs of hybrid electric vehicles?

## History of Hybrid Electric Vehicles

Although the history of HEVs parallels the history of its sibling, the EV, there is one important difference: HEVs function as electric vehicles for short trips, but also offer long-range capability and quick refueling convenience using the existing fuel infrastructure with an on-board internal combustion engine.

Hybrid vehicles, therefore, offer range capabilities similar to the internal combustion engine (ICE) vehicle, which has kept the EV from competing with the ICE for more than a century. Today, interest in HEVs has increased worldwide because the technology offers reduced emissions of pollutants and increased fuel economy, both important concerns of the future.

American engineer H. Piper filed for a patent on a hybrid electric vehicle in 1905. Piper's design called for an electric motor to augment a gasoline engine to allow the vehicle to accelerate to 25 miles per hour in 10 seconds, instead of the usual 30 seconds. By the time the patent was issued, three and one-half years later, internal combustion engines had become powerful enough to achieve this kind of performance on their own. Nevertheless, a few hybrid vehicles were built during this period; a 1912 model is displayed in the Ford Museum in Dearborn, Michigan.[2]

The more powerful gasoline engines, along with equipment that allowed them to be started without cranks, contributed to the decline of the electric vehicle and of the nascent HEV between 1910 and 1920. In the early to mid-1970s, a brief flurry of interest and funding, prompted by the oil crisis, led to the construction of several experimental HEVs in the United States and abroad.

## How Does a Hybrid Electric Vehicle Work?

An HEV is powered by the combination of a battery pack and electric motor—like that of an electric vehicle—and a power generation unit (PGU), which is normally an internal combustion engine. Unlike EVs, HEV batteries can be recharged by an on-board PGU, which needs only to be refueled.

HEVs can be configured primarily in a parallel or a series design.[3] The parallel design enables the HEV to be powered by both the PGU and the electric motor, either simultaneously or separately, whereas the series design uses the PGU to generate electricity, which recharges the HEV's battery pack and powers the vehicle via an electric motor. Both designs allow the battery pack and the PGU to be smaller than those in a typical electric vehicle or internal combustion engine.

### Parallel Design

Most of today's prototype HEVs—as well as the only production HEV, the Toyota *Prius*—use a parallel configuration (see figure 5). A parallel HEV has two propulsion paths, one from the PGU and one from the electric motor. Computer chips control the output of each. An HEV with a parallel configuration has a direct mechanical connection between the power generation unit and the wheels as in a conventional vehicle, but also has an electric motor that drives the

wheels. For example, a parallel vehicle could use the power created
from an internal combustion engine for highway driving and the power
from the electric motor for accelerating.

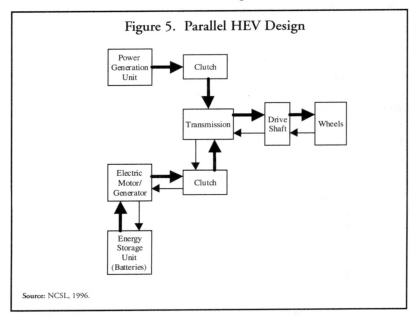

Figure 5. Parallel HEV Design

Source: NCSL, 1996.

Power produced from the PGU also drives a generator, which, in
turn, charges the battery pack as needed. The system to transfer electricity from the generator to the battery pack is exactly like that of an
EV. Alternating current is converted to direct current by the inverter.
HEV parallel designs also use the same regenerative braking features
as EVs.

Some benefits of a parallel configuration versus a series configuration
include:

• The vehicle has more power because both the engine and the
  motor supply power simultaneously.

• Most parallel HEVs do not need a generator.

• Power is directly coupled to the road; thus, the vehicle can operate more efficiently.

## *Series Design*

Many initial designs to test HEVs utilized the series design (see figure 6). Series HEVs use a PGU to power a generator, which either supplies the electric motor with electricity directly or charges the battery pack. Because there is no connection between the PGU and the drive train, all power must be received from the electric motor. The regenerative braking system of the series design is similar to that of an EV. The series configuration is thought to be more suited for city and stop-and-go driving. However, the need for a larger battery pack increases the cost of the vehicle, which has initially put the series design secondary to the parallel configuration.

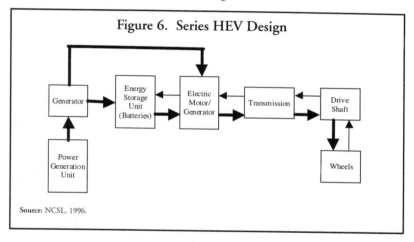

### Figure 6. Series HEV Design

Source: NCSL, 1996.

The benefits of a series configuration over a parallel configuration are:

- The engine never idles, which reduces vehicle emissions.

- The engine drives a generator to run at optimum performance.

- Several options are available for mounting the engine and vehicle components.

- Some series hybrids do not need a transmission.

## Performance and Cost

The key performance advantage of HEVs is fuel economy. HEVs with an efficient electric-drive system, optimally sized power generation unit, on-board energy storage (battery pack), regenerative braking and an effective control strategy can be more fuel-efficient than ICE vehicles. A U.S. Department of Energy HEV Propulsion Project has a near-term fuel economy target of 55 miles per gallon, but 80 miles per gallon is technically feasible.[4]

Like EVs, the full cost of HEVs is estimated to be roughly twice that of a comparable gasoline powered vehicle. But unlike EVs, the market price of the only HEV available is between $15,000 and $16,000. Toyota's *Prius* has an incremental cost of about $3,000 over its comparable Corolla, which sells for just over $13,000. Analysts believe, however, that the real cost of Toyota's HEV may be as much as twice its market price.[5] Toyota hopes that market penetration will bring production costs down and therefore has assumed the initial financial risk for the vehicle. A cutaway view of the Toyota *Prius* and the placement of its key components are pictured in figure 7.

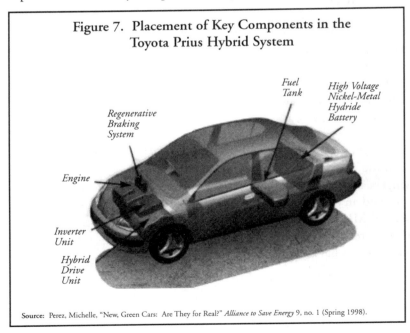

**Figure 7. Placement of Key Components in the Toyota Prius Hybrid System**

Fuel Tank

High Voltage Nickel-Metal Hydride Battery

Regenerative Braking System

Engine

Inverter Unit

Hybrid Drive Unit

**Source:** Perez, Michelle, "New, Green Cars: Are They for Real?" *Alliance to Save Energy* 9, no. 1 (Spring 1998).

Table 3 presents the energy savings realized by operating an HEV such as the *Prius*, based on fuel cost and 10,000 miles driven per year.

| Table 3. Cost of Energy* Assuming 10,000 Miles Driven per Year | | | | | | |
|---|---|---|---|---|---|---|
| | Price per Gallon | | | | | |
| Vehicle | $1 | $1.50 | $2 | $2.50 | $3 | $4 |
| Corolla (30 mpg) | $333 | $500 | $667 | $833 | $1,000 | $1,333 |
| Prius HEV (66 mpg) | $152 | $227 | $303 | $379 | $455 | $606 |
| Energy Savings** | $181 | $273 | $364 | $454 | $545 | $727 |

*Cost of Energy = [10,000 miles per year / miles per gallon] multiplied by the price of fuel

**Energy Savings = Corolla Cost of Energy less Prius Cost of Energy

Source: NCSL, 1999.

## Availability

The only commercially available HEV is the Toyota *Prius*, released to the Japanese market in 1998. Sales of the *Prius* exceeded Toyota's expectations, because the 66 miles per gallon fuel economy appealed to the Japanese, who pay more than $3 per gallon for gasoline. A redesigned Prius is scheduled to be released in the U.S. market some-time in the year 2000.

The Toyota *Prius* has a unique chassis and is slightly smaller in size than the Toyota Corolla. Its features include a capacity of five pas-sengers, a top speed of 100 mph, a 1.5-liter internal combustion en-gine and an electric motor. Its battery pack is made of 248 "D"-cell size Ni-MH batteries—the same size as most flashlight batteries—that are recharged by the PGU via a generator. Toyota estimates that the batteries have a cycle life of 150,000 miles.

DaimlerChrysler and Ford introduced HEV prototypes—the Dodge Intrepid ESX2 and the Ford P2000—at auto shows in 1998. Both use alternative fuels to power the PGU.

The Intrepid HEV uses a parallel design—a 1.8-liter three-cylinder turbo-diesel engine and two permanent-magnet DC electric motors. DaimlerChrysler chose a diesel engine because of its high power-to-fuel economy ratio, which allows the Intrepid to achieve approximately 70 miles to the gallon and generate more than 200 horsepower. DaimlerChrysler plans to release the ESX2 around 2003.

The most significant obstacle that DaimlerChrysler must overcome to meet this release date is incorporating complicated components without adding weight. Developing a car that weighs 40 percent less than today's autos with no cost or performance drop-off is a primary goal of the DaimlerChrysler HEV program.[6] Another barrier is the creation of a smoother transition between the electric motor and the PGU.

The Ford P2000 is a family prototype HEV that averages 63 miles per gallon of fuel. The fuel used is a natural gas derivative, high-cetane Fischer Tropsch fuel. The P2000 uses a parallel configuration, but, unlike the Prius or the Intrepid HEV, it cannot be operated solely on battery power. The PGU is a 1.2-liter direct injection engine made primarily of aluminum (instead of steel). Because aluminum is much lighter than steel, the P2000 weighs 40 percent less than the Ford Taurus.

Like the ESX2, the P2000 will need to overcome some obstacles in order to be sold on the market. Most notably, the fuel substitution must occur. Fischer Tropsch fuel cannot be stored and distributed using the current gasoline infrastructure. In response to this, Ford is developing a fuel cell HEV P2000.

In addition, American Honda plans to introduce its two-passenger Honda VV to the U.S. market. It runs on a combination of a nickel-metal hydride battery pack and a 1-liter gasoline engine. It is expected to average more than 70 miles per gallon.

## Environmental Impact

The increased fuel economy of HEVs reduces the emission of air pollutants, although conclusive HEV emissions data is not yet available. Toyota claims however, that carbon dioxide emissions from the Prius are approximately 160 grams/mile, or half those of its gasoline-powered Corolla. Toyota also reports that the Prius emits 90 percent less nitrous oxides, sulfur dioxide and hydrocarbons than today's average car, which has a fuel economy of 23 miles per gallon.

## Conclusion

Of all the current efforts under way by private industry and by the federal program under the Partnership for a New Generation of Vehicles (PNGV), the most promising candidate appears to be the hybrid-electric/internal combustion engine combination. This technology is advanced and does not require a new storage and delivery infrastructure. It would potentially more than double the average mileage of a vehicle and simultaneously reduce air pollution. However, without a change in paradigm from the single-occupancy vehicle to some other way of transporting people, particularly commuters, hybrid automobiles will not ameliorate gridlock problems in metropolitan areas.

Data proving HEV technology is not widely available and is often proprietary. Policymakers might consider a "wait-and-see" attitude for the HEV; results from Toyota's introduction of the Prius into the Japanese marketplace and consumers' acceptance of the technology will be available in the short-term. It is also important to note that any gains in internal combustion engine technology will improve HEV efficiency. The electric engine in a hybrid vehicle will always allow an HEV to be more fuel efficient and emit fewer pollutants than any gasoline vehicle.

In the United States, it will take much longer—perhaps 15 years—to realize savings from the Prius' fuel economy as long as gasoline sells for between $1 and $2 per gallon. Increases in gasoline prices would shorten this payback time. It remains to be seen—when the Prius goes on sale in the United States sometime after 2000—whether

Americans are willing to pay extra money for a smaller and less powerful automobile in exchange for a reduction in emissions and gas consumption.

Regulator acceptance of an HEV as an Ultra Low Emission Vehicle (ULEV), or even as a zero emission vehicle (ZEV), is possible if HEV emissions can be reduced to the level of power plant emissions associated with charging an EV's battery pack. Current lack of such acceptance by regulators is related to the potential for deterioration of the HEV's engine with time and mileage. Rugged and durable systems will be needed to provide credibility to a claim of long engine life and low emissions.

# 5. FUEL CELL VEHICLES

Fuel cell vehicles are another transportation option that can satisfy California's zero-emission vehicle mandate. However, producing fuel cells at a cost low enough for automobile propulsion is a challenge that has yet to be met.[1]

Commercialization of fuel cell vehicles has been slow because of high production costs. This topic is presently the subject of a heavily financed research and development program among some of the world's largest auto manufacturers, such as DaimlerChrysler, Ford, General Motors and Toyota. Automakers are hopeful that fuel cells eventually may become a viable replacement for the internal combustion engine for single-occupancy vehicles and have invested more than $750 million in a partnership with Ballard Power Systems, the leading developer of the automotive fuel cell.[2]

In light of these dynamic changes in the budding fuel cell industry, it is important to be aware of the current state of fuel cell technology to accurately gauge the viability of the technology on a mass production scale. It must also be realized that fuel cell research and development programs that demonstrate the potential of the technology do not imply its commercial availability and feasibility.

Although some may construe that private investments in fuel cell technology by automakers demonstrates its potential, legislators and other policymakers should ask the following questions before considering fuel cell vehicle technology as a policy option.

- Are fuel cell vehicles priced competitively in the marketplace?

- What primary fuel will be used to power the fuel cell?

- If the primary fuel used to power the fuel cell is a hydrogen rich liquid fuel—such as methanol or natural gas—what will be the cost to implement a new fueling infrastructure?

- How does methanol production affect air quality and how do the emissions associated with reforming the fuel on-board affect the environment?

- If the primary fuel used to power the fuel cell is hydrogen and is to be stored on-board the vehicle, what safety measures must be considered to protect the public welfare?

- What is the complete cost of hydrogen production and a hydrogen infrastructure and how do these increase the real cost of operating a fuel cell vehicle?

- What are the insurance and legal issues associated with increased production, storage and transportation of hydrogen?

## History of Fuel Cells

Sir William Grove constructed the first fuel cell in 1839. While conducting experiments electrolyzing water to produce hydrogen and oxygen, Grove reasoned that he could reverse the process and generate electricity by recombining the hydrogen and oxygen to produce water.

Although the principles of fuel cell operation were demonstrated conclusively by Grove in 1839, it was not until the 1950s that Francis Bacon succeeded in building a device that could generate practical amounts of power over prolonged periods. The largest unit built by Bacon produced 6 kilowatts of power. Building on the success of the Bacon cell, Pratt and Whitney Aircraft began a program sponsored by the U.S. government to develop a fuel cell for the Apollo Space Program. By 1965, fuel cells were routinely used in space flight and still are used on board the space shuttle. There also has been substantial research and development of fuel cells for military applications, such as the propulsion of submarines and unmanned undersea vehicles. For commercial, industrial and utility applications, the private sector and the U.S. Department of Energy (DOE) have worked during the past 30 years to develop fuel cells for generating electricity. As a result, fuel cells now are being commercially sold in 200-kilowatt (kW) units (enough power to supply about 40 homes) for on-site cogeneration of electricity and steam heat. In addition, power plants of up to 11,000 kW of electrical capacity have been built and demonstrated.

The Department of Energy's research and development of fuel cells for transportation began in 1987; they still are in an early stage of development. For vehicular applications, minimizing the size and weight of fuel cells is important. Although there are other technological—as well as infrastructure and economic—hurdles to overcome before fuel cells can be mass-produced, the fuel cell vehicle of the future may provide the same kind of satisfaction expected from a conventional vehicle that uses an internal combustion engine, but without the pollution or the noise.[3]

## How Does a Fuel Cell Work?

Fuel cells use hydrogen ($H_2$) to produce power.

A fuel cell is an electrochemical device, similar to a battery, that produces electricity silently and without combustion. However, where batteries must be recharged to continue power generation, fuel cells must be refueled with hydrogen. Fuel cells produce energy in the form of electricity and heat as long as hydrogen is supplied; heat and water vapor are the cell's only by-products.

With the exception of compressed hydrogen and the direct methanol fuel cell (DMFC), all fuel cell vehicle designs require an on-board reformer to release hydrogen from a hydrocarbon feedstock fuel—such as natural gas, gasoline, methanol or ethanol—to power the fuel cell. Figure 8 presents a schematic view of the fuel cell mechanism, including the fuel reformer.

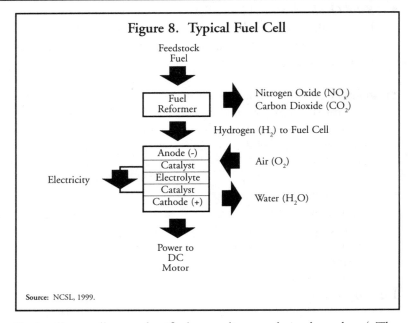

**Figure 8. Typical Fuel Cell**

Feedstock
Fuel

Fuel
Reformer

Nitrogen Oxide ($NO_x$)
Carbon Dioxide ($CO_2$)

Hydrogen ($H_2$) to Fuel Cell

Anode (-)
Catalyst
Electrolyte
Catalyst
Cathode (+)

Air ($O_2$)

Electricity

Water ($H_2O$)

Power to
DC
Motor

Source: NCSL, 1999.

Fuel cells usually are classified according to their electrolyte.[4] The bullets below indicate the major fuel cell types, their convenient abbreviations and their nominal operating temperatures.

- *Proton Exchange Membrane (PEM)*—These cells operate at 200 degrees Fahrenheit (a considerably lower temperature than most engines) and have high power density. Their output can be quickly varied to meet shifts in power demand and they are suited for applications such as automobiles and portable power generators.

- *Phosphoric Acid (PAFC)*—This is the most commercially developed type of fuel cell. It is currently used in such diverse environments as hospitals, nursing homes, hotels, office buildings, schools, utility power plants and airport terminals. PAFC fuel cells operate at a temperature of 392 degrees Fahrenheit.

- *Molten Carbonate (MCFC)*—Molten carbonate fuel cells promise high fuel-to-electricity efficiencies and the ability to consume coal-based fuels. MCFC fuel cells operate at a temperature of 1,202 degrees Fahrenheit.

- *Solid Oxide (SOFC)*—The solid oxide fuel cell could be used in large, high-power applications such as industrial and large-scale central electricity generating stations. SOFC fuel cells operate at a temperature of 1,832 degrees Fahrenheit.

- *Alkaline (AFC)*—Although these cells were used by NASA on space missions, they remain much too costly for commercial use. Companies are examining ways to reduce costs and improve operating flexibility. AFC fuel cells operate at a temperature of 212 degrees Fahrenheit.

- *Direct Methanol Fuel Cells (DMFC)*—DMFC are a relatively new member of the fuel cell family. These cells are similar to the PEM cells in that both use a polymer membrane as the electrolyte, run on liquid methanol and eliminate the need for a fuel reformer.

## Performance

The performance of fuel cells is measured by the efficiency with which they convert hydrogen to electricity, referred to as fuel cell conversion efficiency. The conversion efficiency depends on the electrolyte used in the body of the fuel cell. PAFC and PEM cells operate at relatively low temperatures and are the most likely candidates to be used for vehicle propulsion.

The PAFC is the most developed fuel cell technology and has been used to power fuel cell buses. The PAFC operating temperature is much higher than that of PEM cells, however, and requires more expensive operating components. Moreover, the PAFC reforming technique is complex and requires high capital costs, but its expected efficiency is 40 percent to 45 percent, compared to 36 percent to 39 percent for small diesel engines.

PAFC limitations led to research on alternative fuel cells that use a solid, polymer electrolyte instead of a liquid. These PEM fuel cells now are used to power the Daimler-Benz NECAR3 and Toyota's RAV4 hybrid prototype. Like the PAFC, PEM cells use platinum as a catalyst. The feedstock fuel for these fuel cells can be any hydrogen-rich chemical, including gasoline or methanol.

Currently, the choice fuel to power prototype fuel cell vehicles is methanol, which both the NECAR3 and the RAV4 use in conjunction with a fuel reformer on-board the vehicle. Methanol PEM fuel cells have a fuel cell conversion efficiency of 27 percent, whereas gasoline internal combustion engines have a total efficiency of 17 percent.[5]

## Cost

The American Methanol Institute (AMI) reports that the cost of a complete PEM fuel cell engine is $500 per kilowatt, which includes the fuel cell stack, methanol reformer and associated controls.[6] Approximately 50 kW, or 67 horsepower, is needed to power a small passenger vehicle; therefore, the cost of a small car's fuel cell system is $25,000, based on AMI's estimate. In comparison, the cost of a gasoline internal combustion engine is approximately $50 per kW, or $2,500. Developers estimate the cost of a full power fuel cell system could be in the range of $50 per kW in high-volume production.

Dr. Peter Lehman, director of the Schatz Energy Research Center and professor of Environmental Resources Engineering at Humboldt State University in California, reports that, "kilowatt for kilowatt, a [large stationary] fuel cell is two to three times more expensive than a conventional power plant and about sixty times more expensive than a car engine." Lehman attributes the high cost of fuel cells to the expense of assembling the cells in the laboratory by engineers. Lehman believes their manufacture must make the transition from laboratory to automated factory for the price to be reduced."[7]

DaimlerChrysler reports that the cost of its newest prototype fuel cell vehicle, the NECAR4, is more than $100,000. The vehicle is not yet available for purchase.[8]

## Availability

At present, the only fuel cell-powered vehicles in day-to-day use in the world are in Palm Desert, California. The fleet includes a cherry-red, pint-sized street-ready fuel-cell coupe and three fuel-cell powered golf-carts that use commercially bottled hydrogen. The vehicles are used as commute vehicles and for park maintenance.[9] The vehicles were produced at Humboldt State University's Schatz Energy Research Center (SERC) though a $3.9 million transportation project, to create a fleet of pollution-free vehicles powered by fuel cells—and the infrastructure to support them. Figures 9 and 10 illustrate the SERC fuel cell vehicles.

**Figure 9. The Schatz Energy Research Center's (SERC) fuel cell powered car takes a spin on the streets of Arcata, California.**

Source: Schatz Energy Research Center, 1999.

Figure 10. Workers use the fuel cell powered golf cart built by SERC in the City of Palm Desert's City Park.

Source: Schatz Energy Research Center, 1999.

The coupe debuted on April 24, 1999, at the Clean Cities Celebration in the City of Palm Desert, California, about 800 miles south of the lab where it was made. The fuel cell powered neighborhood electric vehicle (NEV) is a small car that carries two people, runs at a top speed of 35 mph, has a range of 30 miles, can be refueled in two minutes and emits no exhaust other than water. SERC's next step is to construct a hydrogen-generating and refueling station where solar electricity will power the electrolysis of water to produce hydrogen fuel.[10]

The automakers are in the process of developing a fuel cell vehicle that will compete with the internal combustion engine. DaimlerChrysler unveiled its first prototype fuel cell vehicle in 1994—the NECar, or New Electric Car—powered by fuel cells Daimler bought from Ballard Power Systems as part of an approximately $19 million order. Because the NECar had room only for a driver and the fuel-cell system—and tanks of pure hydrogen also mounted inside the vehicle—Daimler continued research and development and in 1996 unveiled the NECAR2.

Soon after Daimler introduced the NECAR2, Toyota unveiled a fuel cell electric vehicle (FCEV) version of its compact RAV4 sport-utility vehicle. In 1997, both Toyota and Daimler introduced new prototype vehicles that use a fuel reformer, using methanol as the primary fuel rather than pure hydrogen stored on-board. These prototypes altered the auto industry's perspective of the viability of fuel cell vehicles, especially when the technology was compared to the progress of battery technology for electric vehicles. Although the latest EVs use batteries that travel only about 150 miles per charge, Daimler's NECAR3 achieves 250 miles on a tank of methanol.

## The NECAR3

The NECAR3 is the third prototype produced by DaimlerChrysler. It is based on the 12-foot-long Mercedes A-class chassis and contains a 50 kW methanol PEM fuel cell designed by Ballard Power Systems. NECAR3 employs a fuel reformer, which vaporizes methanol into hydrogen that is necessary to power the fuel cell.

## The NECAR4

DaimlerChrysler unveiled the NECAR4 in early 1999 and plans to introduce the car to the marketplace in five years. Unlike the NECAR3, NECAR4 is powered by hydrogen stored on-board the vehicle and reaches top speeds of 90 mph with a range of 280 miles. NECAR4 is pictured in figure 11.

**Figure 11. The DaimlerChrysler NECAR4**

Source: DaimlerChrysler, 1999.

Liquid hydrogen is stored in a cryogenically insulated cylinder (similar to a large thermos) at the rear of the NECAR4 under the floorboard. DaimlerChrysler executives report that they are not sure what the cost of the commercial NECAR will be when it reaches the consumer. Ferdinand Panik, DaimlerChrysler's project leader for the NECAR4, notes that hydrogen fuel cell vehicles, due to fueling constraints, are better suited for central fuel depots—such as those used for taxis, buses, ambulances, police cars and company fleets—than for private vehicles.[11]

## The RAV4 Fuel Cell Electric Vehicle (FCEV)

Toyota's next-generation fuel cell electric vehicle (FCEV) technology currently is being developed for the RAV4 platform, and Toyota reports that it has an energy conversion efficiency of more than 60 percent. The FCEV employs a fuel reformer that vaporizes methanol into hydrogen that is necessary to power the fuel cell.

## Fuel Cells in Public Transportation

Three Ballard commercial prototype fuel cell buses were delivered to the Chicago Transit Authority (CTA) in 1997 for a demonstration project where performance, cost and reliability data were collected during a two-year test period. The buses, illustrated in figure 12, were powered by Ballard fuel cells that convert hydrogen directly into electricity. Hydrogen for the demonstration project was provided by Air Products and Chemicals Inc., which built its first commercial hydrogen fueling station at CTA's Pulaski hub for this purpose. Air Products delivered hydrogen to the fueling station as a liquid and pumped it to high pressure using cryogenic liquid pumps. The liquid hydrogen at high pressure then was vaporized and transferred into pressurized cylinders located on the roof of the bus where it was stored. Air Products' hydrogen fueling station was designed to fuel a bus in 15 minutes; with one charge, the average bus travels 250 miles.[12] Yazeed Kyayyat at CTA reports the cost of the demonstration project was $10 million.

Figure 12. CTA / Ballard Power Systems Fuel Cell Buses

Source: Ballard Power Systems, 1997.

## Environmental Impact

The amount of pollution emitted from the tailpipe of a fuel cell vehicle depends on whether a fuel reformer is used. Because all fuel cells require hydrogen for their operation, hydrogen must either be produced on-board the vehicle from a feedstock fuel such as methanol, or produced elsewhere and then stored on-board the vehicle in tanks.

Vehicles like the NECAR4 do not use a fuel reformer; instead, pure hydrogen is stored on-board the vehicle. NECAR4 therefore produces no tail pipe emissions. However, fuel hydrogen must be distributed in tankers as a cryogenic liquid. Its expanded use probably would require distribution in pipelines as a gas, but few hydrogen pipelines now exist and any large-scale distribution system also would require techniques for bulk storage. Other considerations include those associated with the fact that storing hydrogen on-board the vehicle constitutes a safety hazard.

Unlike most other fuels, hydrogen cannot be produced directly by digging a mine or drilling a well; it must be extracted chemically from hydrogen-rich materials such as natural gas, water, coal or plant matter. Accounting for the energy required for the extraction process is critical in evaluating any hydrogen use option. Therefore, when considering emissions produced from vehicles such as the NECAR4, the true cost of producing hydrogen and the environmental impact of this production process must be considered. Production techniques now used include steam reforming of natural gas, cleanup of industrial by-product gases and electrolysis of water.[13]

Vehicles like the NECAR3, however, use a reformer on-board the vehicle that vaporizes methanol into hydrogen, carbon dioxide ($CO_2$) and traces of other pollutants. The drive system of the NECAR3 is virtually emission free. Neither nitrogen oxides nor soot particles are created during conversion of methanol to hydrogen or in the subsequent generation of electrical energy. Due to the efficiency of the fuel cells, DaimlerChrysler reports that $CO_2$ emissions are substantially below those of a diesel passenger car.[14]

The American Methanol Institute reports that in initial dynamometer tests, emissions from a methanol fuel cell vehicle produced no nitrogen oxide or carbon monoxide emissions. Hydrocarbon emissions were 0.005 grams per mile.[15]

## Conclusion

A combination of regulatory pressures, technological potential and old-fashioned competition has accelerated efforts to develop fuel cell vehicles. At present, fuel cell-powered vehicles are in day-to-day use in Palm Desert, California. The vehicles are fueled with commercially bottled hydrogen and used as commute vehicles and for park maintenance. Three Ballard prototype fuel cell buses are in use under a $10 million demonstration program in Chicago, Illinois.

Although fuel cells are technologically well advanced and have been used successfully to power spacecraft, the cost of a fuel cell engine per unit of horsepower is many times greater than that of an internal combustion engine. In the long-term, fuel cells may someday become competitive. However, there is no fuel cell available to economically replace the internal combustion engine in the short-term.

The most successful efforts to date have been achieved by fuel cells powered by pressurized hydrogen carried in a tank on-board a vehicle. Carrying pure hydrogen on board, however, constitutes an explosive hazard. Moreover, producing hydrogen requires a significant amount of energy, is expensive and would require a totally new refueling infrastructure.

Automakers that presently are involved in a research and development program are hopeful that fuel cells eventually may become a viable replacement of the internal combustion engine for single-occupancy vehicles. DaimlerChrysler, Ford, GM and Toyota have invested approximately $750 million in a partnership with Ballard Power Systems, the leading developer of the automotive fuel cell. However, there is no hard evidence that fuel cell vehicles can be economically mass produced in the near future.

# 6. HIGH-EFFICIENCY GASOLINE AND DIESEL VEHICLES

During the last 20 years, gasoline- and diesel-powered internal combustion engines have become cleaner and more efficient. A typical well-tuned car or truck emits about 80 percent less pollution—primarily due to the catalytic converter—than it did in the 1970s, and fuel efficiency (miles per gallon) has increased by 34 percent. Auto manufacturers continue the quest to improve the gasoline engine's efficiency and resultant emissions. The benefits of greater fuel efficiency have been offset, however, by a 50 percent increase in the total number of vehicle miles traveled and by an increase in the number of larger cars and trucks on the road.

Questions that should be asked when considering high-efficiency gasoline and diesel engines as policy options include the following.

- Is the public ready to accept the need for high-efficiency vehicles?

- What incentives can state and local governments provide to make high-efficiency vehicles attractive to the public?

- Is there any reason to promote high-efficiency vehicles as opposed to hybrid electric vehicles, or should the free market take care of this?

52

- Should there be special highway lanes for high-efficiency vehicles?

- How does the emission of pollutants within the state from new internal combustion vehicles compare with emissions from new alternative fuel vehicles?

- What are the purchase price and the total operating cost of high-efficiency internal combustion vehicles compared with alternative fuel vehicles?

- Can the state meet clean air standards without removing existing "high polluters" from the vehicle fleet?

- What policies can reduce air pollution from internal combustion engine vehicles in the short term or intermediate term?

- Are state gasoline taxes reasonable?

## History of High-Efficiency Gasoline and Diesel Vehicles

The first successful type of heat engine was the steam engine built by James Watt during the 18th century. The internal combustion engine is an improved heat engine that was made possible by advances in materials, mechanical skills and knowledge of thermodynamics.

The first practical internal combustion (IC) engine was built by the German firm of Otto and Langen in 1876; manufacture of Otto engines began in the United States in 1878 (the engine that powered the Ford Model T was quite similar to the one built by Nicholas Otto in 1876). In fact, the modern internal combustion engine that powers most of today's automobiles and buses still operates on the same principles as the Otto engine.

The only new concept to compete with the traditional internal combustion engine was the Wankel rotary engine, which was conceived in its commercial form in 1954. The rotary engine primarily was used in the Mazda RX-7 automobile; by 1987 more than 1.5 million

Wankel rotary engines had been sold. Although the rotary engine has some advantages over traditional internal combustion engines—such as fewer parts and smaller size—it does not measure up to the fuel economy of automotive spark ignition (SI) engines and, in the judgment of engineers, does not offer the potential for significant improvement.

## How Does an Internal Combustion Engine Work?

In any internal combustion engine, hot gases that result from the burning of a fuel-air mixture move a piston that generates useful work. Because the internal combustion engine is a self-contained power unit with high efficiency and small bulk, it is used widely to power automobiles, trucks and airplanes.

Examination of a four-stroke cycle illustrates the operation of an internal combustion engine. As shown in figure 13, during the intake stroke a fresh charge of air and fuel is drawn into the cylinder by the partial vacuum created during the descent of the piston. The piston then ascends on the compression stroke (with both intake and exhaust valves closed); the charge is ignited by an electric spark as the end of the stroke is approached. The power stroke follows (with both valves still closed); pressure from expansion of the ignited gas pushes the piston down and moves the crankshaft that powers the car. The exhaust stroke completes the cycle as the piston forces the product of

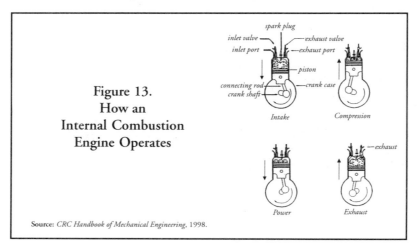

**Figure 13.
How an
Internal Combustion
Engine Operates**

Source: *CRC Handbook of Mechanical Engineering*, 1998.

combustion out of the cylinder through the exhaust valve and into the environment. This is the action that causes pollution.

The two most common reciprocating internal combustion engines are the spark ignition and the compression ignition (CI) or diesel. The basic operation of SI and CI engines has not changed fundamentally since the early 1900s, although major advances have been made in the areas of materials, manufacturing processes, electronic controls and combustion efficiency. Electronic controls, in particular, have played a major role in improving SI engine efficiency through fuel injection and ignition systems that control the combustion process.

The major difference between SI and CI engines is that, in an SI engine, the fuel is ignited by means of a spark plug, whereas in the diesel engine high compression initiates combustion. Electronic control of diesel fuel injection systems also has been commercialized recently and is producing improvements in fuel economy and reduced emissions.

SI engines can operate on a two-stroke or a four-stroke cycle. For the same speed, a two-stroke engine is smaller and lighter than a four-stroke engine of equal output, but has a lower fuel efficiency and higher exhaust emissions, because the intake and exhaust processes overlap. For these reasons, use of two-stroke SI engines has been largely confined to small displacement applications such as motorcycles and marine engines. Despite their greater emissions of noxious gases, however, two-stroke engines—because of their low initial cost—are used widely in developing countries to motorize bicycles and tricycles and have contributed greatly to the air pollution and smog problems of cities such as Bangkok and Manila.

The most common SI engine fuel is gasoline, although alcohol, natural gas and propane also can be used. Diesel fuel is the predominant fuel for CI engines, although they, too, can operate on other fuel, such as natural gas. Both gasoline and diesel fuel are distilled from crude oil.

## Table 4. Corporate Average Fuel Economy (CAFE) Standards versus Sales-Weighted Fuel Economy Estimates for Automobiles and Light Trucks, 1978-98
### (Miles per gallon)

| Model Year | Automobiles CAFE Standards | CAFE Estimates Domestic | CAFE Estimates Import | CAFE Estimates Combined | Light Trucks CAFE Standards | CAFE Estimates Domestic | CAFE Estimates Import | CAFE Estimates Combined |
|---|---|---|---|---|---|---|---|---|
| 1978 | 18.0 | 18.7 | 27.3 | 19.9 | a | b | b | b |
| 1979 | 19.0 | 19.3 | 26.1 | 20.3 | a | 17.7 | 20.8 | 18.2 |
| 1980 | 20.0 | 22.6 | 29.6 | 24.3 | a | 16.8 | 24.3 | 18.5 |
| 1981 | 22.0 | 24.2 | 31.5 | 25.9 | a | 18.3 | 27.4 | 20.1 |
| 1982 | 24.0 | 25.0 | 31.1 | 26.6 | 17.5 | 19.2 | 27.0 | 20.5 |
| 1983 | 26.0 | 24.4 | 32.4 | 26.4 | 19.0 | 19.6 | 27.1 | 20.7 |
| 1984 | 27.0 | 25.5 | 32.0 | 26.9 | 20.0 | 20.0 | 25.9 | 21.5 |
| 1985 | 27.5 | 26.3 | 31.5 | 27.6 | 19.5 | 19.6 | 26.5 | 20.7 |
| 1986 | 26.0 | 26.9 | 31.6 | 28.2 | 20.0 | 20.0 | 25.9 | 21.5 |
| 1987 | 26.0 | 27.0 | 31.2 | 28.5 | 20.5 | 20.5 | 25.2 | 21.7 |
| 1988 | 26.0 | 27.4 | 31.5 | 28.8 | 20.5 | 20.6 | 24.6 | 21.3 |
| 1989 | 26.5 | 27.2 | 30.8 | 28.4 | 20.5 | 20.4 | 23.5 | 20.9 |
| 1990 | 27.5 | 26.9 | 29.9 | 28.0 | 20.0 | 20.3 | 23.0 | 20.8 |
| 1991 | 27.5 | 27.3 | 30.0 | 28.4 | 20.2 | 20.9 | 23.0 | 20.8 |
| 1992 | 27.5 | 27.0 | 29.2 | 27.9 | 20.2 | 20.5 | 22.7 | 20.8 |
| 1993 | 27.5 | 27.8 | 29.6 | 28.4 | 20.4 | 20.7 | 22.8 | 21.0 |
| 1994 | 27.5 | 27.5 | 29.6 | 28.3 | 20.5 | 20.5 | 22.0 | 20.7 |
| 1995 | 27.5 | 27.7 | 30.3 | 28.6 | 20.6 | 20.3 | 21.5 | 20.5 |
| 1996 | 27.5 | 28.3 | 29.7 | 28.7 | 20.7 | 20.5 | 22.1 | 20.7 |
| 1997 | 27.5 | 27.9 | 29.8 | 28.6 | 20.7 | 20.1 | 22.1 | 20.4 |
| 1998 | 27.5 | 28.1 | 28.1 | 28.8 | 20.7 | 20.4 | 23.0 | 20.8 |

a Standards were set separately for two-wheel drive and four-wheel drive light trucks; no combined standard was set in this year.
b Data not available.

**Source:** U.S. Department of Transportation, National Highway Safety Administration, *Summary of Fuel Economy Performance*, Washington, D.C., March 1998 (additional resources: http://www.nhtsa.dot.gov)

# Performance

All automakers are continuously trying to improve the efficiency and fuel economy of conventional SI and CI automobiles. Table 4 shows the average estimated fuel performance of domestic and imported automobiles and light trucks for the 20-year period from 1978 to 1998, as well as the corporate average fuel economy (CAFE) standards. These data show that fuel economy for cars increased from 19.9 miles per gallon in 1978 to 28.8 miles per gallon in 1988. However, as a result of low fuel prices, a lack of increase in CAFE standards, and the demand for less fuel efficient minivans, sport utility vehicles and ever-larger trucks, the fuel economy did not change from 1988 to 1998.

A number of new technologies and engine concepts will be introduced in the very near future. These include advanced electronic controls to improve the combustion process and increase the compression ratio, use of lightweight materials to reduce mechanical friction, and oxidation catalysts and better fuel control to reduce the emission of particulates from diesel engines.

A new engine concept that promises additional benefits for SI engines is the direct injection stratified charge (DISC) engine, which injects fuel directly into the cylinder rather than premixing fuel and air as conventional engines do. The injected fuel is aimed at the spark plug, thus reducing the amount of fuel—though not the amount of air—injected into the cylinder. As a result, these engines have smaller losses and can operate at higher compression ratios. The U.S. Office of Technology Assessment (OTA) estimates that—using currently available technology—improvements in conventional engines can yield further fuel economy increases of up to 15 percent, while commercialization of DISC engines can result in 20 percent to 33 percent increases, compared to current automobile engines. These advances could increase the average fuel economy of vehicle fleets to 40 miles per gallon or more.

Diesel engines, which operate at compression ratios of approximately 20:1 (compared to a gasoline engine's 10:1) have inherently higher thermodynamic efficiencies and thus achieve better mileage than gasoline engines. They are not popular in the U.S. market because, compared with gasoline engines, they are noisier, more prone to vibration and pollute more. Although they have low hydrocarbon (HC) and carbon monoxide (CO) emissions, their nitrogen oxides ($NO_x$) and particulate emissions are relatively high. Compared with current gasoline engines, advanced diesel engine designs can yield approximately a 25 percent gain in miles per gallon (about a 12 percent gain on a fuel energy basis), while direct injection designs may yield as much as a 40 percent gain in fuel economy. The main barrier to expanded diesel use, in the eyes of manufacturers, is the difficulty of developing a suitable catalyst that can satisfy clean air regulations.

In summary, it is believed that substantial improvements in performance and fuel economy can be obtained in the near- and mid-term—without shifting to exotic technologies such as fuel cells or hybrid electric drive trains—using the existing gasoline infrastructure. Except for carbon dioxide ($CO_2$) levels, air pollution from new (1999) model vehicles is insignificant when compared to pollution from older, poorly maintained cars. Furthermore, since emission of $CO_2$ (a greenhouse gas) is virtually inversely proportional to mileage, a doubling of average automobile and truck fuel economy would automatically cut the remaining air pollution (including $CO_2$) in half.

## Cost

A 1994 evaluation by the now-defunct U.S. Office of Technology Assessment indicated that near-term technology developments could yield vehicles with fuel economy at least twice as great as today's average. Using lighter DISC engines, optimized aluminum bodies and low drag coefficient shapes, automobiles that attain approximately 53 miles per gallon at a net additional price of $1,500 are attainable. By the year 2015, the 53-mile-per-gallon advanced conventional vehicle would achieve a 64 percent fuel savings compared with today's typical 33-mile-per-gallon vehicle. By comparison, a hypothetical advanced hybrid vehicle that attains the Partnership for a New Generation of Vehicles' (PNGV) goal of 80 miles per gallon is likely to cost several thousand dollars more.

In view of the fact that internal combustion vehicles are used as the baseline for this study, their cost is reflected by the market price. The cost depends mainly on consumers' choice and varies between approximately $10,000 and $30,000. A typical "comparable gasoline-powered vehicle" in the 1999 market would cost between $15,000 and $20,000, depending on the equipment and extras selected.

Daniel Sperling estimates that the air pollution control equipment necessary to achieve compliance with new emissions regulations will cost no more than $200 extra.[1] Given the intense competition in the automotive market, any cost increases will result from consumers' preference for larger, heavier, more powerful and more accessory-laden vehicles rather than from pollution control equipment. New cars purchased in 1996, for example, were 8 percent heavier and 23 percent more powerful than they were 10 years earlier. The future of this trend may depend on the cost of gasoline, taxes and CAFE standards—matters that are under legislative control.

## Availability

Today's internal combustion engines—although basically similar to those used at the turn of the century—have continuously improved during the past 100 years in efficiency, fuel economy, power-to-weight ratio and pollution control. Availability of high-mileage, low-pollution automobiles is mostly a matter of market demand. The most efficient automobile available today (the four-door GEO sedan) can attain 56 miles per gallon. Current market demand favors large sport utility vehicles that average only about 14 to 15 miles per gallon. If federal or state regulation were to require it, however—or if consumer demand changed as a result of higher gas prices—automakers could provide cars that would achieve, on average, approximately 50 miles per gallon for SI engines and possibly an even higher amount for diesel engines. It should be kept in mind, however, that even if there were a shift in demand to higher performance vehicles or if new legislation required greater efficiency, it would take a considerable amount of time before high-efficiency vehicles would constitute an appreciable percentage of the total automobile fleet.

The car that is expected to be available by approximately 2015 that would achieve between 50 and 60 miles per gallon (for a medium-sized sedan) would require no major technical breakthroughs or innovations, but continued steady progress in the improvement of automobiles that currently are in the research and development stage. Therefore, availability of IC automobiles that can achieve high mileage and low pollution does not depend on new concepts in research and development and could be provided to consumers at a relatively modest cost.

## Environmental Impact

### Exhaust Emissions

Combustion products from internal combustion engines contain several components that are considered hazardous to human health and may contribute to global warming. Hazardous emissions include carbon monoxide (CO), unburned hydrocarbons (UHC), nitrogen oxides ($NO_x$) and particulates from diesel engines. Carbon monoxide production in SI engines results from incomplete combustion, particularly during idling, start-up, acceleration, and frequent start and stop conditions. Fuel maldistribution and poor ignition system maintenance (fouled spark plugs and improper timing) also can cause increased CO production in SI engines; this factor is less significant in diesel engines.

The principal cause of UHC in SI engines is incomplete combustion. When UHCs combine with $NO_x$ in the presence of sunlight, ozone and photochemical oxidants form that can adversely affect human health and cause smog. Certain UHCs also are considered to be carcinogenic.

Nitric oxide (NO) is formed from the combination of nitrogen and oxygen that are present in the intake air under high temperature conditions during combustion. In the presence of additional oxygen in the air, some NO transforms into toxic nitrogen dioxide ($NO_2$). The combination of NO and $NO_2$ is referred to as $NO_x$. In SI engines, $NO_x$ production is affected by the air-to-fuel ratio and spark timing.

Particulates are a troublesome constituent of diesel engine exhaust. The U.S. Environmental Protection Agency defines particulates as any exhaust substance—other than water—that can be trapped on a filter at a temperature of 325 Kelvin or below (126°F). Particulates, because of their small size, can be inhaled and entrapped in the lung walls, thus causing a health concern.

A summary of the total emissions from all U.S. transportation sources is shown in table 5. Apart from greenhouse gases, the most serious pollution comes from the EPA criteria pollutants CO, $NO_x$ and volatile organic compounds (VOC). These data include pollution from all cars on the road and do not show the enormous reductions that have been achieved during this same period in new cars (more than half the cars currently on the road are more than five years old, as shown in table 6[2]).

---

### Table 5. Total Emissions from All U.S. Transportation Needs

Transportation share of carbon dioxide emissions from fossil fuel consumption (in percent):

| | |
|---|---|
| 1984 | 30.5 |
| 1990 | 32.1 |
| 1996 | 32.1 |

Percentage share of carbon dioxide emissions from transportation energy use (1996):

| | |
|---|---|
| Motor gasoline | 61.1 |
| Liquified petroleum gas | 0.1 |
| Jet fuel | 13.4 |
| Distillate fuel | 18.8 |
| Residual fuel | 3.7 |
| Lubricants | 0.3 |
| Aviation gas | 0.1 |
| Natural gas | 2.2 |
| Electricity | 0.1 |

Percentage share of transportation-generated emissions of criteria pollutants (1996):

| | |
|---|---|
| Carbon monoxide | 78.7 |
| Nitrogen oxides | 50.4 |
| Volatile organic compounds | 41.5 |
| PM-10 | 2.8 |
| Lead | 14.6 |

Source: U.S. Department of Energy, 1998.

---

## Table 6. Distribution of Vehicles by Vehicle Age and Household Vehicle Ownership (1994)

| Vehicle age (years) | One-vehicle households | Two-vehicle households | Three-vehicle households | Four-vehicle households | Five-vehicle households | Total |
|---|---|---|---|---|---|---|
| **Vehicle 1** | | | | | | |
| New | 1.45 | 2.28 | 0.76 | 0.56 | 0.14 | 5.23 |
| 2-5 | 5.81 | 8.18 | 3.97 | 1.34 | 0.56 | 20.10 |
| 6-10 | 7.02 | 8.49 | 4.06 | 1.69 | 0.44 | 21.84 |
| 11-15 | 2.54 | 2.58 | 1.46 | 0.42 | 0.12 | 7.17 |
| 16-20 | 1.20 | 0.98 | 0.57 | 0.17 | 0.14 | 3.09 |
| 21 + | 0.46 | 0.35 | 0.16 | 0.03 | 0.02 | 1.05 |
| **Vehicle 2** | | | | | | |
| New | | 1.11 | 0.35 | 0.25 | 0.05 | 1.84 |
| 2-5 | | 4.45 | 2.88 | 1.05 | 0.26 | 8.80 |
| 6-10 | | 6.29 | 3.72 | 1.79 | 0.61 | 12.46 |
| 11-15 | | 2.55 | 1.59 | 0.51 | 0.19 | 4.96 |
| 16-20 | | 1.28 | 0.62 | 0.20 | 0.08 | 2.19 |
| 21 + | | 1.02 | 0.42 | 0.10 | 0.00 | 1.60 |
| **Vehicle 3** | | | | | | |
| New | | | 0.13 | 0.06 | 0.02 | 0.21 |
| 2-5 | | | 1.06 | 0.47 | 0.21 | 1.82 |
| 6-10 | | | 1.00 | 0.97 | 0.34 | 2.45 |
| 11-15 | | | 0.85 | 0.49 | 0.10 | 1.47 |
| 16-20 | | | 0.66 | 0.21 | 0.14 | 1.01 |
| 21 + | | | 0.40 | 0.26 | 0.10 | 0.85 |
| **Vehicle 4** | | | | | | |
| New | | | | 0.02 | 0.00 | 0.02 |
| 2-5 | | | | 0.28 | 0.02 | 0.36 |
| 6-10 | | | | 0.14 | 0.05 | 0.29 |
| 11-15 | | | | 0.15 | 0.23 | 0.42 |
| 16-20 | | | | 0.12 | 0.12 | 0.30 |
| 21 + | | | | 0.15 | 0.08 | 0.27 |
| **Vehicle 5** | | | | | | |
| New | | | | | 0.00 | 0.03 |
| 6-10 | | | | | 0.02 | 0.05 |
| 11-15 | | | | | 0.00 | 0.05 |
| 21 + | | | | | 0.03 | 0.07 |
| Percent Totals | 18.47 | 39.57 | 24.65 | 11.44 | 4.07 | 100.00 |

Source: U.S. Department of Energy, 1997.

These overall statistics—compiled in the *1998 Transportation Energy Data Book*—show that $CO_2$ emissions in the period from 1989 to 1996 have increased from 30.5 percent to 32.1 percent of total fossil fuel emissions. During the same period, the energy consumption of the transportation sector increased from 19.8 quadrillion Btus to 24.6 quadrillion Btus, or from 26.7 percent to 27.4 percent of total U.S. energy consumption, as shown in table 7.[3]

| Table 7. U.S. Consumption of Total Energy by End-Use Sector, 1970-97* (quadrillion Btu) | | | | | |
|---|---|---|---|---|---|
| Year | Transportation | Transportation's percentage of total | Residential and commercial | Industrial | Total |
| 1970 | 16.07 | 24.2% | 21.71 | 28.65 | 66.43 |
| 1971 | 16.70 | 24.6 | 22.59 | 28.59 | 67.88 |
| 1972 | 17.70 | 24.8 | 23.69 | 29.88 | 71.27 |
| 1973 | 18.61 | 25.1 | 24.14 | 31.53 | 74.28 |
| 1974 | 18.12 | 25.0 | 23.73 | 30.69 | 72.54 |
| 1975 | 18.24 | 25.9 | 23.90 | 28.40 | 70.54 |
| 1976 | 19.10 | 25.7 | 25.02 | 30.24 | 74.36 |
| 1977 | 19.82 | 26.0 | 25.39 | 31.08 | 76.29 |
| 1978 | 20.61 | 26.4 | 26.08 | 31.39 | 78.09 |
| 1979 | 20.47 | 25.9 | 25.81 | 32.62 | 78.90 |
| 1980 | 19.70 | 25.9 | 25.66 | 30.61 | 75.96 |
| 1981 | 19.51 | 26.4 | 25.24 | 29.24 | 73.99 |
| 1982 | 19.07 | 26.9 | 25.63 | 26.15 | 70.85 |
| 1983 | 19.13 | 27.1 | 25.63 | 25.76 | 70.52 |
| 1984 | 19.80 | 26.7 | 26.47 | 27.87 | 74.14 |
| 1985 | 20.07 | 27.1 | 26.70 | 27.21 | 73.98 |
| 1986 | 20.81 | 28.0 | 26.85 | 26.63 | 74.30 |
| 1987 | 21.45 | 27.9 | 27.62 | 27.83 | 76.89 |
| 1988 | 22.31 | 27.8 | 28.93 | 28.99 | 80.22 |
| 1989 | 22.56 | 27.7 | 29.40 | 29.35 | 81.33 |
| 1990 | 22.54 | 27.7 | 28.79 | 29.94 | 81.27 |
| 1991 | 22.12 | 27.3 | 29.42 | 29.57 | 81.12 |
| 1992 | 22.46 | 27.3 | 29.11 | 30.58 | 82.15 |
| 1993 | 22.88 | 27.3 | 30.24 | 30.75 | 83.87 |
| 1994 | 23.57 | 27.5 | 30.44 | 31.59 | 85.60 |
| 1995 | 24.07 | 27.6 | 31.27 | 31.86 | 87.21 |
| 1996 | 24.63 | 27.4 | 32.63 | 32.74 | 90.04 |
| 1997 | 24.78 | 27.4 | 32.83 | 32.92 | 90.59 |
| *Average annual percentage change* | | | | | |
| 1970-97 | 1.6% | | 1.5% | 0.5% | 1.2% |
| 1987-97 | 1.5 | | 1.7 | 1.7 | 1.7 |

*Electrical energy losses have been distributed among the sectors.

Source: U.S. Department of Energy, Energy Information Administration, *Monthly Energy Review*, March 1998.

To plan an effective and economical emission control strategy, it is important to know the distribution of emissions from all the vehicles currently on the road. Figures 14, 15 and 16 show the percentage of CO, NO$_x$ and UHC emissions as a function of percentage of a com-

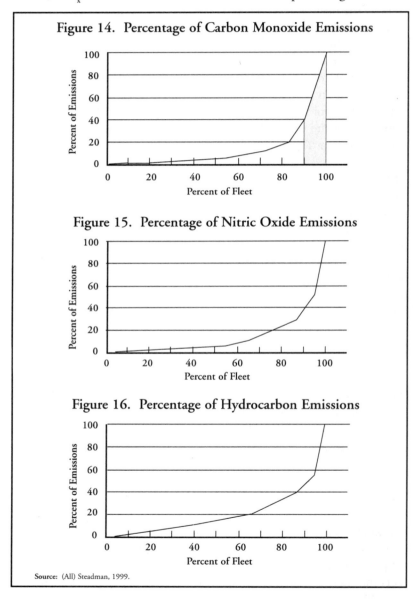

Figure 14. Percentage of Carbon Monoxide Emissions

Figure 15. Percentage of Nitric Oxide Emissions

Figure 16. Percentage of Hydrocarbon Emissions

Source: (All) Steadman, 1999.

mon fleet of consumer-owned vehicles. These measurements were taken in 1997 using remote sensing of 18,000 vehicles in Chicago. To understand the significance of these data, consider the graph for carbon monoxide in figure 14. If a vertical line is drawn at 90 percent of the fleet, it intersects the experimental curve at 40 percent of emissions. This means that if the worst 10 percent of polluters (100 percent to 90 percent of the fleet) were removed from the road, emissions of the pollutant CO would decrease by 60 percent (100 percent to 40 percent of emissions), a result that is shown graphically by the highlighting in figure 14. Similar reduction in the pollutants $NO_x$ and UHC would result if the 10 percent of worst polluters were removed from the vehicle fleet.[4] Appendix D presents additional information regarding this strategic approach to controlling emissions.

It is important to note that the emissions data cited above were obtained by means of remote sensing, because many extreme polluters have passed stationary emissions tests that are performed in accordance with existing regulations. Remote sensing systems are capable of measuring CO and UHC emissions in less than a second as a vehicle passes the sensor. The instrument—a nondispersive infrared detector that simulates the emission reading one would obtain from a traditional exhaust analysis machine—simultaneously records the vehicle's license plate. The cost per measurement is a fraction of that incurred by a conventional test and gives results under real driving conditions. Appendix D presents more information about remote emission sensing.

Given that 90 percent of all cars contribute less than 50 percent of total pollution (and 80 percent of cars contribute less than 30 percent of pollution), an important consideration arises: any effective pollution control program must target gross polluters—which are mostly older and poorly maintained vehicles—rather than new vehicles that do not emit appreciable amounts of pollutants. The pollution attributed to the cleanest 20 percent of cars is less than 5 percent of the total, irrespective of whether the vehicles are fueled by gasoline or any of the alternative fuels. It would, therefore, be prudent to target gross polluters in state programs that are designed to improve air quality instead of emphasizing controls on clean new cars that may become polluters if they are not properly maintained.

Overall, conversion of light duty vehicles to alternative fuels is more expensive and less effective in reducing pollutant emissions than vehicle repair and proper tuning of gross polluting vehicles.

## Controlling Exhaust Emissions Using the Catalytic Converter

The most important emission control device is the catalytic converter, heralded as the main reason that vehicle emissions have declined. Catalytic converters use a catalyst—usually platinum or palladium—to promote reactions at lower temperatures. Many newer SI engines contain a three-way catalytic converter, which permits the treatment of $NO_x$, CO and hydrocarbons in a single device. Maintaining the proper effectiveness of three-way catalytic converters requires monitoring for excess oxygen and controlling the fuel injection. When these monitoring systems are not in good condition or fail, three-way catalytic converters become ineffective.

CI engines operate on a fuel mixture that contains more air than the mixture used in SI engines. For this reason, CI engines cannot use three-way catalytic converters. Instead, they use oxidation catalytic converters to treat CO and hydrocarbons. Particulates and $NO_x$ must be treated in the exhaust system by filters. The lean fuel mixture has an advantage, however, because it aids in the reduction of CO and hydrocarbons. This explains why CI engines generally emit less CO and hydrocarbons—but more $NO_x$ and particulates—than SI engines.

High sulfur content in gasoline fuel limits the effectiveness of catalytic converters. Sulfur inhibits the reaction of hydrocarbons, CO and $NO_x$. Current federal law limits sulfur content in gasoline to 330 parts per million (ppm) by weight, but this law is outdated because catalytic converter technology is much more effective for lower levels of sulfur content.

Table 8 shows emissions levels for different sulfur concentrations. It explains the effect of sulfur concentration in fuel on LEV cars and large passenger trucks that weigh between 3,751 pounds and 5,750 pounds.

**Table 8. Estimated Emissions of LEVs with Increased Concentrations of Sulfur in Fuel (in parts per million [ppm])**

| Pollutant | Carbon Monoxide | | | Nitrogen Oxide | | |
|---|---|---|---|---|---|---|
| Sulfur Concentration in Fuel | 40 ppm | 150 ppm | 330 ppm | 40 ppm | 150 ppm | 330 ppm |
| Cars and Light-Duty Trucks | 4.2 | 6.6 | 7.4 | 0.30 | 0.50 | 0.71 |
| Larger Passenger Trucks | 5.5 | 6.2 | 7.2 | 0.50 | 0.67 | 0.83 |

Source: EPA Staff Paper: *Gasoline Sulfur*, 1996.

In response to these results, the state of California and cities such as Atlanta, Georgia, and Birmingham, Alabama, have enacted more stringent gasoline sulfur requirements. California sets sulfur concentrations at a maximum level of 80 ppm, with an average of 30 ppm. The next phase of the national reformulated gasoline standards—to be implemented in 2000—requires sulfur levels to average 150 ppm.

## Conclusion

Technical improvements have reduced air polluting emissions from new IC engine vehicles enormously at reasonable costs; even greater reductions are imminent. In addition, the improved fuel economy of new cars can have a positive effect in controlling greenhouse gas emissions—such as carbon dioxide ($CO_2$)—through a more efficient combustion process. $CO_2$ emissions for a given fuel are directly proportional to fuel consumption and cannot be reduced by control devices such as catalytic converters. The emission of $CO_2$ can be reduced only by increasing the vehicular mileage (miles per gallon), reducing vehicle travel in SOVs, or switching to fuels such as natural gas. None of these measures have been successfully implemented.

So long as gasoline prices remain low, there is no economic incentive fuel economy have largely been offset by increased travel and a shift from small economical cars to large, heavy sport utility vehicles and trucks that average only 15 miles per gallon or less. The high price of gasoline in other industrialized countries, as shown in table 9, is due largely to higher gasoline taxes in those countries. Table 10 presents gasoline taxes assessed in the United States, but there is no clear evidence that higher gas prices alone can dissuade people from using their cars.

In today's market, fuel economy is less valued than comfort, safety and performance. Car buyers seem to pay little attention to emission characteristics and generally are influenced by purchase price rather than fuel cost. Clean air regulations and increased gasoline prices, however, can significantly change this.

Extensive studies have shown that about 50 percent of the vehicular pollution that causes smog and haze in urban areas is generated by fewer than 10 percent of the worst polluting vehicles; similarly, 80 percent of the pollution is caused by 20 percent of the high-polluting vehicles. Efforts to improve air quality by imposing exhaust limits on new cars and trucks therefore cannot achieve significant results in the short-term unless they are combined with policies that will remove the heavy polluters from the road. State and local governments may want to consider assistance programs for repairs and engine tuning or buy-back programs of polluters, as well as the use of remote sensing systems for easy and economical identification of the polluting vehicles to improve air quality in the short-term. In addition, states must work with the federal government to create procedures to reduce fuel consumption in order to reduce emissions of greenhouse gases. Overall, reducing pollution and gas consumption in the short-term may be made easier and less expensive by supporting improvements of IC engine vehicles than by shifting to exotic alternative fuel vehicle technology. However, some of the necessary legislative steps—such as tightening the CAFE standards and increasing the gasoline tax—may be politically unpopular because they require changes in consumer choice, driver behavior and tax structure.

## Table 9. Gasoline Prices for Selected Countries, 1978-97

| | Current dollars per gallon | | | | | | | | | Average annual percentage change | |
|---|---|---|---|---|---|---|---|---|---|---|---|
| | 1978[a] | 1982[a] | 1986[a] | 1990[b] | 1992[b] | 1994[b] | 1995[b] | 1996[b] | 1997[b] | 1978-97 | 1990-97 |
| China | d | d | d | d | d | d | $1.08 | $0.93[c] | d | d | d |
| India | d | d | d | d | d | d | 2.32 | 2.25[c] | d | d | d |
| Japan | $2.00[c] | $2.60[c] | $2.79[c] | $3.05[c] | $2.59 | $2.28 | 4.56 | 3.77 | $3.28[c] | 2.6% | 1.0% |
| France | 2.15 | 2.56 | 2.58 | 3.40 | 3.69 | 4.14 | 4.02 | 4.41 | 4.22 | 3.6 | 3.1 |
| United Kingdom | 1.22 | 2.42 | 2.07 | 2.55 | 3.28 | 3.31 | 3.21 | 3.47 | 4.25 | 6.8 | 7.6 |
| Germany | 1.75 | 2.17 | 1.88 | 2.72 | 3.84 | 3.34 | 3.91 | 4.32 | 3.87 | 4.3 | 5.2 |
| Canada | 0.69[c] | 1.37[c] | 1.31[c] | 1.92[c] | 2.11[c] | 1.57 | 1.68 | 1.80 | 1.92 | 5.5 | 0.0 |
| United States | 0.66[c] | 1.32[c] | 0.93[c] | 1.04[c] | 1.07[c] | 1.24 | 1.32 | 1.28 | 1.42 | 4.1 | 4.5 |

*Note:* Comparisons between prices and price trends in different countries require care. They are of limited validity because of fluctuations in exchange rates; differences in product quality, marketing practices and market structures; and the extent to which the standard categories of sales are representative of total national sales for a given period.

a  Prices represent the retail prices (including taxes) for premium leaded gasoline. Prices are representative for each country based on quarterly data averaged for the year.

b  Prices represent the retail prices (including taxes) for premium gasoline on January 1 of the year, or the available time period closest to January 1.

c  Regular gasoline.

d  Data are not available.

e  These estimates are for international comparisons only and do not necessarily correspond to gasoline price estimates in other sections of the book.

**Source:** U.S. Department of Energy, Energy Information Administration, *International Energy Annual 1996.* (Additional resources: http://www.eia.doe.gov).

## Table 10. State Motor Fuel Taxes, 1998
### (dollars per gallon or gasoline equivalent gallon)

| State/Jurisdiction | Gasoline | Diesel fuel | Gasohol | CNG | Propane | Methanol | Ethanol |
|---|---|---|---|---|---|---|---|
| Alabama | $0.16 | $0.17 | $0.16 | a | a | $0.16[b] | $0.16[b] |
| Alaska | 0.08 | 0.08 | 0.08[c] | $0.08 | $0.00 | 0.08[b] | 0.08[b] |
| Arizona | 0.18 | 0.18 | 0.00 | 0.10[d] | 0.18 | 0.18 | 0.00 |
| Arkansas | 0.185 | 0.185 | 0.185 | 0.05[e] | 0.165 | 0.185 | 0.185 |
| California | 0.18 | 0.18 | 0.18 | 0.07 | 0.06 | 0.09 | 0.09 |
| Colorado | 0.22 | 0.205 | 0.22 | 0.205 | 0.205 | 0.205 | 0.205 |
| Connecticut | 0.39 | 0.18 | 0.38 | 0.18[f] | 0.18[f] | 0.37b | 0.37b |
| Delaware | 0.23 | 0.22 | 0.23 | 0.22 | 0.22 | 0.22 | 0.23 |
| District of Columbia | 0.20 | 0.20 | 0.20 | 0.20 | 0.20 | 0.20 | 0.20 |
| Florida | 0.04 | 0.04 | 0.04 | a | a | 0.04[b] | 0.04[b] |
| Georgia | 0.075 | 0.075 | 0.075 | 0.075 | 0.075 | 0.075 | 0.075 |
| Hawaii (Honolulu)[g] | 0.325 | 0.325 | 0.325 | 0.325 | 0.22 | 0.325 | 0.325 |
| Idaho | 0.25 | 0.25 | 0.25 | 0.197[h] | 0.181 | 0.25b | 0.25[b] |
| Illinois | 0.19 | 0.215 | 0.19 | 0.19 | 0.19 | 0.19b | 0.19[b] |
| Indiana | 0.15 | 0.16 | 0.15 | a | a | 0.15 | 0.15 |
| Iowa | 0.20 | 0.225 | 0.19 | 0.16[c] | 0.20 | 0.19[b] | 0.19[b] |
| Kansas | 0.18 | 0.20 | 0.18 | 0.17 | 0.17 | 0.20 | 0.20 |
| Kentucky | 0.15 | 0.12 | 0.15 | 0.12 | 0.15 | 0.15 | 0.15 |
| Louisiana | 0.20 | 0.20 | 0.20 | 0.16[i] | 0.16[i] | 0.20b | 0.20[b] |
| Maine | 0.19 | 0.20 | 0.19 | 0.18 | 0.18 | 0.18 | 0.18 |
| Maryland | 0.235 | 0.2425 | 0.235 | 0.235 | 0.235 | 0.235 | 0.235 |

## Table 10. State Motor Fuel Taxes, 1998 (continued)
### (dollars per gallon or gasoline equivalent gallon)

| State/Jurisdiction | Gasoline | Diesel fuel | Gasohol | CNG | Propane | Methanol | Ethanol |
|---|---|---|---|---|---|---|---|
| Massachusetts | $0.21 | $0.21 | $0.21 | $0.089 | $0.089 | $0.21 | $0.21 |
| Michigan | 0.15 | 0.15 | 0.15 | 0.0 | 0.15 | 0.15[b] | 0.025[b] |
| Minnesota | 0.20 | 0.20 | 0.20 | 0.001739[i] | 0.15 | NA | 0.20[b] |
| Mississippi | 0.18 | 0.18 | 0.18 | 0.18[c] | 0.17 | 0.18[b] | 0.18[b] |
| Missouri | 0.17 | 0.17 | 0.17 | a | a | 0.17[b] | 0.17[b] |
| Montana | 0.27 | 0.2775 | 0.27 | | a | 0.27 | 0.27 |
| Nebraska | 0.253 | 0.253 | 0.253 | 0.253 | 0.253 | 0.253 | 0.253[b] |
| Nevada | 0.23 | 0.27 | 0.23 | 0.23[c] | 0.23[c] | 0.23 | 0.23 |
| New Hampshire | 0.18 | 0.18 | 0.18 | 0.18 | 0.18 | 0.18[b] | 0.18[b] |
| New Jersey | 0.105 | 0.135 | 0.105 | 0.0525 | 0.0525 | 0.105[b] | 0.105[b] |
| New Mexico | 0.22 | 0.18 | 0.22 | 0.03[i] | 0.03[i] | 0.22[b] | 0.22[b] |
| New York | 0.08[l] | 0.10[l] | 0.08[l] | 0.08[l] | 0.08[l] | 0.08[l] | 0.08[l] |
| North Carolina | 0.217 | 0.217 | 0.217 | 0.217 | 0.217 | 0.217 | 0.217 |
| North Dakota | 0.20 | 0.20 | 0.20 | 0.20 | 0.20 | 0.20[b] | 0.20[b] |
| Ohio | 0.22 | 0.22 | 0.22 | 0.22 | 0.22 | 0.22[b] | 0.22[b] |
| Oklahoma | 0.16 | 0.13 | 0.16 | a | 0.16 | 0.16[b] | 0.16[b] |
| Oregon | 0.24 | 0.24 | 0.24 | 0.24 | 0.24 | 0.24 | 0.24 |
| Pennsylvania | 0.12[m] | 0.12[m] | 0.12[m] | 0.12[m] | 0.12[m] | 0.12[m] | 0.12[m] |
| Rhode Island | 0.28 | 0.28 | 0.28 | 0.0 | 0.28 | 0.28 | 0.28 |
| South Carolina | 0.16 | 0.16 | 0.16 | 0.16 | 0.16 | 0.16 | 0.16 |
| South Dakota | 0.18 | 0.18 | 0.16 | 0.06 | 0.16 | 0.06 | 0.06 |

## Table 10. State Motor Fuel Taxes, 1998 (continued)
### (dollars per gallon or gasoline equivalent gallon)

| State/Jurisdiction | Gasoline | Diesel fuel | Gasohol | CNG | Propane | Methanol | Ethanol |
|---|---|---|---|---|---|---|---|
| Tennessee | $0.20 | $0.17 | $0.17 | $0.13 | $0.17 | $0.17 | $0.17 |
| Texas | 0.20 | 0.20 | 0.20 | 0.15 | 0.15 | 0.20b | 0.20b |
| Utah | 0.19 | 0.19 | 0.19 | 0.19m | 0.19m | 0.19 | 0.19 |
| Vermont | 0.16 | 0.17 | 0.16 | 0.16 | a | 0.16 | 0.16 |
| Virginia | 0.175 | 0.16 | 0.175 | 0.10 | 0.10 | 0.175b | 0.175b |
| Washington | 0.23 | 0.23 | 0.23 | a | a | 0.23 | 0.23 |
| West Virginia | 0.205 | 0.205 | 0.205 | 0.205 | 0.205 | 0.205 | 0.205 |
| Wisconsin | 0.237 | 0.237 | 0.237 | 0.237 | 0.237 | 0.237 | 0.237 |
| Wyoming | 0.08 | 0.08 | 0.00 | 0.00 | 0.00 | 0.08b | 0.08b |

a Annual flat fee.
b Blends with gasoline only.
c November-February tax rate is $0.02.
d Per 1.25 therm.
e Per 100 cubic feet.
f CNG, LNG and LPG are exempt from motor fuel taxes when used as a vehicle fuel until July 1, 2001.
g For County of Honolulu; for County of Maui, LPG tax is $0.20 per gallon and all other fuels are taxed at $0.18 per gallon; other counties have all fuels taxed at $0.26 per gallon.
h Per therm.
i Optional; flat fee may be paid instead.
j Per cubic foot; LNG is taxed at $0.12 per gallon.
k Per 120 cubic feet.
l Plus a petroleum business tax; the amount varies but is usually approximately $0.12 to $0.14.
m Plus 0.1035 oil franchise tax.

**Source:** J.E. Sinor Consultants Inc., 1998.

# 7. ALTERNATIVE FUEL VEHICLES

Internal combustion engines can be powered by many different fuels, including ethanol, methanol, natural gas in either compressed (CNG) or liquid (LNG) form, hydrogen and reformulated gasoline. During oil shortages—such as, for example, during World War II—even wood and coal have been used as fuels. Recently, interest in alternative fuels (other than gasoline or diesel) for automobiles and light trucks in the United States has increased because of the potential of alternative fuels to ameliorate three problems: 1) unhealthy levels of ozone in urban areas, 2) growing dependence on imported oil, and 3) rising emissions of carbon dioxide and other greenhouse gases from cars and trucks.

Predictions by the U.S. Department of Energy (DOE) in the early 1990s indicated a high potential for the use of alternative fuels in the United States. To date, however, the transportation sector has barely begun to realize their potential. The International Energy Agency (IEA) estimated that the actual use of alternative fuels in 1996 was about 4.6 billion gallons of gasoline equivalent, or approximately 3 percent of the total fuel use for highway transportation. Of this total, 4.2 billion equivalent gallons consisted of oxygenates blended into gasoline, and only 323 million equivalent gallons—or 0.2 percent of all fuel used on highways—were alternative fuels used by alternative fuel vehicles.

Questions that legislators and other policymakers should consider regarding the use of alternative fuel vehicles in their state include the following.

- Is my state in compliance with sections from the Energy Policy Act of 1992 (EPACT)—that require a percentage of all new vehicle acquisitions by specific federal, state and alternative fuel provider fleets to be alternatively fueled?

- If my state is not in compliance with EPACT regarding alternative fuel vehicles, why not?

- What is the primary reason for advancing the use of alternative fuel vehicles in my state—air pollution or energy dependence?

- Are alternative fuel vehicles the best available transportation option to curb air pollution?

- How effective have incentives been in facilitating the purchase and encouraging the use of alternative fuel vehicles? (Appendices E and F present a compendium of federal and state alternative fuel vehicle incentives and regulations.)

## History of Alternative Fuel Vehicles

Since the passage of the 1990 Clean Air Act Amendments (CAAA) and subsequent alternative fuel vehicle (AFV) mandates, AFVs have received considerable attention from state and municipal government agencies, auto manufacturers and fleet operators. It appears, however, that the general public to date has not accepted AFVs. Manufacturers have produced several AFV models in search of the right combination of price, comfort, power, emissions and energy consumption. As shown in table 11, however, of a total 160 million cars on the road in 1998, approximately 400,000 (less than 0.3 percent) were AFVs.[1]

## Table 11. Estimates of Alternative Fuel Vehicles on the Road, 1994, 1996 and 1998

| Fuel Type | Private 1994 | Private 1996 | Private 1998* | State and Local Government 1994 | State and Local Government 1996 | State and Local Government 1998* | Federal Government 1994 | Federal Government 1996 | Federal Government 1998* |
|---|---|---|---|---|---|---|---|---|---|
| LPG a | 169,000 | 167,000 | 178,000 | 43,000 | 43,000 | 45,000 | 33 | 193 | 380 |
| b | 42,000 | 43,000 | 45,000 | 10,000 | 10,000 | 11,000 | 2 | 2 | 2 |
| CNG a | 21,496 | 25,020 | 37,755 | 7,452 | 11,305 | 16,823 | 7,022 | 13,945 | 14,156 |
| b | 2,935 | 5,485 | 9,104 | 2,322 | 4,389 | 7,284 | 0 | 0 | 0 |
| LNG a | 27 | 10 | 12 | 32 | 45 | 74 | 35 | 72 | 181 |
| b | 12 | 77 | 136 | 378 | 453 | 727 | 0 | 6 | 6 |
| M-85 a | 2,675 | 6,633 | 9,302 | 2,410 | 5,958 | 7,329 | 9,291 | 7,668 | 4,733 |
| b | 0 | 0 | 0 | 108 | 6 | 6 | 0 | 0 | 0 |
| M100 a | 0 | 0 | 0 | 0 | 0 | 0 | 0 | 0 | 0 |
| b | 1 | 0 | 0 | 414 | 172 | 172 | 0 | 0 | 0 |
| E-85 a | 58 | 793 | 1,906 | 408 | 1,995 | 4,830 | 139 | 1,748 | 4,136 |
| b | 0 | 0 | 0 | 0 | 0 | 0 | 0 | 0 | 0 |
| E-95 a | 1 | 0 | 0 | 1 | 0 | 0 | 0 | 0 | 0 |
| b | 5 | 4 | 0 | 26 | 357 | 357 | 0 | 0 | 0 |
| Electricity a | 2,047 | 2,451 | 3,398 | 14 | 487 | 764 | 102 | 188 | 400 |
| b | 8 | 32 | 42 | 53 | 113 | 148 | 0 | 9 | 9 |
| Total a | 195,304 | 201,907 | 230,373 | 53,317 | 62,790 | 74,820 | 16,622 | 23,814 | 23,986 |
| b | 44,961 | 48,598 | 54,282 | 13,301 | 15,490 | 19,694 | 2 | 17 | 17 |

a = Light-duty vehicles; b = Heavy-duty vehicles

*Based on plans or projections.

Source: U.S. Department of Energy, Energy Information Administration, *Alternatives to Traditional Transportation Fuels, 1996,* Washington, D.C., December 1997, pp. 16-18.

In 1992, Congress passed the Energy Policy Act (EPACT) that, under section 502-b-2, set a goal of displacing 10 percent of petroleum-based transportation fuels with alternatives by the year 2000, and increasing this to 30 percent by the year 2010. The U.S. Department of Energy (DOE) supports and coordinates AFV acquisition for the federal fleet program; by the beginning of 1996, this effort had placed more than 20,000 AFVs in the federal fleet. DOE's Clean Cities program promotes voluntary commitment and coordinated action by several groups of participating city regions for installation of alternative fuel infrastructure and acquisition of vehicles. By fall 1996, 50 cities and more than 1,000 stakeholder organizations were participating in the program. Although it is too early to reliably assess the success of these programs, progress to date on meeting the goal of displacing 10 percent of conventional transportation fuels in the year 2000 is not encouraging. To meet this goal would have required that AFV sales increase to between 35 percent and 40 percent of total new light vehicle sales between 1995 and 1999; these levels of sales have not been achieved. To reach a 30 percent level of displacement by the year 2010, annual AFV sales would have to comprise 30 percent to 40 percent of total vehicle sales; so far, public acceptance of alternative fuel vehicles has not been sufficient to even begin to meet these goals.

It is believed that enormous changes in the economics of AFVs—as well as improved access to alternative fuel stations and convenience of AFV operation—are necessary conditions for increased public acceptance of AFVs. Major changes in tax policies and air pollution regulations also would be necessary.

## How Does an Alternative Fuel Vehicle Work?

AFVs use an internal combustion engine to generate power just like gasoline vehicles do. Some minor modifications must be made, however. For example, figure 17 shows the components that typically are added or changed to convert a gasoline vehicle to one that can use compressed natural gas. The major challenge is to find adequate space for the large number of gas cylinders needed to achieve a range comparable to gasoline powered vehicles.[2]

## Figure 17. Typical Components of a Compressed Natural Gas Vehicle

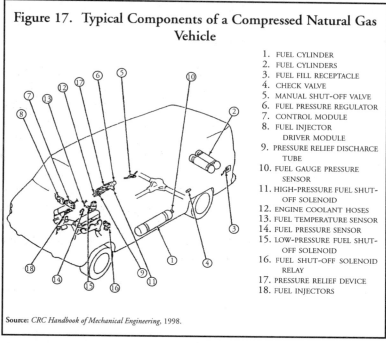

1. FUEL CYLINDER
2. FUEL CYLINDERS
3. FUEL FILL RECEPTACLE
4. CHECK VALVE
5. MANUAL SHUT-OFF VALVE
6. FUEL PRESSURE REGULATOR
7. CONTROL MODULE
8. FUEL INJECTOR DRIVER MODULE
9. PRESSURE RELIEF DISCHARCE TUBE
10. FUEL GAUGE PRESSURE SENSOR
11. HIGH-PRESSURE FUEL SHUT-OFF SOLENOID
12. ENGINE COOLANT HOSES
13. FUEL TEMPERATURE SENSOR
14. FUEL PRESSURE SENSOR
15. LOW-PRESSURE FUEL SHUT-OFF SOLENOID
16. FUEL SHUT-OFF SOLENOID RELAY
17. PRESSURE RELIEF DEVICE
18. FUEL INJECTORS

Source: *CRC Handbook of Mechanical Engineering*, 1998.

In light-duty "flexible-fueled" or "variable-fueled" vehicles, ethanol and methanol are blended with gasoline in the vehicle's fuel tank. The car can be fueled on any mix of the specified alcohol and gasoline up to 85 percent alcohol. For example, an ethanol flexible-fueled vehicle (FFV) could be fueled on 85 percent ethanol (E85) at one refueling and on pure gasoline at the next. A sensor in the fuel line constantly measures the percentage of ethanol or methanol in the fuel and the engine control system adjusts the air/fuel ratio accordingly. All components in the fuel system must be compatible with ethanol or methanol. The fuel injectors must have a higher flow capacity to account for the lower heating value of ethanol and methanol compared to gasoline and the gaskets must be able to resist the corrosive action of the alcohol.

## Performance

Each of the alternative fuels currently under consideration has advantages and disadvantages from a technical and political perspective.  The main drawback of all alternative fuels compared to gasoline is the larger volume required for fuel storage to deliver the same range.  Furthermore, the alcohols are corrosives and are easily contaminated by water.  The gaseous alternative fuels cannot be poured into a tank in open air.  Natural gas requires a large high-pressure tank that is expensive and space-consuming in the vehicle. Table 12 provides a brief overview for the advantages and disadvantages of the alternative fuels specified as meeting the requirements of the federal laws and regulations requiring states to purchase "alternative fuel vehicles" for their fleets.

Natural gas, methanol, ethanol and propane are the most widely used gasoline substitutes used to meet federal regulations that require the use of alternative fuels, although the use of methanol as an alternative fuel option is dwindling.  Each has advantages and disadvantages when used as a fuel in an internal combustion engine.

A comparison of the operating performance of alternative fuels with gasoline is presented in table 13.

The use of alternative fuels such as ethanol and methanol require some changes in the design of vehicle engines to ameliorate problems related to cold weather starting, vapor lock and cold engine driveability. Experience also has shown that the cost of maintenance is higher for engines that use ethanol and methanol than it is for engines that use gasoline.

## Table 12. Advantages and Disadvantages of Alternative Fuels

| Fuel | Advantages | Disadvantages |
|---|---|---|
| **Liquefied Petroleum Gas (LPG)** Liquefied petroleum gas is the most widely used alternative fuel. In the United States, LPG is mostly propane with small amounts of butane and ethane. In 1993, an estimated 350,000 vehicles powered by propane (mostly conversions) were plying the nation's highways. | • Most widely available alternative fuel with an estimated 11,000 refueling sites nationwide.<br>• LPG is nontoxic.<br>• Liquefies at relatively low pressures<br>• One gallon of liquefied propane has about 70 percent of the energy content of gasoline.<br>• Can reduce carbon monoxide and ozone forming hydrocarbon emissions.<br>• Refueling stations are relatively inexpensive. | • 45 percent of LPG in the United States is derived from oil.<br>• Proper detection and ventilation are required for indoor storage and maintenance of vehicles.<br>• Starting problems may occur at very low temperatures due to low vapor pressure.<br>• Perception of a safety problem. |
| **Compressed Natural Gas (CNG)** Natural gas is composed primarily of methane. It is stored on the vehicle under 3,000 to 4,000 pounds per square inch of pressure. An estimated 50,000 vehicles currently are operating on CNG in U.S. fleets. | • High North American resource base.<br>• Natural gas reserves are more globally distributed than oil reserves.<br>• Can reduce all regulated emissions.<br>• Is especially effective in reducing particulate emissions from large trucks.<br>• Less expensive than gasoline.<br>• Eliminates evaporative emissions because the fuel system is sealed.<br>• Can be produced from renewable resources. | • Requires bulky pressure cylinders and high-pressure fuel lines.<br>• Fuel system costs as much as $5,000 more than gasoline fuel system for cars.<br>• Refueling infrastructure is expensive.<br>• Energy storage density is low, making it difficult to achieve adequate range.<br>• Composition of natural gas varies regionally. |

## Table 12.  Advantages and Disadvantages of Alternative Fuels (continued)

| Fuel | Advantages | Disadvantages |
|---|---|---|
| **Methanol**<br>Methanol is an alcohol that can be produced from coal, wood, methane or natural gas. It is often blended with gasoline, e.g., "M85" contains 85 percent methanol and 15 percent gasoline to overcome cold start and poor flame visibility problems. | • Can be produced domestically, but near-term sources are likely to be imports.<br>• Can be produced from renewable resources, but is currently produced predominantly from natural gas.<br>• Can reduce ozone-forming hydrocarbon emissions and particulate emissions.<br>• Eliminates toxic benzene emissions.<br>• A liquid fuel at ambient temperatures. | • May increase formaldehyde emissions.<br>• Corrosive and toxic.<br>• Requires the use of special methanol-compatible materials in fuel system.<br>• Poor flame visibility.<br>• Has a lower energy content than gasoline, therefore requires larger fuel tanks.<br>• Currently is significantly more expensive than gasoline.<br>• Lack of refueling infrastructure.<br>• Engine is difficult to start in cold weather. |
| **Ethanol**<br>Ethanol is an alcohol derived from biomass (corn and other agricultural products such as sugar cane).  Ethanol is often blended with gasoline to avoid taxation as an alcoholic beverage. | • Is produced domestically from renewable resources.<br>• Can reduce carbon dioxide and ozone-forming hydrocarbon emissions.<br>• Eliminates toxic benzene emissions.<br>• A liquid fuel at ambient temperatures.<br>• May increase acetaldehyde emissions.<br>• Has higher energy content than methanol. | • Currently significantly more expensive than gasoline.<br>• Has a lower energy content than gasoline; therefore requires larger fuel tanks.<br>• Lack of refueling infrastructure.<br>• Requires the use of special ethanol-compatible materials in fuel system.<br>• Ability to meet large-scale demand is questionable.<br>• Production from corn or other crops may compete for land with food crops. |

## Table 12. Advantages and Disadvantages of Alternative Fuels (continued)

| Fuel | Advantages | Disadvantages |
|---|---|---|
| **Reformulated Gasoline (RFG)\*** Reformulated gasoline is made by changing the composition of conventional gasoline to reduce emissions. It often contains an oxygenate such as methyl tertiary butyl ether (MTBE). | • Reduces air pollution. • Can be used in all existing cars. • Can use existing refueling infrastructure. | • Slightly more expensive. • Does not reduce oil imports significantly. • May increase engine wear and maintenance costs. |
| **Liquefied Natural Gas (LNG)** Natural gas can be stored on the vehicle as a cryogenic liquid at about -260 F. LNG is used primarily for heavy-duty vehicles. | Same advantages as CNG, plus: • Has higher storage density than CNG so a higher range can be achieved. • Usually has higher methane content than CNG. • Does not require high pressure cylinders for storage. | • Is a cryogenic liquid with special handling requirements. • Requires vacuum-insulated storage tank. • Refueling infrastructure is expensive. • Lack of refueling infrastructure. • Low cetane number for diesel engines. |
| **Electricity** Electricity is stored in a battery bank in the vehicle. The vehicle is powered by one or more electric motors. | • No tailpipe emissions. • Reduces noise pollution. • Can use domestic fuel sources. | • Not cost-competitive. • Limited range per charge. • Limited recharging infrastructure. • May increase sulfur emissions if power is generated by coal. • Potential battery disposal problem. |

\*Reformulated gasoline is considered a "clean fuel" in the Clean Air Act Amendments, but is not considered an alternative fuel in the Energy Policy Act of 1992.

## Table 12. Advantages and Disadvantages of Alternative Fuels (continued)

| Fuel | Advantages | Disadvantages |
|---|---|---|
| **Biodiesel**<br>Biodiesel is a methyl ester that can be made from a variety of products. Most biodiesel used in the United States is made from soybeans. Biodiesel is usually blended with diesel. The most common blend is 20 percent biodiesel, 80 percent conventional diesel. | • Is made from a renewable resource.<br>• Is produced domestically.<br>• Can reduce carbon monoxide, hydrocarbon and particulate matter emissions.<br>• Can be used in existing diesel engines without modifications.<br>• Is nontoxic.<br>• Has energy content comparable to diesel. | • Is several times more expensive than conventional diesel.<br>• May reduce reliability and durability of the engine.<br>• Can increase emissions of oxides of nitrogen.<br>• Needs to be blended with conventional diesel to reduce gelling effect at low temperatures.<br>• May not blend easily with conventional diesel under some conditions. |
| **Dimethyl Ether (DME)**<br>DME can be made from natural gas and is a liquid at relatively low pressures (similar to LPG). It appears to be a good fuel for use in heavy-duty trucks. Prototype engines are currently being produced. | • Can reduce emissions significantly.<br>• Has a high cetane number so it can be used in a diesel engine.<br>• Can be produced from domestic renewable sources. | • No commercially available engines at this time.<br>• Limited fuel supply.<br>• No refueling infrastructure.<br>• Uncertain production cost. |

*Source: CRC Handbook of Mechanical Engineering, 1998.*

| Table 13. Comparison of Alternative Fuel Operating Performance | | | | |
|---|---|---|---|---|
| 👍 Better than gasoline | — Same as gasoline | | 👎 Worse than gasoline | |
| | Natural Gas | Methanol | Ethanol | Propane |
| **Maintenance Characteristics** | | | | |
| Engine wear | — | 👎 | 👎 | — |
| Maintenance costs | — | 👎 | 👎 | — |
| Combustion-chamber deposits | 👍 | 👍 | 👍 | 👍 |
| **Operating Characteristics** | | | | |
| Cold-weather starts | 👍 | 👎 | 👎 | 👎 |
| Vapor lock | 👍 | 👎 | 👎 | — |
| Anti-lock problem | 👍 | 👍 | 👍 | 👍 |
| Convenience of fueling | 👎 1 | 👎 | 👎 | 👎 2 |
| Cold-engine driveability | 👍 | 👎 | 👎 | 👎 |
| Warm-engine driveability | — | — | — | — |
| **Design Characteristics** | | | | |
| Fuel tank capacity | 👎 | 👎 | 👎 | 👎 |
| Compression ratios | 👍 | — | — | 👍 |
| Octane rating | 👍 | 👍 | 👍 | 👍 |
| Fuel tank weight | 👎 | 👎 | 👎 | 👎 |

1 With home refueler, could be better than gasoline.
2 Would be equal to gasoline if infrastructure were equal.
Source: *CRC Handbook of Mechanical Engineering*, 1998.

## Cost

Substituting another fuel for gasoline affects the entire fuel cycle—not only through vehicular performance, but also through changes in fuel handling and safety, storage and distribution, engine material requirements, feedstock requirements and several other factors.

In 1994, the American Petroleum Institute published estimates of the price of crude oil at which various alternative fuels would become competitive. Citing a study by the National Academy of Sciences, API claims that the price of oil would have to increase to $60 per barrel per gallon before ethanol could compete without the current 54 cent per gallon federal tax exemption. For methanol to become competitive, the cost of crude oil would have to exceed $40 per barrel. Synthetic fuels that may be closer to becoming competitive include synthetic oil from Canadian tar sands (at $25 per barrel of oil) and gasoline from coal (at $30 per barrel of crude oil).[3]

An optimistic estimate was provided by Dr. Mark Bohn, vice-president of engineering at Rentech (a company specializing in analyzing and producing synthetic fuels with a Fischer-Tropsch process from various feedstocks—see appendix G), who believes that synthetic diesel fuel could become competitive when the cost of crude oil exceeds $20 to $25 per barrel. It should be noted that estimates are based on engineering analyses with various assumptions, rather than concrete empirical data. Hence, there is disagreement in the scientific community about the accuracy of these estimates and there is an urgent need to provide decision-makers with up-to-date and objective engineering information about the cost of all fuel alternatives for vehicle propulsion.

The price of methanol and ethanol is more than gasoline and there are no indications that this will change. Although compressed and liquid natural gas cost less than gasoline per unit of energy, there currently is a limited infrastructure to deliver these gases to cars. Unlike the other fuels, natural gas currently used in vehicles has no federal excise tax. If it were to become a significant motor fuel, however, it is likely that the federal government would tax it in the future.

## Methanol and Ethanol

**Methanol** is a convenient and familiar liquid fuel that is readily produced by reliable technology from natural gas; it also can be made from coal, although at considerably higher cost and with adverse environmental effects. The most common methanol is M85, a fuel composed of 85 percent methanol and 15 percent unleaded gasoline by volume. Although present world resources of natural gas are plentiful, any significant increase in U.S. methanol consumption would use imports, probably from Saudi Arabia or Chile, where its cost is less than 25 percent of the $2.50 per million Btu charged by domestic producers. Importing the feedstock would remove the attraction of potential energy independence; use of methanol made from natural gas would not reduce emissions of greenhouse gases appreciably (less than 10 percent), while the use of coal as a feedstock to produce methanol would lead to large increases in greenhouse gas emissions. The gasoline equivalent price of methanol is likely to be considerably higher than that of gasoline or diesel fuel for the foreseeable future.

**Ethanol** is another alternative fuel whose use has been proposed by various sources. It is a familiar liquid fuel that provides performance comparable to gasoline in internal combustion vehicles. The most common ethanol is E85, a fuel composed of 85 percent ethanol and 15 percent unleaded gasoline by volume. Many farmers support the use of ethanol as an alternative fuel because corn can be used as a feedstock to produce it.

Currently, however, ethanol production is profitable only because the federal government provides a taxable alcohol mixture income tax credit of up to 54 cents per gallon (depending on the proof of the alcohol used).[4] The income tax credit is taxable—therefore, the value is lowered if the company or individual pays income taxes.[5]

Present law also provides a partial exemption from the federal excise tax on gasoline for gasoline blended in prescribed portions with ethanol. The excise tax exemption is 5.4 cents per gallon of gasoline blended with 10 percent ethanol (gasohol). Gasoline blenders can also use lower amounts of ethanol to meet clean gasoline standards and claim an exemption of 4.26 cents for gasoline containing 7.7

percent ethanol, and 3.18 cents for gasoline containing 5.7 percent ethanol.[6] The total highway motor fuel excise tax rate for gasoline is 18.3 cents per gallon, and 24.3 cents per gallon for diesel fuel.[7]

Gasoline blenders have the option to use the exemption or the alcohol income tax credit (54 cents per gallon of ethanol). The ethanol tax exemption provides the price difference between the higher market price of ethanol when compared to the wholesale price of gasoline.[8] Some states that are interested in promoting the use of corn as a feedstock for ethanol provide further exemption from state taxes, as shown in table 14.

| Table 14. Tax Breaks for Ethanol Producers | |
|---|---|
| State | Ethanol Tax Incentives |
| Alaska | $0.08 per gallon of ethanol (blender). |
| California | E85 and M85 excise tax is one-half of the gasoline tax. Neat alcohol fuels are exempt from fuel taxes. |
| Florida | County governments receive waste reduction credits for using yard trash, wood or paper waste as feed stocks for fuel. |
| Hawaii | 4 percent ethanol sales tax exemption. |
| Idaho | $0.21 excise tax exemption for ethanol or biodiesel. |
| Indiana | 10 percent gross income tax deduction for improvements to ethanol producing facilities. |
| Illinois | 2 percent sales tax exemption for 10 percent volume ethanol blends. |
| Iowa | $0.01 (blender). |
| Minnesota | $0.25 (producer), $0.005 (blender) until Oct. 1, 1997. |
| Missouri | $0.20 (producer). |
| Montana | $0.30 (producer). |
| Nebraska | $0.20 (producer), $0.50 ETBE (producer). |
| North Carolina | Individual income and corporate tax credit of 20 percent for the construction of an ethanol plant using agricultural or forestry products; an additional 10 percent if the distillery is powered with alternative fuels. |
| North Dakota | $0.40 (producer). |
| Ohio | $0.01 (blender), income tax credit. |
| South Dakota | $0.20 (blender), $0.20 (producer); alternative fuels are taxed at $0.06 per gallon. |
| Wyoming | $0.40 (producer). |

Source: U.S. Department of Energy, 1998.

A great deal of controversy exists regarding the amount of energy required to produce ethanol from corn vs. the same amount of energy that ethanol can deliver as a fuel. A 1992 study by David Pimentel indicated that, if ethanol were made from corn grown in the United

States, it would take more Btus of energy to produce the ethanol than the Btus that ethanol can deliver as a fuel.[9] In a 1995 *Solar Today* article, Bardall claimed that, with the current state of technology, 1.3 energy units are delivered by ethanol fuel with an input of 1 energy unit to produce the fuel.[10] A more recent study at Argonne National Laboratory claims that the ration of energy output from corn produced ethanol in the United States compared to the amount of energy necessary to produce the fuel could be even greater than 1.3.[11] Mark Delucchi of the Institute of Transportation Studies at the University of California notes that current knowledge about the corn-to-ethanol fuel cycle is insufficient to make a meaningful assessment of the energy tradeoffs involved.[12]

The environmental effects of increasing corn production for ethanol manufacture are of concern, because growing corn produces soil erosion and is energy and chemically (pesticides and fertilizer) intensive. A U.S. Office of Technology Assessment study also concluded that it is unlikely that given the current technology and fuel use pattern, ethanol production will create any significant greenhouse benefits. It should be noted, however, that the cost of ethanol could decrease significantly if current research and development would lead to ethanol production from wood and lignocellulosic materials. Extensive research and development on this process is under way, but any prognosis on its ultimate success is premature.

Unless used in very dilute form—as, for example, in gasohol—deployment of liquid alternative fuels such as M85 or E85 would require a totally new infrastructure. The cost of building such an infrastructure in all 50 states would be enormous. Along with corrosion and water contamination concerns, there also would be the problem of volume requirements. Compared with gasoline, M85 has just 50 percent of the energy content per gallon. Hence, for the same amount of energy, M85 storage and transportation facilities would have to be twice as large. It also should be noted that the tax structure of alternative fuels is uncertain, especially if substantial incentives were to be considered.

The only large-scale operation of a transportation infrastructure based on ethanol has been conducted in Brazil, using sugarcane as a feedstock. Brazil responded to the 1973 oil crisis by placing its government-owned oil monopoly—Petrobrás—into the ethanol-from-sugarcane business. To entice motorists to change to ethanol, the retail price of ethanol was fixed at 75 percent of the price of gasoline. According to a World Bank study, the subsidy required to buy down the cost of ethanol added $2.7 billion annually to the country's deficit. It has been estimated that in the United States ethanol would cost almost twice as much as gasoline on an energy equivalent basis. It would therefore require large subsidies if it were to be introduced on a large scale.

## Compressed Natural Gas, Liquid Natural Gas and Liquefied Petroleum Gas

Methanol and ethanol currently are more expensive than gasoline and there is no credible evidence that this will change in the near future. On the other hand, on an energy-per-gallon basis, compressed natural gas (CNG) and liquefied petroleum gas (LPG) are less expensive than gasoline. However, an infrastructure to store and deliver natural gas to cars would have to be built. According to a study by R.F. Webb Corporation, to establish the infrastructure to supply LPG for 17 million vehicles (approximately 9 percent of the present U.S. total) would require an investment of $14 billion. There is no estimate from the natural gas industry for the cost of a large-scale natural gas infrastructure, but the cost would be substantial because each refueling station would require a compressor to increase the pipeline pressure from the existing supply system to between 2,400 pounds per square inch (PSI) and 3,600 PSI for storage in an automotive tank. This compression process adds approximately 70 percent to the price of natural gas, according to a report of the California Energy Commission. An estimate of the true cost of natural gas fuel to the consumer also would have to include the amortization of the construction cost of the refueling system.

Since 1992, an experiment with natural gas-powered school buses has been conducted in California by the Antelope Valley school system, located approximately 70 miles northeast of Los Angeles. Combining grants from the California Energy Commission (CEC), the

South Coast Air Quality Managing District (AQMD), Southern California Gas Company and others, Antelope Valley schools chief executive officer Ken McCoy was able to build an alternative fuel school bus fleet complete with an on-site fueling station. This alternative fuel station also supports the city of Lancaster, Calif., which participates in the U.S. Department of Energy's Clean Cities Program. The Southern California Gas Company built both fast and slow CNG fueling stations—valued at $100,000 and $300,000, respectively—at no cost to the Antelope Valley school system.

In El Paso, Texas, Sun Metro, the public transportation authority, operates the world's largest natural gas-fueled mass transit fleet. A combination of state legislation, federal grant funds and the expectation of cost savings provided the incentive to use natural gas. In 1991, Texas enacted House Bill 734, which required all centrally fueled fleets with 15 or more vehicles to convert to alternative fuels. The legislation required mass transit fleets to use alternative fuels in 30 percent of their vehicles by September 1994, with usage rates increasing to 50 percent by September 1996 and to 90 percent by September 1998. These rates applied to all vehicles, not only to new purchases.

In 1994, Sun Metro ordered 35 full-size buses and 22 paratransit vehicles fueled by LNG. New Flier supplied the LNG buses at a cost of $256,000 per bus, compared to a cost of $216,000 for similar diesel buses. The paratransit vehicles were purchased at a cost of $74,000 per vehicle, $12,000 more than a similarly equipped diesel vehicle. Sun Metro also bought 21 support vehicles (vans, minivans, light-duty trucks and sedans); two of these vehicles were fueled with LNG, the rest with CNG. The average cost of a support vehicle was $21,000, about $6,000 more than the cost of a comparable gasoline-powered vehicle.

A summary payback analysis for El Paso's alternative fuel vehicle program is displayed in table 15. The LNG/CNG fueling facility—which can be used for all the 128 vehicles in this particular program—cost $3 million. After the 80 percent matching grants from various federal funds were applied, it took less than one year for Sun Metro to recover the costs from establishing the program. Even without matching grants, however, and assuming that fuel costs remain constant, a payback period of less than five years could have been achieved. Thus, based on the El Paso experience—for applications with a minimal storage and fueling infrastructure requirement—natural gas fuel vehicles appear to be a viable option.

## Table 15. Summary Payback Analysis for El Paso's Alternative Fuel Vehicle Program

### Costs

| Vehicle type | Number | Incremental Cost per Vehicle | Total Investment (in dollars) |
| --- | --- | --- | --- |
| CNG buses | 27 | $59,000 | $1,593,000 |
| LNG buses | 35 | $40,000 | $1,400,000 |
| Paratransit vehicles | 42 | $25,000 | $1,050,000 |
| Support vehicles | 24 | $  6,000 | $4,187,000 |

Vehicles ............................................................................................ $4,187,000
LNG/CNG fueling facilities ................................................................ $3,000,000
*Total cost* ............................................................................................ $7,187,000

80 percent matching grant funds ........................................................ $5,749,600
*Net cost* ............................................................................................. $1,437,400

### Savings

| | |
| --- | --- |
| Fuel | (174,500 gallons per month) ($1.30 - $0.54/DGE) (12 months) = $1,591,440 per year |
| Oil Changes | (64,000 miles/year) (62 buses) (oil change/[12,000 - 6,000] miles) (7 gallons oil/change) ($3.45/gallon of oil) = $7986/year |

*Total Annual Savings* ....................................................................... $1,599,426

### Payback Time

| | |
| --- | --- |
| Before Grant Funds | ($7,187,000) / ($1,599,426 per year) = $4.49 per year |
| After Grant Funds | ($1,437,000) / ($1,599,426 per year) = $0.90 per year |

Source: *Natural Gas Fuels*, 1998.

Compressed natural gas at 3,000 PSI, as currently used in vehicles, has only 25 percent of the volumetric energy density of gasoline. Therefore, for the same range, much larger storage tanks are required, which leads to higher vehicle cost, slower refueling and a more limited driving range. Some of these disadvantages—particularly the range limitation—may be ameliorated by using natural gas in its denser liquefied form (LNG). This requires cooling the gas to –258° F and building insulated storage tanks, however. It also should be noted that large-scale use of natural gas would require extensive imports. Two potential gas suppliers for the U.S. transportation market— Canada and Mexico—could feed their gas into the existing U.S. natural gas supply system. If it became cost effective to ship natural gas in the form of LNG, other countries such as Chile, Saudi Arabia, Algeria, Norway, Nigeria and Indonesia would become potential suppliers, although at a considerably higher cost.

## Availability

Propulsion technologies for alternative fuel vehicles are available for the principal alternative fuels, specifically reformulated gasoline, propane, methanol, ethanol, liquefied petroleum gas and gaseous natural gas.

Although alternative fuel refueling sites have increased in recent years, no adequate networks to support widespread use of any alternative fuels currently are available at retail for vehicle refueling. Therefore, the most promising application for alternative fuels is in situations where a single refueling site can be repetitively and reliably used. This would apply to school buses, public transport systems that use buses, and trucks that transport goods along established routes. State and local governments can assist the introduction of alternative fuels in the transportation sector, but it appears that the programs authorized by Congress will fall substantially short of the year 2010 goal of 30 percent.

If U.S. ground transportation were to switch from oil to some other fuel stock before the peak in world oil production is reached in the next 25 years, enormous changes in engine technology and fuel infrastructure would be required. Demonstration of the feasibility of one or more AFV technologies does not mean that this technology is industrially and economically viable. Although 25 years seems a long time period for planning purposes, it is a short period for the transportation sector to make a major transition in energy sources. Using wood to produce methanol or ethanol is an R&D challenge with an uncertain outcome. Producing synthetic liquid motor fuels from domestic sources such as coal or oil shale is likely to be expensive and not effective in reducing air pollution.

Although in 1998 flexible-fuel vehicles became available to the public, to date AFVs have been used only to meet fleet requirements under the Energy Policy Act (EPACT) and the Clean Air Act (CAA). The major auto manufacturers are offering to the public 1999 model AFVs that run on compressed natural gas, propane and E85 (a fuel mixture of gasoline and up to 85 percent ethanol). Some currently available AFVs are described below by fuel type.

- *E85, flexible-fuel vehicles.* All Chrysler minivans can run on E85 fuel or gasoline and are offered to the public at no extra cost. Chrysler expects to sell more than 250,000 E85 minivans in 1999. The Ford Ranger truck, Ford Taurus sedan and Mazda B3000 pickup also are available with an E85 option for a small incremental cost. Most of these vehicles are classified as transitional low emission vehicles (TLEVs) (any vehicle certified to the low emission vehicle standards specified in 40 CFR part 86). Using E85 fuel in a conventional size tank allows a range of about 250 miles. The low extra cost is the most significant advantage of E85 vehicles. A major problem is the lack of availability of E85 fuel sites. Because only a small number of public E85 fuel sites exist in the United States, the vast majority of E85 drivers refuel with gasoline, and no emission or energy benefit is gained.

- *Compressed natural gas (CNG) vehicles.* These vehicles may be bi-fuel or dedicated CNG, which are the most popular fleet AFV. There are approximately 1,200 public CNG fueling sites in the U.S.[13] Dedicated vehicles run only on natural gas, while bi-fuel vehicles run either on natural gas or gasoline. Because the two fuels cannot be mixed, two separate tanks are needed for bi-fuel vehicles. Ford offers a variety of bi-fuel CNG trucks and one bi-fuel car, the Contour. GM sells a bi-fuel Chevrolet Cavalier, a subcompact car. Operating bi-fuel vehicles with CNG offers a range of between 100 and 180 miles. The Cavalier and Contour have qualified for TLEV classification; the others are awaiting determination. In general, the bi-fuel options cost about $5,000 more than their gasoline counterparts. The Toyota Camry, Honda Civic, Dodge Ram, Ford Crown Victoria and other Ford trucks and vans are available with a dedicated CNG option. Incremental costs are approximately $4,000. All are classified as ultra low emissions vehicles (ULEVs) (a vehicle that meets either EPA's CFV ULEV standards or CARB's California Low Emission Vehicle Program standards), and their ranges vary between 100 and 300 miles.

• *LPG vehicles.* Only Ford offers propane (LPG) trucks and vans in the United States, and all are bi-fuel. These LEV classified vehicles have a range of between 250 and 400 miles, and have an incremental cost of approximately $4,000. Only about 5,000 public propane fueling sites exist in the United States.[14]

Table 16 gives an overview of the availability of AFV vehicles from different manufacturers, and table 17 shows the distribution of refueling sites for each alternative fuel in the different states. It is apparent that the existing infrastructure is nowhere near sufficient to support any of the liquid alternative fuels for interstate vehicular travel.

## Table 16. Overview of Availability of AFV Vehicles From Different Manufacturers

| Model | Model Year (MY) Availability | Fuel | Type | Emission Class |
|---|---|---|---|---|
| *Chrysler Products: (800) 255-2616* | | | | |
| EPIC | MY 1997 (limited) | Electric lead-acid | Minivan | ZEV |
| Minivan | MY 1998 | Ethanol | Minivan | N/A |
| Ram Wagon | Fall 1998 | CNG dedicated | Passenger van | SULEV |
| Ram Van | Fall 1998 | CNG dedicated | Full-size van | SULEV |
| *Ford Products: (800) ALT-FUEL* | | | | |
| Ranger | MY 1997 MY 1998 | Electric lead-acid | Light truck | ZEV |
| Contour (QVM) | MY 1997 MY 1998 | CNG bi-fuel | Compact sedan | Gasoline equivalent |
| Crown Victoria | MY 1997 MY 1998 | CNG dedicated | Full-size sedan | ULEV |
| Econoline | MY 1997 MY 1998 | CNG/LPG dedicated or bi-fuel | Full-size van | Various |
| F-Series | MY 1997 MY 1998 | CNG/LPG dedicated or bi-fuel | Light truck | Various |
| Taurus | MY 1997 MY 1998 | E-85 or M-85 gasoline | Mid-size sedan | TLEV |

## Table 16. Overview of Availability of AFV Vehicles From Different Manufacturers (continued)

| Model | Model Year (MY) Availability | Fuel | Type | Emission Class |
|---|---|---|---|---|
| *General Motors Products: (800)-25Electric, (313) 556-7723 or (800) GM-AFT-4U (CNG)* | | | | |
| EV1 | MY 1997 MY 1998 | Electric lead-acid Nickel-metal hydride (NiMH) option | Sedan two-seater | ZEV |
| Chevrolet S-10 | MY 1997 MY 1998 | Electric lead-acid | Light truck | California certified ZEV |
| GMC Sierra 2500 | MY 1997 MY 1998 | CNG bi-fuel | Medium truck | LEV |
| *Honda: (888) CCHonda* | | | | |
| Honda EV Plus | MY 1997 | Electric NiMH batteries | Sedan | ZEV |
| Civic GX | MY 1998 | CNG dedicated | Compact sedan | ULEV California ILEV Federal |
| *Nissan: (310) 771-3422 (Demonstration fleets only)* | | | | |
| Altra EV | MY 1998 | Electric lithium batteries | Minivan | ZEV |

## Table 16. Overview of Availability of AFV Vehicles From Different Manufacturers (continued)

| Model | Model Year (MY) Availability | Fuel | Type | Emission Class |
|---|---|---|---|---|
| *Toyota: (800) 331-4331 (Press 3 for Alternative Fuel Information) (Fleet sales only)* | | | | |
| RAV4-EV | MY 1998-(U.S.) | Electric lead-acid/NiMH | Sports utility vehicle | ZEV |

Key:
LEV = low emission vehicle.
ILEV = inherently low emission vehicle.
ULEV = ultra low emission vehicle.
ZEV = zero emission vehicle.
TLEV = transitional low emission vehicle.

Source: U.S. Department of Energy, 1998.

Table 17.  Distribution of Refueling Sites for Each Alternative Fuel in the Different States and the District of Columbia (1997)

| State/Jurisdiction | M85 sites | CNG sites | E85 sites | LPG sites | LNG sites | Electric sites | Total |
|---|---|---|---|---|---|---|---|
| Alabama | 0 | 17 | 0 | 114 | 2 | 0 | 133 |
| Alaska | 0 | 1 | 0 | 9 | 0 | 0 | 10 |
| Arizona | 1 | 31 | 0 | 71 | 3 | 40 | 146 |
| Arkansas | 0 | 9 | 0 | 156 | 0 | 0 | 165 |
| California | 66 | 203 | 0 | 219 | 18 | 197 | 703 |
| Colorado | 2 | 45 | 1 | 48 | 3 | 0 | 99 |
| Connecticut | 0 | 22 | 0 | 18 | 0 | 1 | 41 |
| Delaware | 0 | 6 | 0 | 6 | 0 | 0 | 12 |
| District of Columbia | 1 | 8 | 1 | 0 | 0 | 2 | 12 |
| Florida | 3 | 60 | 0 | 222 | 0 | 4 | 289 |
| Georgia | 1 | 89 | 0 | 80 | 3 | 0 | 173 |
| Hawaii | 0 | 0 | 0 | 0 | 0 | 3 | 3 |
| Idaho | 0 | 7 | 1 | 20 | 1 | 1 | 30 |
| Illinois | 2 | 24 | 14 | 163 | 0 | 0 | 203 |
| Indiana | 0 | 47 | 2 | 125 | 3 | 1 | 178 |
| Iowa | 0 | 5 | 10 | 107 | 0 | 1 | 123 |
| Kansas | 0 | 18 | 2 | 38 | 1 | 0 | 59 |
| Kentucky | 0 | 13 | 3 | 35 | 0 | 0 | 51 |
| Louisiana | 0 | 21 | 0 | 44 | 2 | 0 | 67 |
| Maine | 0 | 0 | 0 | 12 | 0 | 0 | 12 |
| Maryland | 2 | 31 | 0 | 21 | 3 | 0 | 57 |
| Massachusetts | 0 | 18 | 0 | 42 | 0 | 4 | 64 |
| Michigan | 2 | 39 | 3 | 187 | 2 | 10 | 243 |
| Minnesota | 0 | 17 | 11 | 125 | 2 | 0 | 155 |
| Mississippi | 0 | 3 | 0 | 75 | 0 | 0 | 78 |
| Missouri | 0 | 11 | 3 | 83 | 0 | 0 | 97 |
| Montana | 0 | 13 | 0 | 48 | 1 | 0 | 62 |
| Nebraska | 0 | 11 | 6 | 47 | 1 | 0 | 66 |
| Nevada | 0 | 13 | 0 | 20 | 0 | 0 | 33 |
| New Hampshire | 0 | 1 | 0 | 31 | 0 | 1 | 33 |
| New Jersey | 0 | 24 | 0 | 37 | 0 | 0 | 61 |
| New Mexico | 0 | 18 | 0 | 46 | 1 | 0 | 65 |
| New York | 18 | 59 | 0 | 100 | 0 | 5 | 182 |
| North Carolina | 0 | 11 | 0 | 72 | 0 | 1 | 84 |
| North Dakota | 0 | 5 | 1 | 17 | 0 | 0 | 23 |
| Ohio | 2 | 70 | 0 | 98 | 1 | 1 | 172 |
| Oklahoma | 0 | 56 | 0 | 56 | 0 | 0 | 112 |
| Oregon | 0 | 9 | 0 | 21 | 1 | 0 | 31 |
| Pennsylvania | 1 | 61 | 0 | 141 | 1 | 1 | 205 |
| Rhode Island | 0 | 3 | 0 | 6 | 0 | 0 | 9 |
| South Carolina | 0 | 3 | 0 | 67 | 0 | 1 | 71 |
| South Dakota | 0 | 5 | 10 | 30 | 0 | 0 | 45 |
| Tennessee | 2 | 7 | 0 | 95 | 0 | 2 | 106 |
| Texas | 0 | 92 | 0 | 862 | 15 | 0 | 969 |
| Utah | 0 | 67 | 0 | 23 | 1 | 0 | 91 |
| Vermont | 0 | 1 | 0 | 40 | 0 | 9 | 50 |
| Virginia | 0 | 30 | 0 | 51 | 3 | 18 | 102 |
| Washington | 2 | 32 | 0 | 69 | 1 | 6 | 110 |
| West Virginia | 1 | 42 | 0 | 21 | 0 | 1 | 65 |
| Wisconsin | 0 | 29 | 3 | 190 | 0 | 0 | 222 |
| Wyoming | 0 | 19 | 0 | 47 | 2 | 0 | 68 |
| Total | 106 | 1,426 | 71 | 4,255 | 71 | 310 | 6,240 |

Source: U.S. Department of Energy, 1998.

## Environmental Impact

A study by Energy Information Agency (EIA) and EPA compares the full cycle—tailpipe and refinery—greenhouse gas emissions of different fuels per vehicle mile traveled.[15]  Interpolated $CO_2$ equivalent results are shown in table 18 for new cars and trucks.  The results indicate that, except for CNG and LPG vehicles, gasoline vehicles emit fewer greenhouse gas emissions (total $CO_2$ equivalent) than methanol or ethanol vehicles.

| Table 18.  Greenhouse Gas Emissions (Grams per Mile)[*] | | | | |
|---|---|---|---|---|
| Fuel | $CO_2$ | $CH_4$ | $N_2O$ | Total $CO_2$ equivalent |
| Gasoline | 347 | 0.35 | 0.074 | 378 |
| Methanol | 383 | 0.55 | 0.075 | 418 |
| Ethanol | 326 | 0.62 | 0.41 | 470 |
| Compressed Natural Gas | 248 | 1.5 | 0.071 | 301 |
| LPG | 264 | 0.27 | 0.071 | 292 |

* $CH_4$ is methane and $N_2O$ is nitrous oxide.  By weight, methane is approximately 20 times more effective and $N_2O$ is 320 times more effective than carbon dioxide at trapping solar energy in the atmosphere and this causes global warming.

Source: U.S. Department of Energy, 1998.

According to a 1999 National Research Council (NRC) study on the ozone forming potential of reformulated gasoline, oxygenates such as ethanol (ETBE) or methanol (MTBE) do not very effectively reduce smog.[16]  Motor vehicle emissions of chemicals that form ozone pollution have decreased in recent years because of better emissions control equipment and components.  Although additives reduce some pollutants from motor vehicle emissions, the oxygenates appear to have little effect on lowering ozone levels.  The NRC study cited found that gasoline blended with ethanol results in more pollutants evaporating from vehicle gas tanks compared to MTBE-blended gasoline.  Furthermore, ethanol blends increase the overall potential of emissions to form ozone.  The study also indicates that the potential is minimal for either additive to lower smog levels. Strict air regulations and improvements to the pollution control systems of vehicles have helped lower ozone levels during the past decade, and as new technologies are incorporated in the future, emissions levels are expected to drop even further.[17]

Furthermore, an intensive investigation of the effects of MTBE conducted by the National Academy of Sciences (NAS) indicates that MTBE may not significantly improve air quality and may cause water pollution. Specifically, the findings of the NAS indicate that:

- MTBE and other oxygenates were found to have no significant effect on exhaust emissions from advanced vehicles.

- Significant risks and costs are associated with water contamination due to the use of MTBE because it is highly soluble in water and will transfer readily to groundwater from gasoline leaks, from storage tanks and other components in the distribution system.

- The economic analysis of the benefits and costs associated with gasoline formulation indicates that non-oxygenated gasoline achieves air quality benefits at less cost than ethanol or MTBE additives. MTBE and other ethers such as ETBE have been used to reduce air pollution. Because the oxygenate content of gasoline fuel is mandated by federal law, most refiners have chosen to meet the federal law.

Although alternative fuels offer some potential to reduce urban ozone and gas toxic emissions, only hydrogen and natural gas offer significant and reliable reductions in vehicle pollution. Methanol and ethanol—in their M85 and E85 mixtures—offer smaller and less quantifiable reduction. The environmental potential for reformulated gasoline is uncertain and less promising. It should be borne in mind, however, that to obtain any of these potential benefits requires vehicle emission standards, strict vehicular maintenance programs, and continuous checking to ensure that the chemical compositions of the alternatives meet standards.

Natural gas can provide performance equal to gasoline, and at a lower level of emissions, with the exception of potentially higher nitrogen oxide ($NO_x$) emissions. In particular, because of its low carbons/hydrogen ratio that produces low carbon dioxide ($CO_2$) emissions per unit of energy, natural gas would yield large ozone benefits for urban areas and achieve moderate greenhouse benefits. Special care must be taken, however, regarding the potential emission of methane—either through the tail pipe or through leakage from the storage and distribution system—because methane is 20 times more effective than $CO_2$ in trapping solar radiation that can cause global warming.

## Conclusion

Despite significant investments of time and money, research has not found the "magic" alternative fuel with the right combination of emission reduction, price, convenience and available infrastructure. Therefore, AFVs have not had a significant effect on the U.S. transportation system. For the most part, these vehicles have been used only for fleets to meet federal mandates under CAAA and EPACT. If not for these mandates however, it is doubtful that many fleets would have bought them.

Although projecting the future costs of new technologies is a highly uncertain business, the alternative fuel vehicles discussed here will likely cost the purchaser a few thousand dollars more than comparable conventional vehicles. Higher vehicle prices could be a major stumbling block to commercializing such vehicles—even in exchange for improved fuel economy and lower emissions—because fuel economy is far less valued than comfort, safety and performance to consumers, and reduced emissions have little value to vehicle owners.

Finally, fuel savings are unlikely to pay for the efficiency improvements unless gasoline prices increase sharply. It should be noted that fuel switching means not only replacing the fuel used by the engine, but also requires the development and deployment of a complete new fuel delivery and storage infrastructure that must be planned and will be expensive to implement.

A state or city could institute experimental demonstration programs, but state and local governments would be well advised to exercise caution before mandating the purchase and deployment of alternative fuel vehicles at percentages greater than those required by federal law. For example, in an effort to reduce gridlock, diminish pollution and provide convenient transportation within the city, Boulder, Colorado, instituted the use of a bus system called, "the Hop." It purchased a number of propane (LPG) fueled mini-buses for this purpose, but the LPG engines overheated under the frequent stop/start conditions required for a city bus and all the engines had to be replaced at a high cost. The buses now operate with CNG as the fuel alternative.[18]

CNG appears to be the most popular alternative fuel because it reduces not only EPA criteria pollutants, but also greenhouse gas emissions. Use of CNG could decrease oil dependency. However, CNG engines are expensive and the refueling infrastructure is available in only a few places. CNG could be a viable option for trucks and mass transport—e.g. buses—that follow a specific route and can be refueled at one or two places. For single-occupancy vehicles, however, the extensive refueling infrastructure needed would be very costly.

None of the liquid alternative fuels will reduce emission of pollutants appreciably more than advanced internal combustion engines with the modern air pollution control equipment. Moreover, the cost of pollution reductions with new AFVs is higher than with conventional new vehicles and neither can resolve pollution and urban smog appreciably, unless the majority of the highly polluting vehicles are repaired or removed from the road. State governments may be able to assist this process by appropriate measures such as buybacks, subsidized repair programs, and/or remote exhaust measuring programs with appropriate follow up. Mandates to buy AFVs are at this time not cost effective, however, and will not significantly reduce air pollution as long as the worst polluting vehicles are on the road.

At this time it appears that the alternative fuel program authorized by Congress under EPACT will fall substantially short of the 30 percent goal for the year 2010. Kelley S. Coyner, the administrator for Research and Special Programs at the U.S. Department of Transportation, has warned against the fragmentation of federal funding that currently is heavily targeted to specific projects. He urged that "... the strategic planning process must consider the feasibility of connecting the separate projects to insure that inter-modal connections are supported, thus contributing to the goal of a national transportation system. The key is that U.S. DOT must foster collaborative enabling research and technology deployment efforts with federal, state, and local governments."[19]

# 8. PUBLIC TRANSPORTATION

Public transportation denotes the ground passenger transportation systems available to the general public. These transportation systems use bus or rail transit services with fixed routes and fixed schedules. The main purposes of public transportation systems are to provide mobility for people who do not have automobiles; to improve the transportation in urban areas; to reduce congestion, pollution, accidents and other negative impacts of single-occupancy vehicles; and to promote healthy urban development patterns with strong downtown areas and concentrated—rather than sprawl—development.

Efficient and well-planned public mass transport systems can reduce pollution, save energy, ameliorate congestion, and provide inexpensive commuter service. However, a poorly planned public transportation system that does not meet the needs of the public can be a waste of money and effort. Experience has shown that public support is necessary for any successful public transportation option.

Questions legislators in state and local governments may wish to ask when considering public transportation as a policy option include the following.

- Is a majority in agreement that building additional highway lanes is only a short-term solution to ameliorating gridlock and easing the adverse effects of urban population growth?

- What are the primary objectives of the proposed public transportation system—serving existing communities, guiding future community development (i.e., growth management strategies), reducing gridlock and/or controlling air pollution?

- Is bus or rail the best option to achieve the objectives of the public transportation system?

- If rail is the best option, should it be, 1) light rail, which must be driven from an electric central station, or 2) commuter rail with a self-propelled system such as a diesel engine or some advanced propulsion system?

- Are there existing rail lines that can be used for part of the proposed public transportation system?

- What are the expected load factors for the proposed public transportation system?

- Is a bus system with designated high-occupancy vehicle (HOV) lines less expensive than a rail system that would be used along the same route?

- What method of financing would fund the construction and development of the public transportation system?

- What are the necessary qualifications for the organization selected to undertake the initial investment study that is required by the federal government?

- Has there been adequate public input into the development of a proposed public transportation system?

## History of Public Transportation

Urban public transport has been a dynamic evolutionary process shaped historically between road and rail advocates. The complex development occurred in an era when the standard of living in the United States increased and the development of mass production made it possible for more people to afford cars. Big business and the federal government responded to the economic opportunities and political pressure of the automobile. Weyrich and Lind of the Free Congress Foundation state that, "… the dominance of the automobile is not a free market outcome, but the result of massive government intervention on behalf of the automobile. The intervention came at the expense of privately owned, privately funded, tax-paying public transit systems."[1] For example, figure 18 depicts the early 20th century commuter train that transported passengers between Boulder, Colo., and Denver, Colo. This option no longer is available to Boulder residents, who must ride a bus if they choose to use public transportation to go to Denver.

### Figure 18. The Denver and Interurban Railway at the Intersection of 12th and Pearl, Boulder, Colorado, circa 1916

Source: Carnegie Branch Library for Local History; Boulder, Colorado, 1916.

In addition to government intervention, private automobiles were preferred because they gave people a sense of freedom to travel anywhere they wanted to go at a time of their own choosing. It also offered people who held jobs in the city the opportunity to live in the country or in suburbs, where public transport was unavailable. Owning a car made it possible to commute between home and work. Engineering innovations such as mass production used by Ford for the Model A automobile, brought the cost of a car within the reach of more people. As Americans became more affluent, for many the car became a status symbol."

Along with these evolutionary factors, which were driven by consumers' preference and affordability of cars, urban electric rail systems in the United States were dismantled in the 1930s by industries that favored road transportation over rail transportation. For example, National City Lines, a holding company made up of interests from the world tire and car industries, bought private electric street car systems in 45 U.S. cities and then closed them down.[2] In response to these actions, a grand jury in 1949 ultimately convicted General Motors, Standard Oil of California, Mack Trucks, Phillips Petroleum and Firestone Tires on a criminal indictment of antitrust conspiracy. By that time, however, the electric urban public transport system had been dismantled.

The continuing influence of automobile, oil and other highway interests has resulted in more federal funding for highways than for public transport. The Federal Highway Administration (FHWA) reports that the net amount used for highway purposes in 1996 was almost $64 billion. Although the data is not finalized, FHWA expects total disbursements for highways in 1998 to reach nearly $106 billion. Of these amounts, nearly one-half of all spending was for capital outlays, such as highway construction, engineering and right-of-way expenditures. All levels of government—including federal, state and local—invested more than $51 billion in 1998 to improve the nation's highways, roads, bridges and streets. FHWA believes that exceeding the $50 billion threshold is an important milestone in highway financing; only a dozen years ago, total capital spending was only slightly more than $26 billion. The 1998 figure represents a $12.5 billion and 13 percent increase since 1995.[3]

In addition to federal support for the construction and operation of the nation's highways, there has been support, mostly by private companies, for convenient parking at places of employment and shopping centers that can be reached only by private automobile. Government supported these trends through tax relief. These measures—as well as federal tax laws such as the oil depletion allowance—have tended to contribute to what some consider the automobile's unfairly gained advantage over other modes of transportation, have perpetuated road transportation by private automobile and have exacerbated urban sprawl. These developments, which at one time seemed the hallmark of affluence and convenience, have resulted in problems that could, at least in part, be remedied by the rebirth of a robust and convenient public transportation system.

## What Are the Public Transportation Technologies?

Public transportation systems have been in existence for many hundreds of years. Today, the primary public carriers are bus or rail transit networks. Vanpools and carpools are other public transportation options.

### Bus Systems

A bus is a rubber-tired passenger vehicle powered by diesel, gasoline, a battery or an alternative fuel engine contained within the vehicle. The bus system consists of a combination of intercity, suburban, and transit buses designed to transport 30 to 70 people on a scheduled and continuing basis. Buses improve public transport by providing convenient and efficient transportation through use of high occupancy vehicle (HOV) lanes incorporated in a city's transportation infrastructure.

### Rail Systems

**Light Rail**—Lightweight passenger rail cars operating as a one- or two-car system on fixed rails in a right-of-way that is not separated from other traffic for much of its travel path. Light rail vehicles are driven electrically; power is drawn from an electric line. This form of travel can be the least polluting of all public transportation modes. Also known as "streetcar," "tramway" or "trolley car."

**Heavy Rail**—Higher speed passenger rail cars operating singly or in trains of two or more cars on fixed rails in separate rights-of-way from which other vehicular and foot traffic are excluded. Labor productivity is considerably lower for trains than for busses. Heavy rail usually is employed for longer commute and travel distances than light rail. Heavy rail can be electricity driven or have its own propulsion system, e.g., a diesel engine.

*Accelerail*—Operates on existing railroad right-of-way, at top speeds ranging from 90 to 150 miles per hour. Typical accelerail systems include tilt trains such as the X-2000 in Sweden, Taldo in Spain, Pendolino in Italy and Metroliners operating between New York and Washington, D.C.

*New High Speed Rail (HSR)*—Operates on almost completely new rights-of-way at speeds of approximately 200 miles per hour. Because new HSR trains can operate on existing track, the system can combine new lines with existing approaches to urban terminals. The French TGV, Japanese Shinkansen and German Intercity Express are examples of new HSR.

*Maglev*—An advanced transport technology in which magnetic forces lift, propel and guide vehicles over a specifically designed guideway. The system uses electric power and control systems, has no wheels or other mechanical parts, and thus minimizes resistance and allows for high acceleration and speed. It can reach cruising speeds of 300 miles or more per hour.

## Vanpools

Vans and/or small buses seating fewer than 25 people that can serve as a commuter ride sharing arrangement, which provides transportation to a group of individuals traveling directly between their homes and their regular places of work within a limited geographical area.

## Carpools

An arrangement where two or more people share the use and cost of privately owned vehicles as they travel together to and from prearranged destinations.

As shown in table 19, the volume of intercity public transport passenger traffic in the United States has decreased enormously in recent years, and a shift has occurred from rail to buses and air carriers. In 1929, for example, railroads accounted for almost 16 percent of all passenger miles traveled; in 1987, this percentage dropped to less than 1 percent. The passenger load carried by buses, on the other

## Table 19. Volume of U.S. Intercity Passenger Traffic
### (millions of revenue passenger-miles and percentage of total)

| Year | Railroads | Pct. | Buses | Pct. | Air Carriers | Pct. | Inland Waterways | Pct. | Private Automobile | Pct. | Private Airplane | Pct. | Total |
|---|---|---|---|---|---|---|---|---|---|---|---|---|---|
| 1929 | 33,965 | 15.50% | 6,800 | 3.10% | — | 0.00% | 3,300 | 1.51% | 175,000 | 79.88% | — | 0.00% | 219,065 |
| 1939 | 23,669 | 7.64 | 9,100 | 2.94 | 683 | 0.22 | 1,486 | 0.48 | 275,000 | 88.73 | — | 0.00 | 309,938 |
| 1944 | 97,705 | 31.52 | 26,920 | 8.68 | 2,177 | 0.70 | 2,187 | 0.71 | 181,000 | 58.39 | 1.00 | 0.00 | 309,990 |
| 1950 | 32,481 | 6.39 | 26,436 | 5.20 | 8,773 | 1.73 | 1,190 | 0.23 | 438,293 | 86.20 | 1,299 | 0.26 | 508,472 |
| 1960 | 21,574 | 2.75 | 19,327 | 2.47 | 31,730 | 4.05 | 2,688 | 0.34 | 706,079 | 90.10 | 2,228 | 0.28 | 783,626 |
| 1970 | 10,903 | 0.92 | 25,300 | 2.14 | 109,499 | 9.24 | 4,000 | 0.34 | 1,026,000 | 86.60 | 9,101 | 0.77 | 1,184,803 |
| 1980 | 11,000 | 0.71 | 27,400 | 1.76 | 204,400 | 13.12 | N/A | — | 1,300,400 | 83.47 | 14,700 | 0.94 | 1,557,900 |
| 1986 | 11,800 | 0.65 | 23,700 | 1.31 | 307,900 | 17.05 | N/A | — | 1,450,100 | 80.30 | 12,400 | 0.69 | 1,805,900 |
| 1987 | 12,300 | 0.66 | 22,800 | 1.22 | 329,100 | 17.58 | N/A | — | 1,494,900 | 79.88 | 12,400 | 0.66 | 1,871,500 |

**Source:** Association of American Railroads, *Railroad Facts*, 1988 Edition.

hand, has remained essentially the same during the past four years, although the percentage of passenger miles traveled using buses has decreased sharply due air carriers, which today account for approximately 18 percent of all passenger miles traveled.

The number of passenger miles traveled by the private automobile grew from 175,000 million passenger-miles in 1929 to 1.5 billion passenger-miles in 1987, which represents an increase in miles traveled of almost 90 percent.

## Performance

In contrast to small vehicle transportation, the financial success, energy savings, pollution reduction and cost per passenger mile of public transportation systems depend less on the propulsion technology than on the demand density. Higher demand densities support greater service frequencies and higher network densities, which decrease user wait and access times. Users of bus or rail transit must spend extra time going to and from stations and waiting at stations. Mass transit services therefore tend to be slower than private automobiles. However, exclusive rights-of-way such as bus lanes or rail tunnels can compensate for the excess time of mass transit. Moreover, transportation cost usually favors mass transit, especially if fuel is expensive and parking for vehicles is scarce and costly.

State legislative action is particularly important for the development of public transportation systems. Engineers can choose from a great variety of options for propulsion systems, vehicle configuration, facility design and operating concepts. However, as illustrated in table 20, the success of a public transportation system mostly depends on the load factor, which is the number of people using the system per vehicle. For example, the vehicle energy intensity (the Btus used per vehicle mile traveled; see note in table 20) of an Amtrak intercity rail system is about 43,000 Btus per vehicle mile traveled, whereas a commuter rail's vehicle energy intensity is twice as high, about 99,000 Btus per vehicle mile traveled. However, because the load factor for the commuter rail is almost twice as high as that for the intercity route, the transport efficiency (the Btus used per passenger mile traveled; see note in table 20) for the two is almost the same.[4]

### Table 20. Load Factor and Energy Use for Transportation Options in the United States, 1996

| Mode of Transport | Energy Use (trillion Btu) | Vehicle-Miles (millions) | Passenger-Miles (millions) | Load Factor | Btu per vehicle mile | Btu per passenger mile |
|---|---|---|---|---|---|---|
| Automobiles | 8,620.8 | 1,467,703 | 2,348,325 | 1.6 | 5,874 | 3,671 |
| Personal Trucks | 4,040.2 | 573,903 | 918,245 | 1.6 | 7,040 | 4,400 |
| Motorcycles | 24.8 | 9,906 | 11,887 | 1.2 | 2,504 | 2,086 |
| Transit Buses | 85.0 | 2,165 | 18,860 | 8.7 | 39,261 | 4,507 |
| Intercity Buses | 23.1 | 1,220 | 28,300 | 23.2 | 18,394 | 816 |
| School Buses | 68.4 | 5,000 | 99,000 | 19.8 | 13,680 | 691 |
| Certificated Air Route | 1773.1 | 4,809 | 434,468 | 90.3 | 368,705 | 4,081 |
| Amtrak Rail | 12.1 | 278 | 5,066 | 18.2 | 43,525 | 2,389 |
| Light and Heavy Rail | 43.0 | 581 | 12,484 | 21.5 | 74,010 | 3,444 |
| Commuter Rail | 23.9 | 242 | 8,371 | 34.6 | 98,760 | 2,855 |

Notes:

*Vehicle energy intensity* demonstrates how efficiently a vehicle utilizes energy for propulsion, and is not dependent on load factor. Naturally, larger vehicles such as buses or rail cars require more energy for propulsion than a smaller car or truck.

*Transport efficiency* demonstrates how efficiently a vehicle utilizes energy when load factor is considered. Although buses or trains require more energy per vehicle-mile traveled than a car or truck, when load factor is considered, the efficiency of buses and rail is greater because they transport more people per vehicle (i.e., they have a higher load factor).

*British Thermal Unit* (Btu) is a measure of energy consumption regardless of whether it is fossil-fuel, nuclear, electric, water power or some other type of energy.

*Passenger miles* are the number of passengers multiplied by the number of miles they travel.

**Source:** Davis, Stacy C., Center for Transportation Analysis, Oak Ridge National Laboratory, U.S. Department of Energy, *Transportation Energy Data Book*, Table 2.12, Edition 18, ORNL-6941, 1998.

Similar data exists for bus service. The transport efficiency of a fully loaded school bus is about 700 Btus per passenger mile, whereas the transport efficiency of a transit bus, because of its much lower load factor, is 4,500 Btus per passenger mile.[5] This and other available data demonstrate that the success and failure of public mass transportation systems depend to a great extent on factors such as demand, network configuration, routing and service reliability. All these factors are related to land use management, which a state legislature can control more effectively than it can the technology used for a propulsion system.

## Cost of Existing Public Transportation Systems

The cost of any public transport system includes the cost of the infrastructure to support it, including the capital and maintenance cost of the equipment and operating costs.

### *Cost of Infrastructure, Including Capital Cost of Equipment*

Capital funds are needed to build a transit infrastructure. Federal law provides for federal funding to be a maximum of 80 percent of the project cost, with the remainder to be provided by state and local governments. However, some projects are entirely funded at the local or state level, and many areas provide more than the minimum requirement; therefore, only 50 percent of transit capital funding comes from the federal government. Transit agencies raise 24 percent from taxes, tolls and fees they levy, plus what revenues they collect from nongovernmental sources. States contribute 13 percent, and local governments contribute 13 percent.[6]

The American Public Transit Association (APTA), which compiles U.S. public transportation data each year, reports that, in 1996, capital funding for public transit projects was approximately $7 billion.[7] Of this amount, 36 percent was for bus related projects, 36 percent for rail modernization, 27 percent for new start transit projects, and 2 percent for planning. Compared to the net collections for highways in 1996, which is reported at $87 billion by the Federal Highway Administration (FHWA), public transportation received less than 10 percent.[8] Tables 21 and 22 present 1996 and 1997 new capital vehicle costs for buses, vans and rail.

## Table 21. Average New Bus and Van Costs, 1996-1997, Thousands of Dollars[9]

| Type of Vehicle | Bus | Trolleybus | Demand Response | Vanpool |
|---|---|---|---|---|
| Number of Orders | 206 | 1 | 98 | 9 |
| Articulated bus (55'-60') | $376 | — | — | — |
| Intercity bus (35'-40') | 343 | — | — | — |
| Large bus (37'6"-42'5") | 262 | — | — | — |
| Long bus (45') | 369 | — | — | — |
| Medium bus (32'6"-37'5") | 241 | $542 | — | — |
| Small bus (27'6"-32'5") | 218 | — | $74 | — |
| Suburban bus (35'-42'5") | 305 | — | — | — |
| Trolley replica bus | 258 | — | — | — |
| Van/Mini (less than 27'6") | 92 | — | 61 | $27 |

Data from American Public Transit Association (APTA) survey of 10 percent of non-rail transit agencies. Cost includes amount paid to manufacturer plus in-house and third-party costs. Not all orders were reported. Each year of a multi-year order is counted as a separate order.

Source: *Transit Fact Book*, American Public Transit Association, February 1998.

## Table 22. Average New Rail Vehicle Costs, 1996-1997, Thousands of Dollars[10]

| Type of Vehicle | Light Rail | Heavy Rail | Commuter Rail Car | Commuter Rail Locomotive | Other |
|---|---|---|---|---|---|
| Number of Orders | 3 | 3 | 20 | 4 | 0 |
| 1-level cab | — | $1,415 | $1,365 | — | — |
| 1-level non-cab | — | — | 1,135 | — | — |
| 2-level cab | — | — | 1,633 | — | — |
| 2-level non-cab | — | — | 1,576 | — | — |
| 3-level cab | — | — | 1,617 | — | — |
| 3-level non-cab | — | — | 1,511 | — | — |
| Diesel | — | — | — | — | — |
| Diesel-electric | — | — | — | $2,180 | — |
| Electric | — | — | — | 5,174 | — |
| Articulated cab | $2,895 | — | — | — | — |

Data from APTA survey of 90 percent of rail transit agencies. Cost includes amount paid to manufacturer plus in-house and third-party costs. Not all orders were reported. Each year of a multi-year order is counted as a separate order.

Source: *Transit Fact Book*, American Public Transit Association, February 1998.

*Operating Costs*

Funds for the operation of public transportation systems come from the area in which the service is provided. APTA reports that, in 1996, operating expenses for public transport in the United States was $18.5 billion. Of this amount, about 38 percent was funded by passenger fares, 22 percent from local governments, and 15 percent came from nongovernment sources and taxes, tolls and fees levied directly by transit agencies. State and federal governments contribute 22 percent and 3 percent, respectively.[9]

The largest types of expense were salaries and wages (47 percent), fringe benefits (25 percent), purchased transportation (10 percent), and fuel and supplies (9 percent). Services, utilities, insurance and other costs made up the remaining 9 percent.[10] APTA reports that public transportation is among the most labor-intensive of governmental services, since labor expenses (salaries and wages, fringe benefits, services and an estimated 75 percent of purchased transportation) account for more than 80 percent of all expenses.[11]

## Cost of New Rail Transportation Systems

The capital costs involved in implementing new rail systems in U.S. cities has hindered their development. In the 1980s, more than $70 million was spent by state and local governments and the private sector on studies for high-speed rail projects throughout the United States. However, except for high-speed rail projects in Texas and Florida, other studies never have evolved beyond the initial planning stages.[12]

In May 1991, the Texas High-Speed Rail Authority awarded a franchise to the Texas TGV Consortium to privately build and finance a 590-mile high-speed rail system between Dallas/Fort Worth, Houston and San Antonio. The project was estimated to cost more than $5 billion, and certain financial benchmarks were established by the High-Speed Rail Authority to ensure that progress was being made to secure financing. Due to the consortium's inability to secure adequate financing, the project died by early 1994, and in 1995, the Legislature abolished the High-Speed Rail Authority.[13]

The Florida Legislature created a High-Speed Rail Commission that was authorized to grant a franchise to build a privately funded and operated high-speed rail network between Miami, Tampa and Orlando. The project would have constructed nearly 300 miles of new high-speed track at an estimated cost of $3.6 billion. This project also died because of inadequate financing.[14]

Charles H. Smith of the Florida Department of Transportation notes, "Unfortunately, none of the high-speed rail projects proposed in the U.S. can generate sufficient project revenue to cover both operating and capital costs. But then, this is not an unusual situation! Few transportation systems in this country are self-supporting. We subsidize the construction and operation of our highways, airports and seaports at enormous levels and often with detrimental consequences for environmental and community assets. Why should we treat efficient high-speed rail service any differently?"[15]

## Environmental Impact

Adverse environmental impacts of public transportation systems are reduced as load factor and energy efficiency increase. Both these measures of effectiveness will increase if convenience to the user improves. As intelligent transportation networks develop, the integration of public transportation systems with more personalized services such as taxis, carpools and vanpools can reduce wait time and improve convenience to the consumer. State legislation can be very effective in many of these areas. Furthermore, private corporations can assist by providing free or reduced cost rail and bus passes rather than financial support for parking.

Figures 19, 20, and 21 show the emissions generated by the use of public transportation and compares their emissions to the single-occupancy vehicle. In each figure, emissions of nitrogen oxides, carbon monoxide and hydrocarbons are reduced by more than 50 percent through the use of public transport.

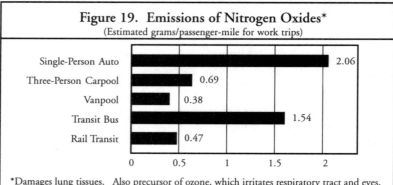

### Figure 19.  Emissions of Nitrogen Oxides*
(Estimated grams/passenger-mile for work trips)

*Damages lung tissues.  Also precursor of ozone, which irritates respiratory tract and eyes, decreases the lungs' working ability and causes both cough and chest pain.

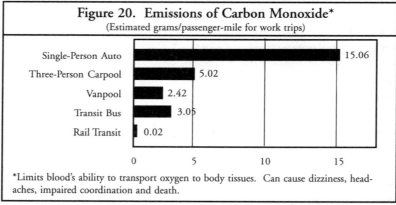

### Figure 20.  Emissions of Carbon Monoxide*
(Estimated grams/passenger-mile for work trips)

*Limits blood's ability to transport oxygen to body tissues.  Can cause dizziness, headaches, impaired coordination and death.

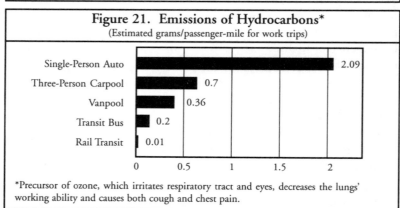

### Figure 21.  Emissions of Hydrocarbons*
(Estimated grams/passenger-mile for work trips)

*Precursor of ozone, which irritates respiratory tract and eyes, decreases the lungs' working ability and causes both cough and chest pain.

Source for figures 19, 20 and 21:  APTA, *Mass Transit—The Clean Air Alternative*, 1991.

# Conclusion

The development of rail or bus mass transit systems could ameliorate gridlock and substantially reduce air pollution. In addition, such systems would be less affected by the expected increase in gas prices after oil production begins to peak. Emerging new propulsion technologies—such as fuel cells and compressed natural gas engines—are easier to implement in large mass transport vehicles than in small single-occupancy vehicles. Moreover, a fully utilized public transportation system will do more to improve energy efficiency and reduce pollution than any policy that continues to rely on alternative single-occupancy vehicles, including fuel cells and EVs.

Creating a successful public transportation system does not depend on the propulsion technology but, rather, on the usage that controls the transport efficiency, pollution and cost. Land use patterns that result in low density housing hinder the development of successful public transportation systems. The future development of better public transportation systems can be greatly assisted by state legislation that uses economic incentives and appropriate land use regulations.

Financial support from the federal government for transportation is concentrated on highway construction and research and development to improve the efficiency and reduce the pollution emitted by single-occupancy vehicles. For example, FHWA estimates total 1998 disbursements for highways to be $106 billion. Of this amount, nearly one-half of all spending was for capital outlays such as highway construction, engineering and right-of-way expenditures.

State and local governments often are forced to abide by and pay for federal mandates related to air pollution and use of alternative fuels. Although these goals are important, they must be supplemented by support for a long-term strategy that includes more emphasis on public transportation and other measures that will reduce reliance on the single-occupancy vehicle as the primary means of ground transportation.

In their book *Sustainability and Cities*, Peter Newman and Jeffrey Kenworthy note five policy techniques for overcoming automobile dependence, including:

- **Quality transit** (including bicycling and walking)—to provide genuine options to the car;

- **Taxing transportation fairly**—to cover external costs and to use the revenues to help build sustainable cities;

- **Growth management**—to prevent urban sprawl and redirect development into urban villages;

- **Urban villages**—to create multinodal centers with mixed, dense land use that reduce the need to travel and that are linked to good transit, and

- **Traffic calming**—to slow auto traffic and create more urban, humane environments that are better suited to other transportation modes.

Newman and Kenworthy also present strategies used in Singapore and Hong Kong in their efforts to overcome dependence on the single-occupancy vehicle. These strategies are included in table 23.

## Table 23. Strategies for Overcoming Automobile Dependence

| Traffic Calming | Favoring Alternative Modes | Economic Penalties | Non-Auto Dependent Land Uses |
|---|---|---|---|
| Low levels of road space to start with and limited new road building for private cars. | Investment in mass rapid transit systems.<br><br>Priority for buses through bus-only lanes and bus-only turns. | High cost of car ownership and use through high taxes on cars and fuel. | City-wide planning based on the integration of high-density, mixed-use nodes at rail stations on rapid transit systems. |
| Pedestrianization and formal traffic-calming schemes. | Buses for surface access to central city through traffic-restriction zone. | Certificates of entitlement to purchase cars (Singapore). | Increasing orientation toward pedestrians and cyclists for local access to nodal centers and to transit. |
| Increasing pedestrian orientation in central area through wide sidewalks, etc. | Heavy parking restrictions. | High parking charges.<br><br>Photo radar | Land use planning totally predicated on encouraging non-auto transportation modes. |
| Photo radar | Effective integration between trains and buses. | High gasoline taxes (Europe) | |
| Speed bumps | Development of circumferential as well as radial rail-transit services. | | |

Source: Newman, Peter, and Jeffrey Kenworthy, *Sustainability and Cities: Overcoming Automobile Dependence*, Island Press, 1999.

# 9. TELECOMMUTING

Telecommuting is the substitution of telecommunications technology for the trip to and from the primary work place, along with the necessary changes in company policy, organization, management and work structure that allow employees to telecommute. In simple terms, it is moving the work to the workers instead of having the workers commute to work.

SBC Communications Incorporated, a global leader in the telecommunications industry, recommends that all companies that are considering telecommuting first ask, "What's in it for us?" With this in mind, legislation in the form of incentives could play an important role in the advancement of telecommuting in American culture. Questions that legislators may wish to ask when considering telecommuting as an option in the larger framework of transportation policy include the following.

- In the state's effort to reduce air pollution and ameliorate traffic congestion, what incentives can be offered to private businesses or not-for-profit organizations that offer their employees the option of telecommuting?

- What telecommuting policies can be instituted for state employees?

- What types of voluntary initiatives can the state advocate in the business community to encourage telecommuting?

120

- Under a telecommuting policy, what legal issues must be considered if an employee is injured or killed while doing business away from the work place?

- How much will telecommuting affect the state's revenue base? Will the use of telecommuting affect state tax law?

## History of Telecommuting

Providing the background for telecommuting are computers, cellular phones, fax machines and advanced communication links such as integrated digital service networks that have removed the necessity for workers to conduct their jobs in central offices. These technological advancements, coupled with America's competitive service economy, allow businesses to consider telecommuting in terms of cost savings. Widespread telecommuting in a service firm reduces the need for office space required to support employees. This reduction in office space offers companies significant cost savings in terms of rent and maintenance.

## What Is Telecommuting?

Telecommuting is the use of telecommunication and computer technologies to replace or reduce traditional commuting to the work place. Telecommuters most often work in service careers such as sales or consulting. Most telecommuting occurs on a part-time basis, with part of the work week spent at the traditional office and the other part spent working at home.

Telecommuting options include:

*Work at Home*—The most popular form of telecommuting is working at home. Employees designate work space at home to conduct business functions one or more days per week.

*Satellite Office*—A remote office location—usually placed within a concentration of employee residences—allows employees from a single company to share office space and reduce the time and expense of traveling to and from the main office facility.

*Hoteling*—An office operation where space is designed for use on a shared, as-needed basis. The work force literally checks into and out of office space to use standard business tools and technologies.

*Neighborhood Work Center*—This space provides work space for employees of different companies in one location. Each company at a neighborhood work center is responsible for the administrative and technical requirements of its employees.

*Virtual Office Mobile Worker*—An airport, hotel, car or even a solitary table can be a work place for the growing number of "mobile workers." Employees who are constantly on the road, using technology to link them to customers, the office or suppliers, are literally, telecommuters.

## Environmental and Social Impacts

Reducing automobile use is a primary benefit of telecommuting. Studies of telecommuters have shown clear and dramatic reductions in all aspects of automobile usage, because telecommuters eliminate two trips per day if they work at home.[1] Environmental and social benefits that appear with reduced automobile use are reduction in rush hour traffic, improved air quality and conservation of liquid fuel energy.

As the number of telecommuters increases across the United States, so will the associated environmental and social gains. According to a survey by Telecommute America, the number of Americans who telecommute from their homes to their places of business rose by 3 million people, or 30 percent, from 1997 to 1999.[2] Other telecommuting statistics also point to a rising trend in its use. A FIND/SVP's 1997 American Internet users survey found that the number of teleworkers rose from 4 million in 1990 to 11 million in 1997. It is estimated that, in 1998, almost 16 million people telecommuted in the United States.[3]

Projects that demonstrate the benefits of telecommuting include those described below.

- A telecommuting pilot program in California demonstrated that productivity increased from between 10 percent to 30 percent among workers who had this option.[4]

- A 1997 telecommunications survey conducted by the Institute of Transportation Studies at the University of California at Davis showed that California commuters spend 300,000 hours daily sitting in traffic. Of those hours, 90,000 are wasted by Bay area commuters alone, at a cost of more than $210 million. It is estimated that, if 10 percent of the work force were to telecommute only once a week, Californians could save more than 1.2 million gallons of fuel and reduce air pollution by almost 13,000 tons.[5]

## Conclusion

Telecommuting has the potential to reduce rush hour traffic, improve air quality and save liquid fuel, although technical data substantiating these claims is not widely demonstrated. State governments can actively participate in the state's promotion of telecommuting for part of the work force, as well as implement telecommuting in state governments. An awareness of the advantages of telecommuting and its potential to reduce traffic congestion, air pollution and fossil fuel consumption is an important step in the deliberations of state governments as they deal with transportation issues in the next century.

For telecommuting to work effectively as a traffic reduction measure, planning and policy efforts must be coordinated between various departments. It is counterproductive for one department to encourage telecommuting while another advocates for additional highway lanes. Strategies to facilitate automobile use can act as a disincentive to telecommuting. Larger highway systems and free work place parking encourage people to remain in their cars.

The International Telework Association and Council (ITAC) launched a far-reaching and intensive telework education and implementation initiative in 1998. Members of Congress were asked to officially declare 1999 as the year of telework and Wednesday, Oct. 27, 1999, as Telework America Day.[6] State legislatures can play an important role in facilitating their state's future participation in this effort.

# 10. Intelligent Transportation Systems

Traditionally, states combat traffic congestion by building new roads or adding lanes to existing highways. Increasingly, however, states are relying on computer-based technology to more effectively use the existing infrastructure. Collectively known as intelligent transportation systems (ITS), advanced information and communication technologies are helping states more efficiently manage their transportation networks. The ambitious goals of ITS are to reduce congestion, improve safety, and create new technologies and new jobs.

States use integrated technology to control and manage traffic, improve transportation safety, dispense travel and transit information, limit environmental pollution, route motor carriers, manage transit systems, quicken toll operations, guide parking, and save money for government agencies and private companies. ITS technologies range from the very sophisticated and very costly to the practical and not so costly; automated highway systems where specially equipped cars, trucks and buses travel together under computer control will be very expensive to implement, whereas electronic payment capabilities at toll booths are less expensive and already in use.

As ITS evolves, state legislators will be increasingly involved in ITS deployment and funding decisions. Questions that legislators and

This section has been abstracted in part from James B. Reed, Janet B. Goehring and Chris Pattarozzi, "Intelligent Transportation in America: Prospects and Perils," *Transportation Series*, no. 1 (January 1996), National Conference of State Legislatures.

other interested parties may wish to ask when considering ITS as a policy option include the following.

- What are the goals that the legislature wishes to address through the use of ITS? Have alternative solutions been considered to meet those goals?

- Are the benefits of the ITS technology clearly defined and tested?

- What is the size of the public investment necessary to fund an intelligent transportation system?

- Will the average consumer be able to afford to purchase or install specific ITS technologies?

- Is a majority of the legislature in agreement that ITS is only a short-term solution to ameliorating gridlock and dampening the effects of urban population growth, and that it may possibly stimulate single-occupancy vehicle use?

- Has the legislature considered a coordinated effort to implement ITS among all levels of state government, the federal government, geographical lines and the private sector?

- What are the privacy issues associated with ITS? (For example, information generated by ITS will contain "real time" information about the location of vehicles—and, possibly, drivers and passengers—at any given time.)

## History of Intelligent Transportation Systems

The field of intelligent transportation systems gained attention in 1991, when Congress authorized $660 million over six years to research, develop and test ITS under the banner of the Intelligent Vehicle-Highway Systems Act of 1991, a part of the Intermodal Surface Transportation Efficiency Act (ISTEA). This act authorized a program of research, development and operational testing to establish ITS as a component of the nation's surface transportation system. The program strives to enhance the capacity, efficiency and safety of the federal-aid highway system and the states' efforts to attain mandated air quality goals, while also reducing the societal, economic and environmental costs associated with traffic congestion. As a result, projects began to proliferate across the country to test and deploy new ITS technologies.

As a part of TEA-21, authorized in 1998, a total of $1.282 billion in contract authority is provided for fiscal years 1998 to 2003 to fund ITS programs. Of this total, $603 million is targeted to research, training and standards development. Programs to accelerate integration and interoperability in the metropolitan and rural areas and to deploy commercial vehicle ITS infrastructure are established and funded at $482 million and $184 million, respectively. Funding for metropolitan areas is limited primarily to integration of infrastructure.

Many states have embraced ITS and are actively involved in planning and implementing ITS projects. Several states are represented on the ITS American Coordinating Council, which oversees the development of a national ITS program. State and local participation is a key to the success of any ITS architecture because states have the primary responsibility for managing traffic and building, operating and maintaining surface transportation systems.

## Intelligent Transportation System Technologies

ITS technologies range from the very sophisticated and very costly (automated highway systems) to the more practical and not as expensive (electronic payment systems). Categories of ITS are listed in italics in figure 22. The categories—in ITS lingo—commonly are referred to as user services bundles; specific services are referred to as user services. Appendix H presents descriptions of ITS user service technologies as defined in the U.S. Department of Transportation's ITS Architecture.

# Figure 22.  Intelligent Transportation System Categories

| User Services Bundles | User Services |
|---|---|
| *Travel and Transportation Management* | En-Route Driver Information<br>Route Guidance<br>Traveler Services Information<br>Traffic Control<br>Incident Management<br>Emissions Testing and Mitigation<br>Demand Management and Operations<br>Pre-Trip Travel Information<br>Ride Matching and Reservation<br>Highway-Rail Intersection |
| *Public Transportation Operations* | Public Transportation Management<br>En-Route Transit Information<br>Personalized Public Transit<br>Public Travel Security |
| *Electronic Payment* | Electronic Payment Services |
| *Commercial Vehicle Operations* | Commercial Vehicle Electronic Clearance<br>Automated Roadside Safety Inspection<br>On-Board Safety Monitoring<br>Commercial Vehicle Administration<br>  Process<br>Hazardous Materials Incident Response |
| *Emergency Management* | Emergency Notification and Personal<br>  Security<br>Emergency Vehicle Management |
| *Advanced Vehicle Control and Safety Systems* | Longitudinal Collision Avoidance<br>Lateral Collision Avoidance<br>Intersection Collision Avoidance<br>Vision Enhancement for Crash Avoidance<br>Safety Readiness<br>Pre-Crash Restraint Deployment<br>Automated Highway System |

**Source:** *LEAP-Learning from the Evaluation and Analysis of Performance of Intelligent Transportation Systems*, California PATH (a joint venture between the University of California at Berkeley, Calif. Department of Transportation and private industry), http://www.path.berkeley.edu/~leap, 1999.

## *ITS Architectures*

When ITS became available, communities often used an individual technology to provide one particular service. As ITS grew more sophisticated, however, communities linked technologies and applications so that individual systems could provide many services.

Today, these links between ITS technologies and applications—collectively known as "architectures"—integrate services across the country and play a vital role in the national transportation network. Architectures allow diverse electronic systems and applications to be tied together, providing a unified framework for an ITS strategy. Architectures also allow ITS programs to be added in phases that reflect each area's needs and available funding.

Greater compatibility between ITS systems through an architecture— either within a particular jurisdiction or among many jurisdictions— helps ITS work more efficiently and allows a cohesive, long-range vision. An architecture can show the complete travel picture, including possible traffic management and public transit options, and can help provide better and more up-to-date information. The National ITS Architecture coordinated efforts among traffic, transit, and police, fire and rescue forces to improve overall management of a transportation network.

## Cost

The public and private sectors have committed several million dollars in ITS research and implementation during the past 10 years. LEAP-ITS reports that some of the most mature technologies— the most prominent of these are traffic surveillance and control technologies—have been tested and deployed within the existing transportation infrastructure. However, information about the results from such tests is limited and usually scattered in several publications. With few exceptions, these results have not been pooled and compared across test sites to draw conclusions about the most cost-effective technologies to implement and the circumstances in which they work best. A similar situation occurs with deployed technologies, where evidence of benefits usually is anecdotal and costs are "lost" in the implementing agency's accounting system.[1]

Even with this dilemma of scattered data among ITS projects, it is clear that the cost of purchasing, demonstrating, implementing and maintaining ITS technologies can be very high and due to the wide range of available technologies, must be evaluated on a project by project basis due to the wide range of technologies available. ITS demonstration and testing projects are a necessary and often costly step in the ITS implementation process. If an ITS demonstration project is successful and significant funding is available, it may be implemented into the ITS architecture. Although ITS technology often is readily available, the application of the technology must be tested and refined for specific localities and traffic conditions.

LEAP-ITS reports that the cost per transaction of an electronic toll collection (ETC) system—a mature ITS technology—is estimated to range between $0.05 and $0.10. In comparison, the cost per transaction of a manual collection system is approximately $0.086. Cost projections estimated for the Pennsylvania Turnpike Authority indicate that a full ETC interchange can cost as little as one-quarter to one-fifth that of a conventional cash toll interchange. In terms of operational costs, while a conventional interchange requires 25 full-time employees (assuming four toll booths) at a cost of up to one-third of the toll collection revenue, the ETC option would require only one maintenance person and account support.[2]

Several examples are provided of ITS demonstration and testing projects for various states, along with their completion dates and final costs. The projects listed are demonstration and testing projects only; therefore, the cost required to maintain and operate an ITS system must be added to any amount provided below.

*Examples of ITS Demonstration and Testing Projects and their Costs*

**Connecticut Freeway Advanced Traffic Management Systems (ATMS)**
**Completed:** December 1996
**Total Cost:** $1,380,000

This ATMS project evaluated the use of roadside mounted radar detectors in combination with closed circuit television (CCTV) for incident detection and verification. The ATMS uses 44 radar detectors (wide- and narrow-beam) and compressed video.[3]

**Multi-State Electronic One-Stop Shopping Operational Tests**
**Completed:** Not complete as of February 1999
**Expected Total Cost:** $7,874,856

This project—based in 15 western states—demonstrates a microcomputer-based vehicle one-stop credential purchasing process that reduces public and private sector time and costs; streamlines administrative processes and speeds up turnaround times; improves consistency and uniformity; extends access and availability; and ensures all commercial vehicle operators uniform access to one-stop shopping without causing substantial expenditures or establishment of new bureaucracies.[4]

**Boston Smart Traveler**
**Completed:** December 1994
**Total Cost:** $3,395,000

The project tested the public acceptance and potential traffic impacts of a telephone-based audiotext traffic information service. Travelers can call from home or office or from cellular phones at any time by dialing (617) 374-1234 or *1, respectively. In using touch tone prompts, travelers hear traffic reports on their chosen links; these reports are updated minute by minute. SmartRoute also provides radio and TV reports (WODS-FM and Channel 5, WCVB-TV) in the Boston area.[5]

**MTA Baltimore Smart Bus**
**Completed:** December 1996
**Total Cost:** $8,100,000

This project involved implementation of an automatic vehicle location (AVL) system to provide bus status information to the public while simultaneously improving bus schedule adherence and labor productivity. The system will be expanded to include all 900 Baltimore transit buses. Global positioning system (GPS) inputs are replacing LORAN-C technology for vehicle location. Following a performance test of equipped versus non-equipped buses, figures reflected a 23 percent improvement in on-time performance by the AVL-equipped buses.[6]

**New Jersey TRANSMIT (TRANSCOM) Project**
**Completed:** January 1998
**Total Cost:** $3,438,500

This test evaluated the use of automatic vehicle identification (AVI) technology as an incident detection tool. The system consists of AVI "tag" readers that allow vehicles equipped with transponders to serve as traffic probes to identify potential incidents by comparing actual to predicted travel times between readers. TRANSCOM, a consortium of 14 transportation and public safety agencies in New Jersey, New York and Connecticut, works to improve interagency response to traffic incidents.[7]

**Chicago ADVANCE Project**
**Completed:** December 1996
**Total Cost:** $31,000,000

The primary purpose of the ADVANCE project was to assess the feasibility of providing dynamic route guidance (DRG) and to assess its effect on travel time for drivers who are familiar with the arterial network in the suburbs northwest of Chicago. The test was managed by the Illinois DOT. Deleuw Cather & Company was the system integrator, and designed and operated the traffic information center (TIC). The TIC software was written by the University of Illinois at

Chicago. Motorola provided the in-vehicle navigation units. A number of auto companies donated test vehicles.[8]

## Conclusion

Intelligent transportation systems are new technologies that can help states better manage their transportation networks. ITS consists of both proven, or mature technologies, as well as unproven and more sophisticated technologies. For the short-term, ITS offers a variety of technologies that can reduce congestion and enhance safety; long-term possibilities include automated highway systems. ITS also can improve public transit service through better scheduling and routing. Development of ITS will be of some assistance in transportation policy planning, but is only part of a long-term solution.

ITS offers the potential to improve the flow of traffic and reduce fuel waste due to gridlock and start-and-stop traffic conditions in metropolitan areas. However, ITS applications are not fully developed or widely accepted. At this time, the benefits and costs of deploying ITS have not been clearly demonstrated, and it may be difficult for state legislators to clearly assess the potential of the wide range of ITS technologies to reduce gridlock and air pollution.

# 11. Summary Observations

The transport of people and goods is a key element of modern industrial society. Since the turn of the century when oil was discovered and the internal combustion engine was developed, automobiles and trucks powered by internal combustion engines have taken the place of horse drawn carriages and railroads as the most widely used means of ground transportation. Today, more than 97 percent of the fuel used for transportation in the United States comes from oil.

Almost all the current ground transportation options considered by the federal and state governments deal with ameliorating traffic problems within the next five to 10 years, but none of them have an intermediate or long-term perspective that can simultaneously deal with increased air pollution, a substantial rise in the cost of oil and growing gridlock in metropolitan areas. An urgent need exists to seek a comprehensive long-term approach to the transportation of goods and people in a time frame beyond the next decade. To assist legislators in determining the effect of a given vehicle technology on the various transportation issues discussed in this book, table 24 displays these interactions in a matrix. Obviously, no single approach to solving the total transportation dilemma is feasible, but a combination of approaches may lead to appropriate solutions.

Table 24 summarizes the potential effects of using a particular ground transportation technology, based on the qualitative assessments made in this book. For additional information that supports this matrix, refer to the chapter in this book that describes the given technology option. The authors wish to stress that additional analysis is necessary to present a more precise assessment based upon concrete engi-

134

## Table 24. Summary of Potential Transportation Effects

| | Electric Vehicles | Hybrid Vehicles | Fuel Cell Vehicles | Alternative Fuel Vehicles | High Efficiency Gasoline/Diesel Engines | Telecommuting | Intelligent Transportation | Public Transportation |
|---|---|---|---|---|---|---|---|---|
| Air Quality Improvement | Some | Some | Major | Some | Some | Major | Some | Some |
| Oil Consumption Reduction | Major | Some | Major | Some | Some | Major | Some | Some |
| Gridlock Reduction | None | None | None | None | None | Major | Some | Major |
| Infrastructure Requirement | Major | None | Major | Major | None | None | Some | Major |
| Commercial Availability | Now | Soon | Distant | Now | Soon | Now | Soon | Now |
| Can Become Renewable | Maybe | Maybe | Maybe | Maybe | No | N/A | N/A | Maybe |
| Disposal Problem | Yes | Yes | Unsure | No | No | No | No | No |
| Require New Safety Regulations | Maybe | Maybe | Yes | No | No | No | Maybe | Some |

Source: NCSL, 1999.

neering data to describe the quantitative effects of using an alternative transportation technology. The quantitative effects of each technology option depend largely on the number of people who use the technology. With this in mind, the descriptors—"great," "some," "none," etc.—are based on the original criteria used in this book to analyze each transportation option (see "Approach to Analysis"), which requires that alternatives attract a mass-market audience to make significant inroads in solving national goals, such as reductions in air pollution, gridlock and dependence on foreign oil.

The evidence presented in this transportation technology assessment for the short-term (2000 to 2005) and intermediate-term (2005 to 2020) suggests four primary observations.

- The most realistic transportation options for the time frame between now and the projected peak of world oil production are improved mileage vehicles, such as hybrid electric vehicles and high-efficiency gasoline and diesel engines.

- Except for hybrid electric vehicles, all alternative fueled vehicles—including electricity, fuel cells, ethanol, methanol, and natural gas—require a new infrastructure that will take time, effort and money to construct if it is to serve the general public in an efficient manner. The lead time involved in the construction of a new infrastructure inhibits public acceptance of new technologies.

- To soften the impact of potentially sharp price increases in gasoline for the general public as well as reduce air pollution and ameliorate gridlock, the development of public transportation and intelligent transportation systems and the increased use of telecommuting will be important considerations.

- Based on evidence from other countries where gasoline costs as much as $4 per gallon, there is little reason to believe that an increase in the cost of fuel alone will dissuade people from using their automobiles. It is more likely that, when gridlock becomes so severe that it takes more time to commute by car than by public transport, people will be willing to give up the automobile and switch to public transportation. This change in behavior can be assisted by making public transport affordable and convenient to the majority of people, particularly in metropolitan areas. This process also can be assisted by appropriate land use and public transportation planning and taxation.

It should be emphasized that the analysis presented in this book deals with ground transportation options for the time period between 2000 and 2020. Despite many encouraging stories in the press regarding new transportation technologies, hard data is lacking to support the many expectations that they purport. Research and development on alternative transportation options will continue to be pursued vigorously and may at some future time provide transportation options that are not considered here. Hence, the conclusions presented herein should be periodically updated and reevaluated as new results become available.

Other specific conclusions concerning specific transportation technology options include the following:

- Financial support by the federal government for transportation is concentrated on highway construction and research and development to improve the efficiency and reduce the pollution emitted by single-occupancy vehicles. State governments often are forced to abide by and pay for federal mandates related to air pollution and use of alternative fuels. Although these goals are important, they should be supplemented by development of a long-term strategy that includes more emphasis on public transport and other measures that will reduce reliance on the single-occupancy vehicle as the primary means of ground transportation.

- The current cost of electric vehicles is roughly twice that of a traditional vehicle of the same size. The mileage and range offered by electric vehicles between battery recharging is considerably less and the upkeep and maintenance cost are appreciably higher than for a similar size gasoline powered vehicle.

- Hybrid electric vehicles can reduce emissions of pollutants, decrease gasoline consumption appreciably and increase fuel economy almost twofold compared to conventional gasoline powered vehicles. Hybrid electric vehicles also can function nationwide with the current gasoline infrastructure, but are more expensive to purchase and operate than conventional gasoline powered vehicles.

- Fuel cells are technically able to provide the performance and range of gasoline engines, but cost many times more per unit power than a gasoline or hybrid electric power source. Current fuel cell vehicles use hydrogen as the fuel; no infrastructure exists to transport and store this potentially explosive gas. Hydrogen for fuel cells can be produced from methanol or natural gas on board the vehicle by a reformer. This technology, however, is still a research and development challenge for a transportation vehicle that is not likely to be an economically viable option within the oil peaking time frame.

- Natural gas can be useful as a fuel for the mass transport of people and goods over established routes that can be serviced with a minimal of new storage and distribution infrastructure.

- None of the alternative fuels under consideration at this time appears to offer a realistic substitute in price and convenience for gasoline or diesel in a regular-sized car in the near future without technical breakthroughs; these breakthroughs are difficult to predict.

- Alternative fuels such as ethanol and methanol have not been successful in the marketplace on a wide scale and there is only a minimal infrastructure for either of them in place. Moreover, although these fuels can be produced from renewable biomass stock, the current production methods use natural gas as the base. Hence, the mileage obtained with ethanol or methanol should include to the energy content of the natural gas used in the production of these fuels, not just the energy content of the derived liquid fuel.

- Almost all the alternative fuel vehicles will ameliorate air pollution to a certain extent, but claims of zero tailpipe emissions are misleading. Pollution is emitted in the production of electric power necessary to charge the batteries of electric vehicles and in the cryogenic refrigeration necessary to liquefy hydrogen to the temperature necessary for transporting it.

- A comparison of the cost of producing ethanol or methanol with synthetic gasoline or diesel fuel suggests that it would be less expensive per unit of energy to produce synthetic gasoline and diesel from coal or natural gas than it would be to produce ethanol from corn or methanol from natural gas. It is suggested that an in-depth engineering study be conducted to provide conclusive evidence on the actual production cost of liquid fuel from coal in order to plan for a long-term ground transportation future that would continue to use the existing fuel delivery infrastructure.

- There is no evidence that oxygenates such as MTBE, ETBE or ethanol mixed with gasoline, reduce air pollution. However, leakage of MTBE from storage tanks and pipelines can dissolve in water and produce a health hazard. A recent report by the National Academy of Sciences indicated that, from a technical point of view, there is no reason for the federal government to require states to continue the use of oxygenates, including gasohol, either during the winter or at any other time.

- Federal mandates that require the states to purchase alternative fuel vehicles and reach a certain percentage of alternative fuel vehicles in their fleet in the future should be revisited because there are no indications that these regulations are the most effective way to improve air quality. Moreover, dual fuel vehicles— that are considerably more expensive than gasoline vehicles— have not lived up to their promise. Most drivers find it difficult to locate fueling stations for ethanol, methanol and natural gas, and fill their vehicles with gasoline most of the time.

- Individual car buyers who are considering buying an alternative fuel vehicle should be aware of the limited infrastructure available and the extra cost involved in buying, operating and maintaining an alternative fuel vehicle. This could be accomplished by providing informational stickers similar to those used to alert buyers of the energy efficiency of household appliances such as refrigerators and domestic hot water heaters.

- Recent engineering advances in pollution control devices, especially catalytic converters, have reduced harmful emissions from new cars and trucks to the point where smog and haze could be eliminated in metropolitan areas if the 10 percent of the worst polluting vehicles that are responsible for more than 50 percent of all air pollution were removed from service or properly repaired. However, regulation of the tail pipe emission control systems should be continued because even the cleanest of new automobiles can become bad polluters over time if they are not properly maintained.

- All major automobile manufacturers are developing engines that will reduce pollution and improve vehicle mileage. Current expectations by major manufacturers are that high-efficiency vehicles will achieve somewhere between 50 miles per gallon and 70 miles per gallon and appreciably reduce emissions of most major pollutants.

- Technologies such as cell telephones, lap-top computers and the internet have made it possible in all cases to move more work to the worker rather than the worker to the work place. Experience with telecommuting has shown that rush hour traffic as well as air pollution can be reduced and worker productivity increased by appropriate telecommuting systems.

- Intelligent transportation systems are a recent addition in the options available to improve transportation systems. Although not a major contributor to solving statewide transportation problems, intelligent transportation systems can improve traffic flow, ameliorate congestion and reduce pollution in local areas.

- The gridlock caused by single-occupancy vehicles in the nation's big cities is estimated to cost Americans on the order of $74 billion per year in lost time and wasted fuel. Serious additional gridlock can arise when the fueling and storage infrastructure is not adequate. State highway planners can consider the use of high occupancy vehicle lanes to mitigate congestion for the short- and medium-term, at relatively low cost and high potential value.

• Adding more lanes to existing roads can ameliorate gridlock in the short-term, but is not an effective long-term solution to the transportation problems confronted by states.

• Public transport systems that use buses and rail will be needed to help reduce congestion and soften the impact of high fuel cost on low-income Americans. The success of public transport in reducing pollution, gridlock and high commuting costs depends more on external factors—such as land use patterns, convenience, route location and public acceptance—than on the propulsion system. However, large vehicles such as buses and trucks are more suitable for the deployment of new or alternative propulsion systems such as fuel cells and compressed natural gas engines than are single-occupancy vehicles.

• Public input is imperative in the planning of any transport system. The most important criteria for the success of public transportation systems are the vehicle load factor and the energy use per passenger mile. The most energy efficient urban public transportation option is a well-designed light rail system.

# APPENDIX A. WORLD OIL PRODUCTION FORECASTS

## What Is the Oil Production Peak?

When exploratory drilling finds a crude oil reservoir, the earth's internal pressure forces the oil to the surface. For the average reservoir, the amount of oil flowing to the surface increases as more wells are drilled and a larger portion of the reservoir is accessed. However, as time goes on, the reservoir pressure declines, oil production reaches a peak and then declines as shown in figure 23. The apex of the oil production from the reservoir occurs roughly after one-half the oil

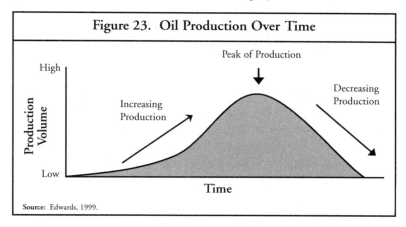

Figure 23. Oil Production Over Time

Source: Edwards, 1999.

---

Information contained in this appendix was supplied by John D. Edwards, former Latin American exploration operations manager for Shell Oil Company and currently an adjunct professor at the University of Colorado at Boulder.

has been taken from the well. The behavior of a single, average oil well is typical of the oil flow from all oil wells in a region or a country.

In 1956, oil geologist M. King Hubbert formulated the behavior of a typical oil well analytically and predicted that oil production in the United States would peak about 1973. His prediction has been borne out, and oil production in this country has declined since that time. Figure 24 illustrates U.S. oil production from 1900 to 2050.

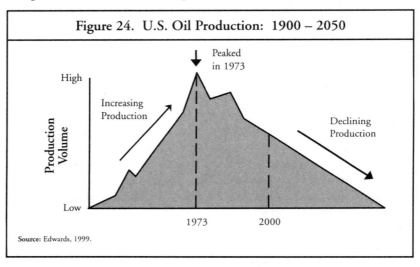

**Figure 24. U.S. Oil Production: 1900 – 2050**

Source: Edwards, 1999.

Using the analysis of M. King Hubbert, scientists in the solar energy field predicted in the 1970s that the world would run short of oil by the turn of the century. These predictions came from people with no experience in the oil and gas industries, but they were reported in the media as though they were based upon hard data from peer reviewed technical analyses. In view of the fact that now, at the turn of this century, the supply is plentiful and the price is low, many people question the predictions made at this time regarding the future peaking of world wide oil supply. This is what psychologists call the 'cry wolf syndrome.' However, the people predicting a future peak in the availability of crude oil today are not promoters of solar energy—as in the 1970s—but instead are experts associated with oil companies all over the world.

Using available data, oil companies and geologists predict that global oil production will peak somewhere between the year 2000 and 2025. Table 25 presents a summary of the dates at which oil experts expect the world to reach its peak in oil production. It is important to note that the difference between the most optimistic and most pessimistic projection is only 25 years.

### Table 25. Date of Peak World Oil Production According to Various Experts

| Name or Organization | Predicted Year of Peak in Global Oil Production |
|---|---|
| 1. P. Appleby (1996)<br>British Petroleum-Amoco, England | 2010 |
| 2. C. Campbell (1998)<br>Petroconsultants, Switzerland | 2005 |
| 3. F. Bernabe (1998)<br>ENI, Italy | 2000 - 2005 |
| 4. R. Duncan and W. Youngquist (1998)<br>Institute on Energy and Man, U.S.A. | 2006 |
| 5. J. Edwards (1997)<br>University of Colorado, U.S.A. | 2020 |
| 6. OECD International Energy Agency* (1998) | 2010 - 2020 |
| 7. L. Ivanhoe (1995)<br>Colorado School of Mines, U.S.A. | 2000 |
| 8. J. Laherrere* (1999)<br>Petroleum Consultant | 2010 - 2020 |
| 9. J. MacKenzie (1996)<br>World Resources Institute, U.S.A. | 2007 - 2019 |
| 10. W. Schollnberger (1998)<br>British Petroleum-Amoco, England | 2020 |
| 11. R. Udall and S. Andrews (1999)<br>Colorado School of Mines, U.S.A. | 2005 - 2025 |
| 12. J. Van der Veer (1997)<br>Royal Dutch Shell Oil Company, England | 2020 |

* (Includes Venezuelan heavy oil, Canadian tar sand oil and oil from oil shales.)

# Appendix B. 1999 Model Electric Vehicles

## General Motors EV-1

- **Availability:** Available for lease in Southern California, the San Francisco Bay Area, Los Angeles, Phoenix and Tucson.
- **Price:** Manufacturer's suggested retail price (MSRP) is $33,395. In California, the lease is $400 per month for 36 months. The lease is $550 per month for 36 months in Arizona. The disparity is due to higher government incentives in California than in Arizona. Start-up costs average about $2,900. This includes first-month lease payment, taxes, registration and charger installation. Although the EV-1 chassis is not available with a gasoline-powered engine, GM's Saturn SC1 is similar. The MSRP on the SC1 is around $15,000. For comparative purposes, an incremental cost of more than $18,000 is associated with the EV-1.
- **Features:** The EV-1 has all the standard features of conventional gasoline powered cars: air conditioning, radio, dual airbags, anti-lock brakes, traction control, cruise control, and power windows, locks and mirrors. In addition, the EV-1 has regenerative braking.
- **Battery information:** The EV-1 uses 26 valve-regulated lead-acid modules and one accessory battery made by Delco. This pack weighs 1,175 pounds and has a maximum storage capacity of 16.2 kWh. The range of the EV-1 under optimal conditions is 90 miles. Cold temperatures, hilly terrain and use of air conditioning may drastically reduce this range. According to GM,

146

driving the EV-1 in the city consumes 0.3 kWh per mile. High-way driving uses 0.25 kWh per mile.

- **Charging information:** A $2,000, 220-volt inductive charger is installed at the user's house. At 70 degrees Fahrenheit, it takes 90 minutes to charge from 20 percent to 80 percent battery capacity. Three hours is needed for a full charge. The EV-1 also can be charged using a standard 110-volt electric outlet with a portable charger located in the trunk. This method takes 15 hours to achieve full charge.

- **Performance:** A 137-horsepower engine allows the EV-1 to reach 30 miles per hour (mph) in less than 3 seconds and 60 mph in 9 seconds. The top speed is governed at 80 mph. A 1994 proto-type EV-1 reached 183 mph.

- **Other Information:** General Motors offered nickel-metal hydride batteries in the 1999 EV-1.

## Ford Ranger EV Pickup

- **Availability:** The Ranger EV Pickup is initially targeted toward fleet customers. Fleet operators in California, the Southwest, the Southeast and the Northeast are using the Ranger EV in 1998.

- **Price:** Not including tax credits or incentives, the Ranger EV costs $32,795 MSRP. The base price for a regular Ranger Pickup is $14,500 MSRP, so there is an incremental cost of approximately $18,000.

- **Features:** Features are the same as the gasoline-powered Ranger, but include an on-board charger and regenerative braking.

- **Battery information:** Thirty-nine 8-volt modules make up the Ranger EVs lead-acid battery pack, which holds 23 kilowatt-hours of electricity, and under optimal conditions can travel 58 miles. Ford estimates the range is more likely 50 miles under "real world miles"—an estimate based on city and highway driving, air conditioning usage and other factors that may affect energy consumption. This corresponds to 0.46 kWh per mile.

- **Charging information:** The Ranger EV uses conductive charging.

- **Performance:** A 90-horsepower, three-phase motor enables the Ranger EV to reach speeds of 75 mph (governed) in drive mode and 65 mph in economy mode. It can go from zero to 50 mph in 12.5 seconds and has a payload of 700 pounds.

- **Other information:** The 1999 Ranger EV has a Ni-MH battery pack option. This increases the payload to 1,250 pounds and the range to nearly 100 miles.

## Chrysler EPIC Electric Minivan

- **Availability:** This is a fleet vehicle and is available for lease only in California.
- **Features:** Standard, plus an on-board charger and regenerative braking.
- **Price:** This minivan costs $450 per month, or $38,750 MSRP. The EPIC Minivan is the electric version of the Dodge Caravan and the Plymouth Voyager. A similar Voyager has an MSRP of approximately $19,500. An incremental cost of over $19,000 is associated with the EPIC.
- **Battery and charging information:** Uses lead-acid batteries from Horizon. This is the third battery system used in the EPIC Minivan. It has a specific power of 153 watts per kilogram, a specific energy of 45 watt-hours per kilogram, a capacity of 29 kWh and is charged by conductive means. The battery pack enables the EPIC Minivan to travel an estimated 68 miles (combined city and highway).
- **Performance:** Top speed is governed at 80 mph and it can reach 60 mph in 16 seconds from standstill. The electric engine generates 100 horsepower and can hold five people or carry an 800-pound payload.
- **Other information:** The 1999 Epic Minivan will represent Chrysler's second chassis design and fourth battery pack. It will use 28 12-volt Ni-MH batteries that should last four to six years under normal use. This will increase payload to 925 pounds and range to 90 miles. Charge time will vary from six to eight hours using the on-board charger. It is compatible with the new 440-volt public chargers. Chrysler says that the Ni-MH batteries are not as affected by cold weather as the previous model's lead-acid batteries were.

## Chevrolet S-10 Electric Pickup

- **Availability:** Available for fleets nationwide.
- **Price:** The S-10 gasoline-powered truck has an MSRP of $12,100. The Electric S-10 is suggested at $34,289, an incremental cost of $22,100. This does not include tax credits or incentives.
- **Features:** Standard, plus an on-board charger and regenerative braking.
- **Battery and charger information:** Twenty-six Delco lead-acid batteries power the S-10, the same used in the EV-1. It also uses an inductive charging system. This corresponds to a range of 40 to 60 miles and an energy usage of approximately 0.32 kWh per vehicle mile traveled.
- **Performance:** Can go from zero to 50 mph in 10.3 seconds, has a payload capacity of 950 pounds and is governed at a top speed of 70 mph. Electric engine generates 114 horsepower.
- **Other information:** A nickel metal-hydride battery pack powers the 1999 model. This increases performance (range 80 miles, top speed 78 mph, payload 950 pounds) and has an energy capacity of 32.2 kWh. The 1999 S-10 EV will use 0.4 kWh per mile traveled.

## Honda EV Plus (*DISCONTINUED, MAY 1999*)

- **Availability:** Fleets in California and New York can lease the EV Plus.
- **Price:** The MSRP is $53,999, which explains its availability only for lease at $455 per month for three years. This includes comprehensive and liability insurance. An in-house charger is installed at a one-time fee of $1,600 to $2,300, depending on the difficulty of installation.
- **Features:** Standard, plus an on-board charger and regenerative braking.
- **Battery and charging information:** The EV Plus uses 24 nickel metal-hydride batteries, which explains the high MSRP. It takes eight hours for a full conductive charge with the 220-volt in-house charger. The battery pack holds 34 kWh of electricity, enabling the EV Plus to go 100 miles between charges. In other

words, the EV Plus uses approximately 0.34 kWh per mile traveled.

- **Performance:** The EV Plus engine produces 66 horsepower. It takes 17.7 seconds to go from zero to 60 mph and reaches a top speed of more than 80 mph. It holds four people or a payload of 700 pounds.

## Nissan Altra EV

- **Availability:** A small electric van available for fleet users in California. Nissan plans to introduce the Altra EV to the consumer market in 2000.
- **Price:** Not available.
- **Features:** Standard, plus an on-board charger and regenerative braking.
- **Battery and charging information:** The Altra EV currently is the only vehicle powered by lithium-ion batteries. Twelve modules make up the battery pack, which can be charged inductively in about five hours. Nissan estimates the "fuel economy" to be 0.30 kWh per mile for the highway and 0.342 kWh per mile for city driving. The Altra EV has a vehicle range of about 120 miles.
- **Performance:** The Altra generates 83 horsepower, has a maximum speed of 75 mph, goes from zero to 50 mph in 12 seconds, and can handle a payload of 820 pounds.

## Toyota RAV4 EV

- **Availability:** This vehicle is available for fleet use throughout the United States.
- **Price:** The MSRP is $42,000; lease price is $457 per month (before incentives).
- **Features:** Standard, plus an on-board charger and regenerative braking.
- **Battery and charging information:** Twenty-four Ni-MH batteries provide 27.36 kWh of energy to power the RAV4 EV and provide a range of 120 miles. This corresponds to a fuel economy of 0.232 kWh per mile. A 220-volt conductive charger is stored

in the trunk. Six to eight hours of charging will restore the battery pack to full capacity. The battery pack is covered by a three-year warranty.

- **Performance:** The RAV4 EV generates 67 horsepower, has a maximum speed of 79 mph, travels from zero to 60 mph in 17 seconds, and has an 827-pound payload capacity.

# Appendix C. Regional Vehicle Emissions Produced by Electric Vehicles

An electric vehicle (EV) is called a zero emission vehicle (ZEV) because it emits no tailpipe emissions. However, this classification can be misleading. To properly quantify the emissions produced by an EV, the power source used to charge the EV's battery pack must be considered. If fuels like nuclear, hydroelectric or renewables are used to charge the battery pack, an EV is close to "zero emission" because these fuels emit very little to no pollutants at the electricity generation plant. However, when coal or natural gas is the fuel used to create the electricity for charging, there can be significant emissions associated with operating EVs. Coal-burning and gas power plants emit pollutants like sulfur dioxide ($SO_2$), nitrous oxides ($NO_x$) and carbon dioxide ($CO_2$). Natural gas power plants emit about half as much $CO_2$ and $NO_x$ as coal-burning facilities per kilowatt-hour (kWh) and virtually no $SO_2$. Carbon monoxide (CO) emissions are negligible in both.

The Clean Air Act Amendments (CAAA) of 1990 called for the reduction of $SO_2$ power plant emissions from 15.6 million tons per year in 1990 to 8.95 million tons per year by 2000 ($SO_2$ is the pri-

---

The emissions calculations and text in this appendix were prepared by Chad Kimbell.

mary cause of acid rain). In 1995, emissions dropped to 11.6 million tons, primarily because nearly half the power generators switched to low sulfur coal.[1] The CAAA also directed EPA to study and issue standards for $NO_x$ emissions from electricity generation ($NO_x$ causes ground-level ozone formation as well as acid rain). EPA promulgated regulations that affect boiler technology in efforts to limit $NO_x$ emissions. Presently, no regulations are in effect to control $CO_2$ emissions from utilities. Although $CO_2$ does trap heat as effectively as methane, nitrous oxide or chlorofluorocarbons (CFCs), the amount of $CO_2$ emitted makes it the most important greenhouse gas.

Table 26 compares the emissions associated with charging EVs to those from gasoline powered vehicles in the western region of the United States. Gasoline vehicle emissions, shown in italics, include tailpipe, production and refining emissions, and are otherwise known as the total fuel-cycle emissions. Because the electricity fuel mixture varies greatly across the country, EV emission values are shown on a regional basis.

| Table 26. Western Region Emissions (grams per mile) | | | | | | | | |
|---|---|---|---|---|---|---|---|---|
| Electric Vehicle | $CO_2$ | $SO_2$ | NOx | CO | Gasoline Vehicle | $CO_2$ | $SO_2$ | NOx | CO |
| GM EV1 | 46 | 0.1 | 0.14 | 0 | *GM Saturn SCl* | *340* | *0.1* | *1.0* | *9* |
| Ford Ranger EV | 85 | 0.1 | 0.25 | 0 | *Ranger* | *430* | *0.1* | *1.3* | *12* |
| Toyota RAV4 EV | 42 | 0.1 | 0.12 | 0 | *Toyota Rav4* | *390* | *0.1* | *1.1* | *10* |
| Honda EV Plus | 63 | 0.1 | 0.18 | 0 | *Honda Civic* | *310* | *0.1* | *0.9* | *8* |
| S-10 Electric | 74 | 0.1 | 0.22 | 0 | *S-10 Pickup* | *500* | *0.1* | *1.4* | *13* |
| Chrysler EPIC | 76 | 0.1 | 0.22 | 0 | *Plymouth Voyager* | *470* | *0.1* | *1.4* | *13* |
| Altra EV | 55 | 0.1 | 0.16 | 0 | *Nissan Sentra/Quest* | *400* | *0.1* | *1.2* | *11* |

Source: NCSL, 1999.

The western EV emission values are much lower than those in any other region. Electricity in this region is generated primarily by hydroelectric, nuclear and natural gas plants. For every mile driven by an EV—as compared to a gasoline vehicle—in the west, $CO_2$ and $NO_x$ emissions are reduced by 80 percent to 90 percent. $SO_2$ emissions remain about the same.

On the other hand, EV usage in the midwest (table 27) and the south (table 28) result in a much different outcome. Carbon dioxide emissions can be reduced by 30 percent to 50 percent, and, in most cases, $NO_x$ can be reduced by 15 percent to 45 percent. However, driving an EV in the midwest or south may actually increase $SO_2$ emissions by 1 gram per mile (GPM) to 3 GPM—a 2,500 percent to 3,500 percent increase over conventional gasoline powered vehicles. This dramatic increase in $SO_2$ emissions can be attributed to the fact that coal is the primary fuel for power generation in the midwest and south. In most areas of this region, the coal used contains high concentrations of sulfur. This dramatic increase in $SO_2$ emissions may substantially increase acid rain in the midwest and south.

| Table 27. Emissions for the Midwest (grams per mile) | | | | | | | | | |
|---|---|---|---|---|---|---|---|---|---|
| Electric Vehicle | $CO_2$ | $SO_2$ | NOx | CO | Gasoline Vehicle | $CO_2$ | $SO_2$ | NOx | CO |
| GM EV1 | 190 | 1.8 | 0.8 | 0 | GM Saturn SC1 | 340 | 0.1 | 1.0 | 9 |
| Ford Ranger EV | 360 | 3.3 | 1.6 | 0 | Ranger | 430 | 0.1 | 1.3 | 12 |
| Toyota RAV4 EV | 180 | 1.6 | 0.8 | 0 | Toyota Rav4 | 390 | 0.1 | 1.1 | 10 |
| Honda EV Plus | 260 | 2.4 | 1.2 | 0 | Honda Civic | 310 | 0.1 | 0.9 | 8 |
| S-10 Electric | 310 | 2.8 | 1.4 | 0 | S-10 Pickup | 500 | 0.1 | 1.4 | 13 |
| Chrysler EPIC | 320 | 2.9 | 1.4 | 0 | Plymouth Voyager | 470 | 0.1 | 1.4 | 13 |
| Altra EV | 150 | 2.1 | 1.0 | 0 | Nissan Sentra/Quest | 400 | 0.1 | 1.2 | 11 |

Source: NCSL, 1999.

| Electric Vehicle | $CO_2$ | $SO_2$ | NOx | CO | Gasoline Vehicle | $CO_2$ | $SO_2$ | NOx | CO |
|---|---|---|---|---|---|---|---|---|---|
| GM EV1 | 160 | 1.8 | 0.6 | 0 | *GM Saturn SCI* | *340* | *0.1* | *1.0* | *9* |
| Ford Ranger EV | 300 | 3.3 | 1.0 | 0 | *Ranger* | *430* | *0.1* | *1.3* | *12* |
| Toyota RAV4 EV | 150 | 1.6 | 0.5 | 0 | *Toyota Rav4* | *390* | *0.1* | *1.1* | *10* |
| Honda EV Plus | 220 | 2.4 | 0.7 | 0 | *Honda Civic* | *310* | *0.1* | *0.9* | *8* |
| S-10 Electric | 260 | 2.9 | 0.9 | 0 | *S-10 Pickup* | *500* | *0.1* | *1.4* | *13* |
| Chrysler EPIC | 270 | 2.9 | 0.9 | 0 | *Plymouth Voyager* | *470* | *0.1* | *1.4* | *13* |
| Altra EV | 190 | 2.1 | 0.7 | 0 | *Nissan Sentra/Quest* | *400* | *0.1* | *1.2* | *11* |

**Table 28. Emissions for the South (grams per mile)**

Source: NCSL, 1999.

The mountain region (table 29) also uses coal as the primary power fuel source, although the coal used in this region is low-sulfur. Even so, EVs will increase $SO_2$ emissions by 0.4 gpm to 0.8 gpm, or 600 percent to 900 percent over gasoline engines. $CO_2$ and $NO_x$ emissions are similar to those in the midwest and the south. Despite a more diverse fuel mix, the northeast (table 30) has higher $NO_x$ and $SO_2$ emission values than the mountain region, but lower carbon emission values. High-sulfur coal is the culprit.

It is important to note that these figures represent only what is emitted inside each region's borders. Imported electricity is not included. For example, if the mountain region burns coal to make electricity and exports it to the western region, the mountain region, not the western region, will experience increased emissions.

## Table 29. Mountain Region Emissions (grams per mile)

| Electric Vehicle | $CO_2$ | $SO_2$ | NOx | CO | Gasoline Vehicle | $CO_2$ | $SO_2$ | NOx | CO |
|---|---|---|---|---|---|---|---|---|---|
| GM EV1 | 210 | 0.4 | 0.7 | 0 | GM Saturn SC1 | 340 | 0.1 | 1.0 | 9 |
| Ford Ranger EV | 390 | 0.8 | 1.4 | 0 | Ranger | 430 | 0.1 | 1.3 | 12 |
| Toyota RAV4 EV | 190 | 0.4 | 0.7 | 0 | Toyota Rav4 | 390 | 0.1 | 1.1 | 10 |
| Honda EV Plus | 280 | 0.6 | 1.0 | 0 | Honda Civic | 310 | 0.1 | 0.9 | 8 |
| S-10 Electric | 340 | 0.7 | 1.2 | 0 | S-10 Pickup | 500 | 0.1 | 1.4 | 13 |
| Chrysler EPIC | 340 | 0.7 | 1.2 | 0 | Plymouth Voyager | 470 | 0.1 | 1.4 | 13 |
| Altra EV | 250 | 0.5 | 0.9 | 0 | Nissan Sentra/Quest | 400 | 0.1 | 1.2 | 11 |

Source: NCSL, 1999.

## Table 30. Emissions for the Northeast (grams per mile)

| Electric Vehicle | $CO_2$ | $SO_2$ | NOx | CO | Gasoline Vehicle | $CO_2$ | $SO_2$ | NOx | CO |
|---|---|---|---|---|---|---|---|---|---|
| GM EV1 | 120 | 1.1 | 0.3 | 0 | GM Saturn SC1 | 340 | 0.1 | 1.0 | 9 |
| Ford Ranger EV | 220 | 2.0 | 0.6 | 0 | Ranger | 430 | 0.1 | 1.3 | 12 |
| Toyota RAV4 EV | 110 | 1.0 | 0.3 | 0 | Toyota Rav4 | 390 | 0.1 | 1.1 | 10 |
| Honda EV Plus | 170 | 1.5 | 0.5 | 0 | Honda Civic | 310 | 0.1 | 0.9 | 8 |
| S-10 Electric | 200 | 1.7 | 0.5 | 0 | S-10 Pickup | 500 | 0.1 | 1.4 | 13 |
| Chrysler EPIC | 200 | 1.8 | 0.6 | 0 | Plymouth Voyager | 470 | 0.1 | 1.4 | 13 |
| Altra EV | 150 | 1.3 | 0.4 | 0 | Nissan Sentra/Quest | 400 | 0.1 | 1.2 | 11 |

Source: NCSL, 1999.

## Calculation Procedure for Tables 26-30.
The following procedure was used for the EV emissions calculations in tables 26-30 of this appendix.

### Table 31. Utility Electricity Generation (EG) and Total Emissions (by region)

|  | EG (kWh) | $CO_2$ (g) | $SO_2$ (g) | NOx (g) |
|---|---|---|---|---|
| Northeast | 3.7423E+11 | 1.65947E+14 | 1.47E+12 | 4.599E+11 |
| Midwest | 7.9042E+11 | 5.55548E+14 | 5.119E+12 | 2.426E+12 |
| South | 1.3593E+12 | 7.99552E+14 | 8.834E+12 | 2.705E+12 |
| Mountain | 2.6693E+11 | 2.02987E+14 | 4.338E+11 | 7.164E+11 |
| West | 2.8018E+11 | 4.6998E+13 | 7.83E+10 | 1.377E+11 |
| California | 1.1471E+11 | 3.24864E+13 | 3.6E+09 | 8.1E+10 |
| Hawaii | 6420000000 | 4.1067E+12 | 1.71E+10 | 9E+09 |

Notes: This data was obtained from the Energy Information Administration (EIA), a U.S. Department of Energy subsidiary. It was converted into system international (SI) units, kilowatt-hours (kWh) and grams (g). The regions contain the following states:

*Northeast*—Connecticut, Maine, Massachusetts, New Hampshire, New Jersey, New York, Pennsylvania, Rhode Island and Vermont.

*Midwest*—Illinois, Indiana, Iowa, Kansas, Michigan, Minnesota, Missouri, Nebraska, North Dakota, Ohio, South Dakota and Wisconsin.

*South*—Alabama, Arkansas, Delaware, District of Columbia, Florida, Georgia, Kentucky, Louisiana, Maryland, Mississippi, North Carolina, Oklahoma, South Carolina, Tennessee, Texas, Virginia and West Virginia.

*Mountain*—Arizona, Colorado, Idaho, Montana, Nevada, New Mexico, Utah and Wyoming.

*West*—California, Oregon, Washington and Alaska. Hawaii is listed separately.

Sources: U.S. Department of Energy, Energy Information Administration, "Net Generation from U.S. Electric Utilities by Selected Prime Mover, Census Division, and State, 1996 and 1997," URL=http://www.eia.doe.gov/cneaf/electricity/epav1/epav1t9.txt; U.S. Department of Energy, Energy Information Administration, "Estimated Emission from Fossil-Fueled Steam-Electric Generating Units at U.S. Electric Utilities by Fossil Fuel, Census Division, and State, 1994," URL=http://www.eia.doe.gov/cneaf/pubs_html/epa_1994/volume2/table25.html; U.S. Department of Energy, Energy Information Administration, "U.S. Electric Power Industry Net Generation, 1990 Through June 1998," URL=http://www.eia.doe.gov/cneaf/electricity/epm/epmt3.txt.

## Table 32. EV Fuel Economy
### (in kWh per mile)

| | |
|---|---|
| GM EV1 | 0.25 |
| Ranger EV | 0.46 |
| Rav4 EV | 0.23 |
| Honda EV Plus | 0.34 |
| S-10 Electric | 0.40 |
| EPIC Minivan | 0.41 |
| Nissan Altra EV | 0.30 |

Note: These values were either provided by the automakers or were calculated from the equation: (battery pack charge capacity in kWh) / (range in miles).

## Table 33. Utility Emissions
### (grams per kWh)

| Region | $CO_2$ | $SO_2$ | NOx |
|---|---|---|---|
| Northeast | 443 | 3.9 | 1.2 |
| Midwest | 703 | 6.5 | 3.1 |
| South | 588 | 6.5 | 2.0 |
| Mountain | 760 | 1.6 | 2.7 |
| West | 168 | 0.3 | 0.5 |
| Hawaii | 640 | 2.7 | 1.4 |

Note: Utility emissions per kWh are found by dividing the total grams of emitted pollutant by the total amount of electricity generated in kWh.

Tables 34, 35, 36, 37, 38 and 39 show a regional comparison of the power plant emissions associated with charging an EV's battery pack. This is found by the equation: (utility emission per kWh) x (EV fuel economy) x 1.1. The last figure in this equation, 1.1, represents an energy loss of 10 percent as electricity travels from the utility to the EV battery.

### Table 34.  Emissions for the Northeast Region
### (grams per mile)

| Vehicle | $CO_2$ | $SO_2$ | NOx | CO |
|---|---|---|---|---|
| GM EV1 | 122 | 1.08 | 0.34 | 0 |
| Ford Ranger EV | 224 | 1.99 | 0.62 | 0 |
| Toyota RAV4 EV | 112 | 0.99 | 0.31 | 0 |
| Honda EV Plus | 166 | 1.47 | 0.46 | 0 |
| S-10 Electric | 195 | 1.73 | 0.54 | 0 |
| Chrysler EPIC | 200 | 1.77 | 0.55 | 0 |
| Altra EV | 146 | 1.30 | 0.41 | 0 |

### Table 35.  Emissions for the Midwest Region
### (grams per mile)

| Vehicle | $CO_2$ | $SO_2$ | NOx | CO |
|---|---|---|---|---|
| GM EV1 | 193 | 1.78 | 0.84 | 0 |
| Ford Ranger EV | 356 | 3.28 | 1.55 | 0 |
| Toyota RAV4 EV | 178 | 1.64 | 0.78 | 0 |
| Honda EV Plus | 263 | 2.42 | 1.15 | 0 |
| S-10 Electric | 309 | 2.85 | 1.35 | 0 |
| Chrysler EPIC | 317 | 2.92 | 1.38 | 0 |
| Altra EV | 146 | 2.14 | 1.01 | 0 |

### Table 36.  Emissions for the South Region
### (grams per mile)

| Vehicle | $CO_2$ | $SO_2$ | NOx | CO |
|---|---|---|---|---|
| GM EV1 | 162 | 1.79 | 0.55 | 0 |
| Ford Ranger EV | 298 | 3.29 | 1.01 | 0 |
| Toyota RAV4 EV | 149 | 1.64 | 0.50 | 0 |
| Honda EV Plus | 220 | 2.43 | 0.74 | 0 |
| S-10 Electric | 259 | 2.86 | 0.88 | 0 |
| Chrysler EPIC | 265 | 2.93 | 0.90 | 0 |
| Altra EV | 194 | 2.14 | 0.66 | 0 |

### Table 37. Emissions for the Mountain Region
### (grams per mile)

| Vehicle | $CO_2$ | $SO_2$ | NOx | CO |
|---|---|---|---|---|
| GM EV1 | 209 | 0.45 | 0.74 | 0 |
| Ford Ranger EV | 385 | 0.82 | 1.36 | 0 |
| Toyota RAV4 EV | 192 | 0.41 | 0.68 | 0 |
| Honda EV Plus | 284 | 0.61 | 1.00 | 0 |
| S-10 Electric | 335 | 0.72 | 1.18 | 0 |
| Chrysler EPIC | 343 | 0.73 | 1.21 | 0 |
| Altra EV | 251 | 0.54 | 0.89 | 0 |

### Table 38. Emissions for the West Region
### (grams per mile)

| Vehicle | $CO_2$ | $SO_2$ | NOx | CO |
|---|---|---|---|---|
| GM EV1 | 46 | 0.08 | 0.14 | 0 |
| Ford Ranger EV | 85 | 0.14 | 0.25 | 0 |
| Toyota RAV4 EV | 42 | 0.07 | 0.12 | 0 |
| Honda EV Plus | 63 | 0.10 | 0.18 | 0 |
| S-10 Electric | 74 | 0.12 | 0.22 | 0 |
| Chrysler EPIC | 76 | 0.13 | 0.22 | 0 |
| Altra EV | 55 | 0.09 | 0.16 | 0 |

### Table 39. Emissions for Hawaii
### (grams per mile)

| Vehicle | $CO_2$ | $SO_2$ | NOx | CO |
|---|---|---|---|---|
| GM EV1 | 176 | 0.73 | 0.39 | 0 |
| Ford Ranger EV | 324 | 1.35 | 0.71 | 0 |
| Toyota RAV4 EV | 162 | 0.67 | 0.35 | 0 |
| Honda EV Plus | 239 | 1.00 | 0.52 | 0 |
| S-10 Electric | 281 | 1.17 | 0.62 | 0 |
| Chrysler EPIC | 288 | 1.20 | 0.63 | 0 |
| Altra EV | 211 | 0.88 | 0.46 | 0 |

## Table 40. 30 Miles Per Gallon Gasoline Car Emissions
### (grams per mile)

| Pollutant | Emissions |
|-----------|-----------|
| $CO_2$ | 347 |
| $SO_2$ | 0.074 |
| NOx | 1.0 |
| CO | 9.25 |

Note: These values are taken from an EIA report on auto emissions. It is based on the following: unleaded gasoline, 30 miles per gallon fuel efficiency and the total fuel cycle. The total fuel cycle emissions include not only tailpipe emissions but emissions from gas leaks and flares, feedstock recovery and transmission, and fuel production and distribution. The vehicle does not have any special emissions control devices.

Source: U.S. Department of Energy, Energy Information Administration, "Alternatives to Traditional Fuels 1994-Volume 2, Greenhouse Gas Emissions," URL=http://www.eia.doe.gov/cneaf/pubs_html/attf_94v2/chap3.html.

## Table 41. Gasoline Vehicle Emissions
### (grams per mile)

| Vehicle | Miles Per Gallon | $CO_2$ | $SO_2$ | $NO_x$ | CO |
|---------|------------------|--------|--------|--------|-----|
| GM Saturn SC1 | 31 | 336 | 0.07 | 1.0 | 9 |
| Ranger | 24 | 434 | 0.09 | 1.3 | 12 |
| Toyota RAV4 | 27 | 386 | 0.08 | 1.1 | 10 |
| Honda Civic | 34 | 306 | 0.07 | 0.9 | 8 |
| S-10 Pickup | 21 | 496 | 0.11 | 1.4 | 13 |
| Plymouth Voyager | 22 | 473 | 0.10 | 1.4 | 13 |
| Nissan Sentra/Quest | 26 | 400 | 0.09 | 1.2 | 11 |
| GM Geo Metro | 47 | 221 | 0.05 | 0.6 | 6 |

Note: This table estimates the total fuel cycle emissions from some common gasoline vehicles. The fuel efficiencies are interpolated from manufacturers' data. It assumes 60 percent city driving and 40 percent highway driving. The emission estimates assume a linear relation between fuel efficiency and emissions. It does not include any extra emission control devices these models may have. These devices have no reduction effect on $CO_2$ emissions, but have been found to initially reduce $SO_2$ and $NO_x$ levels.

The equation is (the 30 mpg emission) / [(the car's fuel efficiency) / (30 mpg)].

The Altra EV chassis is smaller than the Quest but larger than the Sentra, so the Altra is compared to a vehicle that is half Sentra and half Quest. The Geo Metro is included for comparison because it is the most efficient gasoline vehicle today.

# Appendix D. Identification of Polluting Vehicles by Remote Sensing

Air pollution violations have been decreasing nationwide (U.S. Environmental Protection Agency [EPA] statistics) and measured average on-road motor vehicle emissions have been getting smaller year by year. (Bradley, Stedman and Bishop, Chemtech, July 1999). This arises because the newest vehicles are built with low emissions and remain in that condition for a considerable length of time (Report by AIAM, 1997 among other sources discussed on the EPA web page under M6.EXH.008).

Adding zeros to an already skewed distribution makes it even more skewed, thus the average becomes a less relevant number and the total is dominated by an ever-smaller fraction of gross polluters. Many of these vehicles find various ways to cheat upon or avoid state and local inspection and maintenance (I/M) requirements (Stedman, Bishop, Slott and Aldrete, Env. Sci Tech. 1997 and Stedman, Bishop and Slott ibid. 1998)

Apparently, the U.S. EPA recognizes these facts and is formulating the new version of the MOBILE model so that emissions reduction credits from traditional I/M programs will be reduced by about a

This appendix was prepared by Dr. Donald Stedman, professor of chemistry at the University of Denver and foremost expert on identifying polluting vehicles by remote sensing.

factor of two (Ward's Automotive Report, May, 1999). An extensive program measured more than 18,000 on-road vehicle emissions in Chicago in a single week in 1997 and 1998 (Popp et al., presented to CRC San Diego, April 1999). The measurements include on-road emissions in mass of emissions per mass/volume of fuel burned for carbon monoxide, nitrogen oxide and hydrocarbons.

The average emissions for CO, HC and NO were 160, 12, and 16 gm/gallon, respectively. The average emissions of these pollutants for cars less than two years old were 3, 4 and 3, while the highest-emitting 10 percent in each group emitted 860, 50 and 15 gm/gallon for the same three gases.

For CO, which has been shown to be very good indicator of a broken vehicle, (Gorse et al., SAE, Fuels and Lubricants Conference, October 1993) only 10 percent of the vehicles produce 61 percent of the emissions. Similar data are found in IM240 analysis. In Colorado, IM240 failing vehicles average 80 gm/mile of CO, while passing vehicles average about 12 gm/mile. In the first few years after purchase, new cars averaged only 4 gm/mi.

All these statistics point to the fact that programs that treat all vehicles as equal (fuel changes, I/M programs, etc.) are unlikely to be cost-effective. An agency that can devise a program that succeeds in motivating continuous maintenance of well-tuned vehicles (and immediate repair of broken ones) so that they do not fail in use has the potential for significant further air quality improvements. Tighter new car standards also are shown by this logic to be of little value because new car emissions are already so low as to be irrelevant to air quality.

According to Lacey et al., (*ITS World*, September 1997) a single, unmanned remote sensor can carry out more than 3,000,000 emissions readings per year. In Colorado, 77 IM240 lanes with 310 employees make 772,835 emission tests per year (CDPHE, *Air Quality Control Commission report to the State Legislature*, 1998). The cost of the remote sensing sign, complete with remote sensor, is about $300,000. A single remote sensor with a van with necessary options sells for about $180,000. A complicating element is the fact that the company that manufactures and sells most of the sensors under exclusive license from the University of Denver is ESP (which recently purchased Envirotest). ESP is reported to make most of its income on scheduled off-road emissions testing programs in competition with remote sensing. How that conflict of interest situation emerged is discussed in the 1996 university lecture available on the web at www.du.edu under academics, departments, chemistry, don Stedman.

According to Klein and Koskenoja, *CATO Institute Policy Analysis No. 249*, Feb. 7, 1996: "A detailed examination of how a remote sensing program could be implemented in Los Angeles indicates that remote sensing would prove far more effective and about five times less costly than the current ... program." "Pseudoscientific evaluations are one of the most powerful tools used to sell I/M programs to the general public" writes Paul Coninx in a 1998 Fraser Institute (www.fraserinstitute.ca) *Critical Issues Bulletin* on the subject of vehicle emissions testing.

Lawson, et al., in *Program for the use of Remote Sensing Devices to Detect High Emitting Vehicles* (April 1996 report to South Coast Air Quality Management District) state that if roadside remote sensing had been able to pull over every passing high-emitting vehicle (HEV) for repairs, the identification costs would have been $9 per HEV. This should be contrasted with typical IM240 programs with approximately a 5 percent failure rate and a $20 cost per test, which result in a $400 cost for each HEV identified.

On-road remote sensing of gross polluters is being used routinely in Texas to supplement the Dallas/Fort Worth and Houston emission testing programs, and similarly in Phoenix, Arizona, although with some difficulties. It also is being used in Taiwan to replace an unsuccessful I/M program. The Missouri program recently has initiated a contract for a "clean-screen," in which on-road remote sensing is used to identify and allow low-emitting cars to waive their routine emission testing. However, this approach is not a low-cost method of identification of high polluters.

# Appendix E. Alternative Fuel Vehicle Fleet Buyer's Guide Federal Incentives/ Regulations Section

The information in this appendix is current as of September 15, 1998. The most current information can be obtained through the Alternative Vehicle Fleet Buyer's Web site at http://www.fleets.doe.gov.

## United States (Federal)

### Overview

The main federal incentives for the purchase or conversion of individual alternative fuel vehicles (AFVs) are the federal income tax deductions of $2,000 to $50,000 for clean fuel vehicles, and the income tax credit of up to $4,000 for electric vehicles (EVs). An income tax deduction also is available for the installation of refueling or recharging facilities for AFVs.

Except for the federal tax credits and deductions, most of the federal incentives are programmatic grants oriented toward large investments such as infrastructure and larger purchases. The lead federal agencies for AFV programs are the U.S. Department of Treasury (Internal

---

This appendix was prepared by Kathleen E. Gatliffe, ASME intern at NCSL.

    165

Revenue Service), the U.S. Department of Energy (DOE), the U.S. Department of Transportation (DOT), and the U.S. Environmental Protection Agency (EPA).

The information listed below is organized according to the federal agency responsible for enactment or enforcement. Please contact that agency for more information.

## Highlights

A $2,000 to $50,000 federal income tax deduction is available for the purchase or conversion of qualified clean fuel vehicles.

Up to $4,000 federal tax credit is available for 10 percent of the purchase price of an EV.

***U.S. Internal Revenue Service (IRS)*** U.S. Department of Treasury, 1111 Constitution Avenue, NW, Room 5214, CC:PSI:8, Washington, D.C. 20224.

**Federal Tax Deduction.** This is a deduction for clean fuel vehicles and certain refueling properties. A tax deduction for the purchase of a new original equipment manufacturer (OEM) qualified clean fuel vehicle, or for the conversion of a vehicle to use a clean-burning fuel, is provided under the Energy Policy Act of 1992 (EPACT), Public Law-102-486, Title XIX-Revenue Provisions, Sec. 179A. The amount of the tax deductions for qualified clean fuel vehicles is based on the gross vehicle weight (gvw) and types of vehicles as follows:

- Truck or van, gvw of 10,000 lbs. to 26,000 lbs. = $5,000
- Truck or van, gvw more than 26,000 lbs. = $50,000
- Buses, with seating capacity of 20 or more adults = $50,000
- All other vehicles, off-road vehicles excluded = $2,000.

The tax deduction for clean fuel vehicles is available for business or personal vehicles, except EVs eligible for the federal EV tax credit. The deduction is not amortized and must be taken in the year the vehicle is acquired. A tax deduction of up to $100,000 per location is available for qualified clean fuel refueling property or recharging property for EVs. The equipment must be used in a trade or business.

**Electric Vehicle Tax Credit.** A tax credit for the purchase of qualified EVs and hybrid electric vehicles (HEVs) is provided under EPACT Public Law-102-486, Title XIX-Revenue Provisions, Sec. 30, Credit for Qualified Electric Vehicles. The size of the credit is 10 percent of the cost of the vehicle, up to a maximum credit of $4,000. Beginning in 2001, the size of the credit is reduced by 25 percent per year until the credit is fully phased out. To qualify for the credit, the vehicle must be powered primarily by an electric motor drawing current from batteries or other portable sources of electric current. All dedicated, plug-in only EVs qualify for the tax credit. All series and some parallel HEVs meet these qualifications. The tax credit for EVs is available for business or personal vehicles.

The dollar amount for the Clean Fuel Vehicle tax deductions and credits will be reduced after the year 2001 according to the following schedule: 2002—25 percent reduction, 2003—50 percent reduction, and 2004—75 percent reduction. These deductions and credits are available between December 20, 1993, and December 31, 2004. For more information call the toll-free order desk at (800) 829-3676, and ask for publication #535, Business Expenses.

*U.S. Department of Energy (DOE)* 1000 Independence Avenue, SW, Washington, DC 20585. General telephone number: (202) 586-5000.

**Energy Policy Act of 1992 (EPACT).** Congress passed EPACT, or Public Law 102-486, on October 24, 1992, to accelerate the use of alternative fuels in the transportation sector. With EPACT in place, DOE's primary goals are to decrease the nation's dependence on foreign oil and increase energy security through the use of domestically produced alternative fuels. DOE's overall mission is to replace 10 percent of petroleum-based motor fuels by the year 2000 and 30 percent by the year 2010. EPACT mandates federal, state and alternative fuel provider fleets to purchase AFVs.

Federal fleets must follow guidelines established in Executive Order 12844 (April 21, 1993) and subsequently reinforced by Executive Order 13031 (December 13, 1996). An AFV guide for federal fleets is located at http://www.whitehouse.gov/WH/EOP/OMB/html/mheda/afvguide.html. State and fuel provider fleets must meet the requirements outlined in the Alternative Fuel Transportation Program, Final Rule [10 CFR Part 490], located at the Web site: http://www.afdc.doe.gov/ottdocs/fprovrule.pdf.

**Clean Cities Program.** DOE's Clean Cities Program coordinates voluntary efforts between locally based government and industry to accelerate the use of alternative fuels and expand AFV refueling infrastructure.

**Federal Incentives.** EPACT establishes an incentive program for the purchase of AFVs and conversion of conventional gasoline vehicles to alternative fuels. Through federal tax incentives, companies and private individuals can offset a portion of the incremental costs associated with the purchase or conversion of an AFV.

**State and Alternative Fuel Provider Fleets AFV Credits Program.** Congress created the credits program to encourage fleets or covered fleet operators to use AFVs early and aggressively. Credits are allocated to state fleet operators and covered alternative fuel provider fleet operators when AFVs are acquired over and above the amount required, or earlier than expected. Since credits can be traded and sold, fleets have the flexibility to acquire AFVs on the most cost-effective schedule without impeding the achievement of EPACT national oil displacement goals. Please see the AFV Acquisition and Credits Web site for more information on the credits program at www.ott.doe.gov/credits, or call the National Alternative Fuels Hotline at (800) 423-1DOE or (800) 423-1363.

**Advanced Notice of Proposed Rulemaking (ANOPR).** DOE published an ANOPR for AFV acquisition requirements for private and local government fleets on Friday, April 17, 1998. Programs potentially created by the ANOPR would help ensure that DOE meets its energy replacement goals. Public feedback will be incorporated into the rulemaking, which must be finalized by January 1, 2000. A copy of the ANOPR is available on the *Federal Register* website at http://www.access.gpo.gov/su_docs/aces/aces140.html or directly from the website at http://www.ott.doe.gov/pdfs/anopr.pdf.

**State Energy Program.** States will promote the conservation of energy, reduce the rate of growth of energy demand, and reduce dependence on imported oil through the development and implementation of a comprehensive State Energy Program. The State Energy Program is the result of the consolidation of two formula grant programs—the State Energy Conservation Program and the Institutional Conservation Program. The State Energy Program includes provisions for competitively awarded financial assistance for a number of state-oriented special project activities, including alternative fuels. See individual state and local incentives for more information. In addition to funding for special project activities, states may choose to allocate base formula funds to program activities to increase transportation efficiency, including programs to accelerate the use of alternative transportation fuels for government vehicles, fleet vehicles, taxis, mass transit and privately owned vehicles. For more information, contact the State Energy Office or the DOE Regional Office for the local region, listed under the Points of Contact section of each state, or contact Ron Santoro at DOE Headquarters at (202) 586-8296.

**DOE/Urban Consortium Funds.** DOE's Municipal Energy Management Program has funded about 300 projects that demonstrate innovative energy technologies and management tools in cities and counties through the Urban Consortium Energy Task Force (UCETF). Each year the task force requests proposals from urban jurisdictions, including cities, counties, and recognized tribal governments. After a review process, UCETF funds those projects that best define and demonstrate innovative and realistic technologies, strategies and methods that can facilitate urban America's efforts to become more energy efficient and environmentally responsible. In the past, many AFV projects have received funding from UCETF. The RFPs are available from the website at http://pti.nw.dc.us.

**Petroleum Violation Escrow (PVE) Account.** Oil overcharge funds, also known as petroleum violation escrow (PVE) funds, became available as a result of oil company violations of the federal oil pricing controls that were in place from 1973 to 1981. Several companies paid fines or funds settlements that have been made available to the states for use in energy efficiency programs. These funds may be used in one or more of three federal energy-related grant programs: the State Energy Program and the Weatherization Assistance Program (administered by DOE), and the Low-Income Home Energy Assistance Program, which is administered by the Department of Health and Human Services. A portion of the funds also may be used for a broader range of energy-related programs, at the discretion of the state and with DOE review. To date, more than $4 billion in oil overcharge (PVE) funds has been made available to the states. Please contact the State Energy Office for more information.

*U.S. Department of Transportation (DOT)*   Federal Highway Administration (FHWA) and Federal Transit Administration (FTA), 400 7th Street, SW, Washington, DC 20590. General telephone number: (202) 366-4000.

**Congestion Mitigation and Air Quality (CMAQ) Improvement Program.** The CMAQ program was reauthorized in the recently enacted Transportation Equity Act for the 21st Century (TEA-21). The primary purpose of the CMAQ program remains the same: to fund projects and programs in nonattainment and maintenance areas that reduce transportation- related emissions. However, TEA-21 made some changes to the CMAQ program, which are included in interim guidance that was published in the *Federal Register* on Oct. 26, 1998. This information can be obtained from the *Federal Register Online* at the Government Printing Office website: http://www.access.gpo.gov.

The interim guidance provides 1) informational items on issues related to the reauthorized CMQ program, 2) new provisions regarding eligible geographic areas under TEA-21, and 3) guidance related to projects now eligible for CMAQ funds. With the exception of the issues discussed in the interim guidance, all provisions of the CMAQ policy guidance issued on March 7, 1996 (61 FR 50890, Sept. 27,

1996), continue to apply. For further information contact state or local FHWA representatives.

**Section 3 Discretionary and Formula Capital Program.** This program provides funding for the establishment of new rail projects, improvement and maintenance of existing rail projects, and the rehabilitation of bus systems. Funding is not specifically designated for AFVs, but the funds provided by this program may be used to purchase alternative fuel buses. For most projects funded through Section 3, FHWA will pay 80 percent of the total project costs. For more information, contact the regional FHWA office for the state.

*U.S. Environmental Protection Agency (EPA)* 401 M Street, SW, Washington, DC 20460. General telephone number: (202) 260-2090.

**Clean Air Act Amendments of 1990.** The Clean Air Act (CAA) was passed in 1970 to improve air quality nationwide. Congress amended the law in 1990, passing the Clean Air Act Amendments of 1990 (CAAA), which created several initiatives to reinforce one of the original goals of the CAA: to reduce mobile source pollutants. CAAA sets emissions standards for stationary and mobile sources. The CAAA establishes targets, standards and procedures for reducing human and environmental exposure to a range of pollutants generated by industry and transportation.

**The Clean Fuel Fleet Program (CFFP)** is an initiative implemented by the EPA in response to the CAAA. The CFFP requires fleets in cities that have significant air quality problems to incorporate vehicles that will meet clean fuel emissions standards. For more information about requirements, covered fleets, and affected areas, visit one of the following EPA Web sites: http://www.epa.gov/OMSWWW or http://www.epa.gov/oms/eff.htm.

**National Low Emission Vehicle (NLEV) Program.** The NLEV program, effective March 2, 1998, is a voluntary program between the EPA, nine of the Ozone Transport Commission (OTC) states, and the automobile manufacturers. The program is designed to reduce unhealthy levels of smog and other toxic air pollutants formed from vehicle tailpipe emissions. Automobile manufacturers will provide cars and light-duty trucks that are cleaner burning than currently required by law. For model year 1999, vehicles will be available in Connecticut, Delaware, Maryland, New Hampshire, New Jersey, Pennsylvania, Rhode Island, Virginia and the District of Columbia, and elsewhere across the country by 2001.

Documents relating to this program are available on the website at http://www.epa.gov/OMSWWW/lev-nlev.htm.

**Air Pollution Control Program.** This program, known as Section 105 grants, assists state and municipal agencies in planning, developing, establishing, improving and maintaining adequate programs for prevention and control of air pollution or implementation of national air quality standards. States and municipalities may receive up to 60 percent in federal funds to implement their plans. Requests for application forms and completed applications are submitted to the appropriate EPA regional grants administration branch.

**Pollution Prevention Grants Program.** This program supports the establishment and expansion of state pollution prevention programs and addresses various sectors of concern such as energy, transportation, industrial toxins, and agriculture. Funds available under this grant/cooperative agreement are awarded to support innovative pollution prevention programs that address the transfer of potentially harmful pollutants across all media—air, land and water. State agencies are required to contribute at least 50 percent of the total cost of their project. For more information, contact the Pollution Prevention Coordinator in the EPA regional office.

State agencies are required to contribute at least 50 percent of the total cost of their project. For more information, contact the Pollution Prevention Coordinator in the EPA regional office.

## Utilities/Private Incentives

Ford Motor Company is offering a $2,000 incentive on its dedicated F-Series natural gas vehicles (NGVs) and dedicated and bi-fuel Econoline NGVs. Incentives for the Crown Victoria NGV range from

$1,500 to $2,025, depending on the purchase of Ford's extended range package. Other incentives include $1,500 for the bi-fuel propane F-Series pickup and bi-fuel propane Econoline van, and $1,000 for the Taurus flexible fuel vehicle (FFV). For more information about pricing and incentives for fleets, contact Ford at 800-ALT-FUEL or at http://www.fleet.ford.com.

# Appendix F. Overview of State Alternative Fuel Vehicle Incentives and Regulations

### Alaska
Fuel containing 10 percent alcohol by volume is exempt from an $0.08 per gallon tax. Fuels with a minimum oxygen content of 2.7 percent by weight are required under state statute to be used in Anchorage from November 1 through March 1. This requirement is currently being met with ethanol-blended fuels. For more information, contact Barbara Shepherd, Alaska Department of Environmental Conservation, at (907) 465-5100.

### Alabama
The Alabama Department of Economic and Community Affairs provides technical assistance to state fleet managers to meet the EPACT mandate. The state road tax for propane vehicles and NGVs is paid through a flat-fee sticker in place of the per-gallon tax on gasoline. Several Alabama natural gas utilities support natural gas vehicle (NGV) programs and will offer incentives on a case-by-case basis.

### Arkansas
The state established an 11-member Alternative Fuels Commission

---

This appendix was prepared by Kathleen E. Gatliffe, ASME intern at NCSL.

to promote the development of alternative fuel use in the state. The major incentive for alternative fuel vehicles (AFVs) in Arkansas is a rebate available from the Arkansas Energy Office for conversions or original equipment manufacturer (OEM) incremental costs for AFVs. Additional state and private incentives are also available.

### Arizona

Arizona has several forms of rebates and incentives available for the purchase and use of alternative fuel vehicles (AFVs), including an income tax reduction, vehicle license tax reductions and fuel tax reductions. For example, a $1,000 tax credit is available for the purchase or conversion to AFVs and a $1,000 grant is available for home or small business refueling equipment and installation appliances. Grants of up to $100,000 are available for the construction of public AFV refueling stations. SB 2001 allocated $2.9 million to be distributed to school districts to pay for the conversion of buses and vehicles to alternative fuels or to pay for the incremental cost of an AFV over a gasoline or diesel vehicle. For more information about these programs, contact Bill Biesemeyer, Department of Commerce Energy Office, at (602) 280-1430.

### California

California has a wide variety of incentives for alternative fuel vehicles (AFVs). The California Energy Commission's (CEC) Zero Emission Vehicle Demonstration Program has allocated $1.7 million (half from CEC funds and half from air district funds) to provide incentives for the purchase of or conversion to AFVs. The program provides a $5,000 buy-down incentive to purchasers or lessees of qualifying electric vehicles (EVs) in five California air districts—the Bay Area, Sacramento, San Diego County, Santa Barbara County and Ventura. Other highlights include a $5,000 incentive toward the purchase or lease of qualified zero emission vehicles (ZEVs) for public and private fleets and individuals, a $5,000 incentive toward the purchase or lease of qualified ZEVs, $200 to $800 incentives for AFVs that operate 75 percent of the time in the Sacramento air district, a $1,000 incentive for dedicated natural gas vehicles or certified low-emission vehicle (LEV) conversions through July 1999. For more information, contact Jerry Mason at (805) 645-1479 or (805) 645-1444-fax.

## Colorado

The Governor's Office of Energy Conservation (OEC), in partnership with the Colorado natural gas and propane fuel providers and the U.S. Department of Energy (DOE), offers a rebate program of up to 80 percent of fuel option cost per vehicle. Colorado also offers a generous state tax credit to vehicle owners who convert or purchase an alternative fuel vehicle (AFV). The OEC, in partnership with the Colorado alternative fuels industry and DOE, offers rebates to qualified fleets and individuals switching to alternative fuels. All public and private fleets and individuals are eligible, except fleets operated by the federal government and fuel suppliers. House Bill 1169 (1998) provides financial incentives for clean fuel vehicles (CFVs). This bill modifies and extends the existing income tax credit (HB 92-1191) for private sector fleets, and provides cash rebates to public sector and nonprofit fleets. In addition, the bill adds an income tax credit for the construction of alternative fuel refueling facilities. The tax credit and rebates will be administered by the Colorado Department of Revenue. Fuel tax exemptions for CNG or LPG are included in HB 88-1161. Instead of paying the $0.22 per gallon tax on gasoline, owners of gaseous-fueled vehicles purchase an annual tax decal for $70, $100 or $125, based on the gross vehicle weight rating. All CNG and LPG vehicles must display a current fuel tax decal in the front window. For more information about the Clean Fuel Fleet Program and the credit program, contact Macie LaMotte Jr., environmental protection specialist, at (303) 692-3133, (303) 782-5693-fax, write to the Colorado Department of Public Health and Environment, APCD-MS-B1, 4300 Cherry Creek Drive South, Denver, Colo. 80222.

## Delaware

The Delaware Energy Office administers the state's funding from the petroleum violation escrow (PVE) settlements (also known as the oil overcharge funds), which can be used to finance vehicle conversions and the incremental costs of purchasing alternative fuel vehicles (AFVs) for state, county or municipal fleets. Delaware also is participating in the National Low Emission Vehicle Program, beginning with the 1999 model year. Delaware has received a State Energy Program Special Projects Grant to implement a multi-state AFV rebate program in conjunction with the Philadelphia, Pennsylvania, and North New

Jersey Clean Cities Programs. For more information, contact Suzanne Sebastian, Delaware State Energy Office, at (302) 739-5644, (302) 739-6148- fax, or email ssebastian@state.de.us.

## Florida

Statewide incentives for private sector alternative fuel vehicles (AFVs) include a tax exemption for electric vehicles (EVs). The Gold Coast Clean Cities Coalition operates a $2.5 million low-interest revolving loan fund for AFVs in Broward, Dade and Palm Beach counties. The State Energy Office also is using $2 million in oil overcharge funds (also known as petroleum violation escrow [PVE] funds) to assist state agencies to meet AFV fleet requirements by paying for conversion or incremental costs for dedicated original equipment manufacturer (OEM) AFVs. The State Energy Office has $1.1 million available for grants to local governments in the Gold Coast Clean Cities Coalition for AFVs. For more information, call Jacky Klein, Florida Energy Office, at (850) 922-6086.

## Georgia

The state of Georgia offers a $1,500 tax credit for purchase or lease of clean alternative fuel vehicles (AFVs) and access to high occupancy vehicle (HOV) lanes for single-occupancy automobiles that operate on alternative fuels and have the clean alternative fuel vehicle tags (see laws and regulations). Clean AFV tags are available through the Department of Motor Vehicles for qualifying vehicles. The Atlanta Clean Cities Coalition has a legislative committee that coordinates a joint effort among numerous AFV interests and works to educate legislators about the use of clean alternative fuel vehicles. Propane sold in bulk is exempt from a $0.045 per gallon excise tax when sold to a consumer distributor. The state of Georgia also offers a tax credit of up to $1,500 for the purchase of a dedicated AFV that is federally certified to the low emission vehicle (LEV) standard. This program is available only to individuals or companies that are not covered by the state's Clean Fueled Fleet Program. Vehicle purchase or lease must take place on or after January 1, 1998. Only a limited number of counties qualify for vehicle registration. For more information, contact the Georgia Environmental Protection Division at (404) 363-7028.

## Hawaii

Hawaii has income tax deduction incentives for the use of alternative fuel vehicles (AFVs), which are identical to those found in the federal income tax deductions for the installation of clean fuel vehicles and refueling property. Propane used as a vehicle fuel also is taxed at a lower rate than gasoline. State income tax deductions of $2,000 to $50,000 are available for the installation of refueling stations. The state provides income tax deductions, identical to the federal income tax deductions, for the installation of clean fuel refueling property provided in the Energy Policy Act of 1992. For additional information, contact Maria Tome, Hawaii State Energy Office, at (808) 587-3809.

## Idaho

Idaho offers an excise tax exemption for the use of biodiesel or ethanol. Montana Fuel offers a wide range of assistance, including alternative fuel comparisons, financial analysis and technical assistance for customers wishing to convert to compressed natural gas (CNG). In 1987, the governor issued an executive order that all state vehicles must be fueled with E10 (10 percent ethanol) whenever possible. For more information about Idaho alternative fuel projects, contact K.T. Hanna, Department of Water Resources, at (208) 327-7978, (208) 327-7866-fax, or email khanna@idwr.state.id.us.

## Illinois

Illinois offers a rebate of 80 percent on the conversion or 80 percent of the incremental costs of alternative fuel vehicles (AFVs), up to $4,000 per vehicle. Additional utility and private incentives are also available. A State Energy Program (SEP) grant from the U.S. Department of Energy will provide for rebates for 50 AFVs for eligible municipalities and state of Illinois vehicles. SEP also provides leverage for the establishment of alternative refueling facilities at selected public sites.

Illinois has adopted an Employee Commute Options Program in which 25 percent of all staff of companies of 100 or more employees must participate in a rideshare program. The program sets forth a maximum ratio of vehicles to employees in each area. AFVs initially will count as one-half of a vehicle. A 1987 executive order requires state vehicles to use E10. Public transportation authority districts with a population greater than 50,000 are required to use ethanol blends. All vehicles leased by any state college or university must operate on gasoline blended with E10, whenever it is available. For more information, contact Dave Loos, Department of Commerce and Community Affairs, at (217) 785-3969.

## Indiana

The state of Indiana offers a Small Business Energy Initiative Grant Program, which may be used to pay for the incremental cost of alternative fuel vehicles (AFVs) or for installing AFV refueling stations. Several Indiana utility companies support AFV projects and offer rebates for the conversion of vehicles to run on natural gas. Southern Indiana Gas and Electric and Citizens Gas and Coke offer $1,000 rebates for conversions. For more information from the Indiana Department of Commerce, contact Victoria Scott at (317) 232-8955, or Niles Parker at (317) 232-8970.

## Iowa

Iowa offers lower fuel taxes for ethanol and compressed natural gas (CNG). The Iowa Department of Natural Resources also provides low-interest loan financing for alternative fuel vehicle (AFV) conversions and purchases for state and local governments, school districts, community colleges and nonprofit organizations. The Department of Natural Resources marketing encourages the use of alternative fuels and has funded public refueling sites for 85 percent ethanol blends (E85). For more information contact Ward Lenz at (515) 281-8518, (515) 281-6794-fax, email wlenz@max.state.ia.us, or visit the website at http://www.state.ia.us/governments/dnr.

## Kansas

The state of Kansas offers a state tax credit to fleets of 10 or more vehicles for conversion or purchase of alternative fuel vehicles (AFVs). Kansas offers an income tax credit for taxpayer expenditures for qualified AFV property, conversion equipment and refueling property purchased after Jan. 1, 1996. The tax credit is available to anyone who operates a fleet of 10 or more vehicles with an average fleet fuel consumption of at least 2,000 gallons per year. For more information contact Otto Sitz at (785) 271-3117, (785) 271-3268-fax, email

ositz@~kc.state.ks.us, or visit the Web site at http://
www.kcc.state.ks.us/.

## Kentucky

A rebate of up to $1,000 per vehicle is available from Western Ken-
tucky Gas for CNG conversion costs or incremental costs for purchasing an original equipment manufacturer (OEM) natural gas vehicle (NGV). Kentucky does not have any mandates or incentives
for alternative fuels, but does sponsor some demonstration projects,
including a small biomass demonstration program. The Kentucky
Division of Energy provides information about a range of alternative
fuels, helps publicize demonstration projects, and promotes networks
of people who work with alternative fuels. The Kentucky Division of
Energy received a grant from the U.S. Department of Energy to install four CNG refueling stations in Kentucky that will be open to
the public. For more information, contact the Division of Energy,
Natural Resources Cabinet via John Stapleton or Geoff Young at (502)
564-7192, (502) 564-7484-fax, email stapleton_j@nrepc.nr.state.ky.us
or young_g@nrepc.nr.state.ky.us, or visit the website at http://
www.state.ky.us/agencies/nrepc/dnr/energy.dnrdoe.html.

## Louisiana

The state of Louisiana offers an income tax credit for 20 percent of
the incremental or conversion costs for alternative fuel vehicles (AFVs)
or refueling stations. For additional information about the tax credit,
contact the Louisiana Department of Natural Resources via Sam
Stuckey (504) 342-2122, or call the Louisiana Department of Revenue and Taxation at (504) 925-4611.

## Maryland

Maryland has several tax incentives to encourage the use of alternative fuel vehicles (AFVs). State income tax credits are available for the
costs of purchasing or converting vehicles to alternative fuels. Refueling and recharging equipment for AFVs are exempt from property
tax. Electric vehicles (EVs) are exempt from the motor fuels tax, and
the conversion costs for clean fuel vehicles are exempt from sales tax.
Several utilities in Maryland actively promote AFVs. Potomac Electric Power Co. has a special rate for off-peak charging of EVs. Mary-

land is participating in the National Low Emission Vehicle Program, beginning with the 1999 vehicle model year.

## Massachusetts
Massachusetts offers two Congestion Mitigation and Air Quality (CMAQ)-funded incentive programs for AFVs: 1) an electric vehicle (EV) leasing program for commuters in an intermodal context to commute from home to public transportation transfer stations and 2) a program for municipal and state fleets that covers the acquisition cost differential between AFVs and their conventional vehicle counterparts. For more information, call David Rand, transportation program manager at the Division of Energy Resources, (617) 727-4732, ext. 138.

## Maine
The state of Maine provides a partial tax exemption for the purchase of clean fuel vehicles from January 1, 1999, through Jan. 1, 2006. Maine has adopted the California vehicle exhaust emissions requirements. For more information, contact Danuta Drozdowicz, Department of Environmental Protection, at (207) 822-6317.

## Michigan
Michigan did not have incentives for AFVs at the time of publication. In compliance with the Energy Policy Act of 1992, Michigan Governor John Engler established an interdepartmental task force to analyze issues related to the development of AFVs in Michigan. The Michigan State Plan for Alternative Fueled Vehicles was completed in 1996. For more information about the findings of this task force, contact John Sarver at (517) 334-7234 or (517) 882-1685-fax.

## Minnesota
Minnesota offers incentives for the production of ethanol. Several Minnesota natural gas utilities also offer incentives for the purchase or conversion of natural gas vehicles (NGVs), including a $250 to $1,000 rebate from Minnegasco, Northern States Power and others. The greatest success in Minnesota to date has been the expansion of the E85 (85 percent ethanol fuel) infrastructure that includes a total of 11 fueling sites throughout the state with other sites in planning stages. The state fleet currently has a total of 270 flexible fuel vehicles

capable of using E85 fuel.   Minnesota does not offer any incentives for alternative fuel vehicles (AFVs). For additional information, contact Jan Reak at (651) 297-5648 or email jreak@dpsv.state.mn.us, or contact Mike Roelofs, Minnesota Department of Public Service, at (651) 297-2545 or email mroelofs@dpsv.state.mn.us.

### Missouri
Missouri currently does not offer financial incentives for alternative fuel vehicles (AFVs).  Thirty percent of all state vehicles must be operated solely on alternative fuels by July 1, 2002. These AFV phase-in goals currently are being considered for revision to reflect the passage of the Energy Policy Act of 1992 and the current status of AFV infrastructure in the state  For more information, contact Cindy Carroll, Missouri Division of Energy, at (573) 751-4000 or email nccarrc@mail.dnr.state.mo.us.

### Mississippi
Mississippi does not have any mandates or incentives for AFVs at this time, although policy language is included in the state energy plan. For more information about Mississippi's alternative fuel programs, contact Marilyn Wash, Mississippi State Energy Office, at (601) 359-6600, (601) 359-6642-fax, or email mwash@mississippi.org.

### Montana
The primary incentive for alternative fuel vehicles (AFVs) in Montana is a 50 percent income tax credit that is available for conversion costs for vehicles to operate on alternative fuels. Up to $500 also is available for the conversion of vehicles under 10,000 lbs. gross vehicle weight (gvw), and up to $1,000 is available for heavier vehicles. Several utility companies in Montana offer incentives for purchase of or conversion to natural gas vehicles.  Contact Bob Frantz, Montana Department of Environmental Quality, at (406) 444-6764, for additional information about Montana AFV programs.

### Nebraska
The state of Nebraska offers low-cost and no-cost loans for conversion of fleet vehicles, incremental costs of original equipment manufacturer (OEM) alternative fuel vehicles (AFVs), and installation costs for refueling facilities. Metropolitan Utilities Distribution also offers

a $500 rebate for conversions and purchases of OEM compressed natural gas (CNG) vehicles. For additional information, contact John (Jack) Osterman at (402) 471-2867.

### New Hampshire

New Hampshire has mandates requiring public and private entities to purchase a percentage of inherently low emission vehicles (ILEVs). In addition, New Hampshire is participating in the National Low Emission Vehicle Program beginning in vehicle model year 1999. New Hampshire has no incentives to promote the use of alternative fuel vehicles. For more information about New Hampshire alternative fuel programs, contact Jack Ruderman, Governor's Office of Energy and Community Services, at (603) 271-2611.

### New Jersey

New Jersey has lower taxes on the sale of liquefied petroleum gas and compressed natural gas (CNG) than for gasoline. The Board of Public Utilities, Division of Energy, is using $1.5 million in oil overcharge funds (also known as petroleum violation escrow [PVE] funds) to convert vehicles to alternative fuels for use by state agencies. The New Jersey Board of Public Utilities, Division of Energy, with support of a pilot grant from the U.S. Department of Energy (DOE), is providing $320,000 to assist the cities of Newark, Jersey City, Elizabeth and other stakeholders on the North Jersey Clean Cities Program to convert vehicles to CNG or propane, or to purchase original equipment manufacturer vehicles. Proposed legislation would provide several tax incentives for alternative fuels and AFVs, including a sales tax exemption, a motor fuels tax exemption and a corporate tax credit for vehicle conversions. For more information, contact Ellen Bourbon, North Jersey Clean Cities Program coordinator and New Jersey Division of Energy Alternative Fuels project manager, at (609) 984-3058.

### New Mexico

New Mexico currently offers a lower sales tax for alternative fuels than the sales tax on gasoline. The Energy, Minerals and Natural Resources Department (EMNRD) administers a Transportation Program, which provides grant funds on a competitive basis for projects

including the incremental cost of alternative fuel vehicle (AFV) purchases. For more information, contact Louise Martinez, EMNRD -
Energy Conservation and Management Division, at (505) 827-1129.

## Nevada

Nevada offers a private fleet incentive program through the Nevada
State Energy Office to fleets in the Las Vegas area. This program will
pay up to $3,500 per vehicle, after the private entity pays the first
$1,500 per vehicle for the conversion to natural gas, up to two ve-
hicles per fleet. No incentives currently are available from the state
for the use of alternative fuel vehicles.

## New York

New York has several sales tax exemptions for various alternative fuel
vehicles (AFVs). In addition, several state agencies fund alternative
fuel projects on a case-by-case basis, including The New York State
Energy Research and Development Authority (NYSERDA), the Department of Environmental Conservation (DEC) and the New York
Power Authority. Many of the state's utility companies also offer assistance for AFV projects on a case-by-case basis. NYSERDA continues to co-fund AFV research and demonstration projects on a case-
by-case basis. Projects must be innovative, show a New York component, meet NYSERDA's technical requirements and not duplicate
projects previously demonstrated in New York. For additional information about NYSERDA's programs, contact Ruth Horton at (518)
862-1090, ext. 3306 or (518) 862-1091-fax.

New York has adopted regulations establishing a centrally fueled clean
fuel fleet program. This regulation applies to motor vehicle fleets
operating vehicles with a gross vehicle weight rating between 6,000
lbs. and 26,000 lbs, in areas of New York state designated as severe
nonattainment with the national ambient air quality standard for
ozone (See 6 NYCRR Part 210). New York established a six-year,
$40 million comprehensive Alternative Fuel Vehicle Fleet Demon-
stration Program to learn the practical requirements of operating
AFVs, determine their costs and assist potential users to adapt to the
use of these vehicles. New York has adopted California's low emission vehicles program.

## North Carolina
Several North Carolina utilities support alternative fuel vehicle projects on a case-by-case basis. Since 1987, the state has provided a corporate or personal income tax credit for the construction of certain new ethanol fuel plants in the state. In 1991, legislation was enacted that requires state agencies to study the use of alternative fuels in state-owned vehicles and establish a CNG demonstration project. For more information about North Carolina's Alternative Fuel Program, contact Gary Lew, Department of Commerce, Energy Division, (919) 733-2230, (919) 733-2953-fax, or email glew@energy.commerce.state.nc.us.

## North Dakota
The governor has proclaimed that all state vehicles must be fueled with 10 percent ethanol by volume (E10) when possible. In practice, E10 is used at state refueling stations only when the price is within $0.02 per gallon of gasoline. For more information about North Dakota alternative fuel programs, contact Kim Christianson, Office of Intergovernmental Assistance, at (701) 328-2094.

## Ohio
At the time of publication, Ohio did not offer any incentives for AFVs other than an income tax credit for 10 percent ethanol by volume (E10). For more information, contact Jeff Westhoven at the Ohio Office of Energy at (614) 466-6776, (614) 728-2400-fax, email GSA_westhovn@ohio.gov, or visit the website at http://www.odn.ohio.gov/gsa/oes.

Under House Bill 201 (1992), Ohio has established an Alternative Fuels Advisory Council to evaluate the use of alternative fuels in the state. To obtain a copy of the council's report, contact Gordon Proctor at (614) 644-8241, (614) 466-1768-fax, or contact Christy Collins at (614) 644-7085, (614) 466-1768-fax, or email ccollins@odot.dot.ohio.gov.

## Oklahoma
Oklahoma's main incentive for alternative fuel vehicles (AFVs) is a state income tax credit of 50 percent of the cost of converting vehicles to alternative fuels and 10 percent of the total vehicle cost, up

# <cite>...

to $1,500, to individuals who buy an original equipment manufacturer (OEM) AFV. In addition, the state of Oklahoma has both public- and private-sector loan funds to cover the cost of conversions or the incremental costs of an OEM AFV. For more information about state programs, contact Jeanie Robards, Oklahoma Department of Central Services, at (405) 521-4687, emaileanie_robards@dcs.state. ok.us,or visit the website at http://www.dcs.state.ok.us/okdcs.nsf/ htmlmedia/alternative_fuels.html.

**Oregon**
The Business Energy Tax Credit is the major state incentive for alternative fuel vehicles (AFVs) in Oregon. A tax credit of 35 percent is available for AFVs and alternative fuel fueling stations. The Oregon Department of Energy also offers a small-scale loan program for conservation and renewable resource related projects that may be used for AFV projects. All the natural gas utilities in Oregon will work with customers to facilitate the tax credit program for natural gas vehicles. HB 765 (1990) requires that after July 1, 1994, the state may purchase only vehicles designed to operate on alternative fuels except in areas where the fuels are not economically available. State government vehicles are required to be capable of burning alternative fuels to the maximum extent economically possible. Contact Sylvia Billa, Oregon Department of Energy, at (503) 378-5981 for more information.

**Pennsylvania**
Pennsylvania has several incentives for promoting alternative fuel vehicles (AFVs), including tax exemptions and registration fee exemptions for electric vehicles (EVs). The main incentive for all AFVs is the Alternative Fuels Incentive Grants (AFIG) Program, offered by the Pennsylvania Department of Environmental Protection. The AFIG Program currently offers to pay 40 percent of the cost for converting vehicles to alternative fuels, 40 percent of the incremental cost for the alternative fuel option on a new factory-equipped vehicle, and 40 percent of the costs to install refueling equipment. For additional information about the grants program, contact Sandy Rudy, Pennsylvania Department of Environmental Protection, Office of Pollution Prevention and Compliance Assistance, at (717) 772-8912 or email rudy.sandy@dep.state.pa.us.

## Rhode Island

The state of Rhode Island offers several incentives and tax credits for alternative fuel vehicles (AFVs) and their infrastructure. Providence Gas also provides rebates for natural gas vehicle projects on a case-by-case basis. An Alternative Transportation Fuel Study Committee was established in 1992 to conduct a study of alternative transportation fuels. For more information, contact Janice McClanaghan at (401) 222-3370, (401) 222-1260-fax, email janicem@gw.doa.state.ri.us, or visit the website at http://www.riseo@state.ri.us.

## South Carolina

In South Carolina, Piedmont Natural Gas Co. offers a promotional rate for natural gas used to fuel vehicles. South Carolina Electric and Gas Co. also has installed a compressed natural gas (CNG) refueling station in Columbia, South Carolina. South Carolina does not offer any incentives for alternative fuel vehicles (AFVs). For more information, contact Patricia Tangney at (803) 737-8030, (803) 737-9846-fax, email ptangney@drd.state.sc.us, or visit the website at http://www.state.sc.us/energy/.

## South Dakota

The state of South Dakota offers a reduced fuel tax for alternative fuels. A South Dakota utility company also offers incentives for converting to compressed natural gas (CNG) on a case-by-case basis. For more information, contact Dale Knapp at the Governor's Office of Economic Development at (605) 773-5032.

## Tennessee

United Cities Gas provides rebates for the conversion of vehicles to natural gas, and for the purchase of original equipment manufacturer (OEM) natural gas vehicles (NGVs) on a case-by-case basis.

At this time, Tennessee does not offer any incentives for alternative fuel vehicles. For more information about Tennessee alternative fuel programs, contact Terry Ellis, Department of Economic Development, at (615) 741-6671, (615) 741-5070-fax, or email tellis@mail.state.tn.us.

## Texas

Incentives and grants are available on a case-by-case basis from several sources in Texas. Funds also are available on a limited basis through the Congestion Mitigation Air Quality federal grant program. Senate Bill (SB) 200 (1995) set forth clean fuel vehicle requirements for certain mass transit, local government and private fleets in each of the state's nonattainment areas. The affected fleets will be required to ensure that their fleet vehicles are certified to the U.S. Environmental Protection Agency's (EPA) low emission vehicle (LEV) standards in accordance with a schedule. Fleets may use any vehicle/fuel combination that is certified by EPA standards.

## Utah

Utah offers a tax credit and a loan program as incentives for the purchase of alternative fuel vehicles (AFVs). The state provides a 20 percent tax credit—up to $500—for each new AFV registered in Utah, and a 20 percent tax credit—up to $400—for the cost of conversion equipment for compressed natural gas (CNG), liquefied petroleum gas (LPG) and electric vehicles (EVs). The Office of Energy Services offers a loan program for the purchase of dedicated AFVs or the conversion of AFVs, or for the construction of refueling facilities for AFVs. The Office of Energy Services also provides technical assistance and information about AFV conversions. For additional information, contact Ran Macdonald, Utah Department of Environmental Quality, at (801) 536-4071.

## Virginia

The Commonwealth of Virginia provides a number of incentives for alternative fuel vehicles (AFVs), including no-charge licensing for AFVs and exemption from high occupancy vehicle (HOV) lane-use restrictions for AFVs. Virginia has several tax incentives, including a tax credit to 10 percent of the federal clean fuel tax deduction, a 1.5 percent sales tax reduction for AFVs and an AFV fuel tax reduction. In addition, the Virginia Alternative Fuels Revolving Fund provides loans to local governments and state agencies for the conversion of publicly owned motor vehicles to alternative fuels. Several Virginia utility companies support AFV programs and offer incentives on a case-by-case basis. The Virginia Alternative Fuels Revolving Fund provides grants to local governments and state agencies for the conversion of publicly owned motor vehicles from gasoline and diesel fuels to alternative fuels. Contact Tom Finan, Virginia Department of Transportation, at (804) 786-1508, for more information.

## Vermont
Vermont Gas Systems will provide assistance on a case-by-case basis to customers wishing to convert to natural gas vehicles. Private and public sponsors also operate the EVermont project, which has focused on improvement of battery thermal management and cabin heating and cooling in electric vehicles. In addition, Vermont has received funding from the U.S. Department of Energy's Heavy-Duty Alternative Fuel Vehicle (AFV) Program and is testing a compressed natural gas bus in school bus service. At this time, Vermont does not offer incentives for AFVs. For more information, contact Tom Frank at (802) 828-4035, (802) 828-2342-fax, email franks@psd.state.vt.us, or visit the Web site at http://www.state.vt.us/psd.

## Washington
Washington offers a fuel tax reduction for propane and natural gas vehicles (NGVs), infrastructure development for compressed natural gas (CNG) vehicles from oil overcharge funds (also known as petroleum violation escrow [PVE] funds) and a state highway tax fuel reduction. Puget Sound Energy offers qualified fleets access to its CNG refueling stations by arrangement. Washington Natural Gas also provides technical support and assistance to help customers convert to NGVs. For more information about Washington alternative fuel programs, contact Kim Lyons, WSUEP at (360) 956-2083, (360) 956- 2217-fax, email lyonsk@energy.wsu.edu, or visit the Web site at http://www.energy.wsu.edu.

## Wisconsin
Wisconsin municipalities are eligible to apply for competitive cost sharing grants for the added costs of alternative fuel vehicles (AFVs). The maximum grant is $4,500 per auto and $15,000 for trucks, vans or buses. Each municipality is limited to a total of $50,000. Several utilities in Wisconsin actively promote natural gas vehicles (NGVs), including cash rebate offers from Wisconsin Gas and Wisconsin Electric for the purchase or conversion of NGVs. For further information, contact Kim Kujoth, UWM Center for Alternative Fuels, at

(414) 229-3881, or contact Jennifer Nelson, Alternative Fuels Task Force, at (608) 267-2715.

**West Virginia**
Compressed natural gas (CNG) and liquefied petroleum gas (LPG) powered vehicles are required to pay an annual fee, based on gross vehicle weight (gvw), instead of motor fuel excise taxes. The fee is $85 for light-duty vehicles. Electric, LPG and CNG vehicles are exempt from emission control inspections. Grant allowances were established under law with vocational and technical institutes to certify clean fuel mechanics. However, no funds have been appropriated for this grant program.

**Wyoming**
Montana-Dakota Utilities Co. provides incentives for the conversion of vehicles to compressed natural gas (CNG) on a case-by-case basis. Wyoming does not have any incentives for alternative fuel vehicles; however, the state does have a demonstration project using $225,000 in oil overcharge funds (also known as petroleum violation escrow funds) to convert vehicles at municipalities and state fleets to alternative fuels. The State Energy Office is funding a demonstration project involving conversion of four state motor vehicle maintenance service vehicles to CNG. For additional information, contact Dale Hoffman, Division of Economic and Community Development, at (307) 777-7716.

**District of Columbia**
The District of Columbia is participating in the National Low Emission Vehicle Program, beginning with the 1999 model year. Many utilities and private organizations also offer incentives, while state incentives for alternative fuel vehicles (AFVs) are pending approval. The District of Columbia does not offer any incentives for AFVs. The Clean Fuel Fleet Program included an initiative for the district to develop AFV incentives such as income tax credits for AFVs, motor fuels exemptions and preferential parking. However, the D.C. City Council has not implemented the measure. For more information, contact George Nichols, Clean Cities coordinator, Metropolitan Washington Council of Governments, at (202) 962-3355; Sam Wiggins, District of Columbia Department of Consumer and Regu-

latory Affairs, at (202) 645-6093; or Charles Clinton, District of Columbia Energy Office, at (202) 673-6710.

# APPENDIX G. FISCHER-TROPSCH TECHNOLOGY TO PRODUCE GASOLINE AND DIESEL FUEL

It is well known that gasoline and diesel fuels can be produced from many feedstocks—including coal, natural gas, solid waste and biomass—by a catalytic conversion process. This process was patented in 1927 in Germany by two engineers, Franz Fischer and Hans Tropsch, and is widely referred to as Fischer-Tropsch conversion. The process can be used to produce synthetic gasoline and diesel fuels with very low sulfur and aromatic content, as well as excellent auto ignition characteristics. Recent engineering advances indicate that up-to-date technology can produce diesel fuels that soon could be economically competitive with diesel fuels produced from crude oil.

The Energy Policy Act of 1992 was intended to stimulate production of alternative fuel technologies in the United States to reduce the nation's dependence on imported oil. The Fischer-Tropsch technology is a chemical gas-to-liquid conversion process that has been successfully used to produce high-quality gasoline and diesel fuel from coal, natural gas, municipal waste and biomass feedstock. German industries developed the process during World War II to produce motor fuels that were used by the Hitler war machine. During the apartheid regime, South African industry further developed Fischer-Tropsch processes successfully to synthesize transportation fuels from its domestic coal reserves. The South African energy company, Sasol, built a synthetic fuel plant in 1955 and provided synthetic fuels to the entire country during the oil embargo in the 1970s and 1980s. Today Fischer-Tropsch diesel is widely used as a transportation fuel and also is blended for use with petroleum derived diesel to achieve low sulfur content specifications. Sasol has recently developed a cobalt based catalyst and slurry phase distillation reactor technology that has produced diesel fuel economically. Lana Van Wyk of Sasol informed NCSL that the company recently has shifted to natural gas as the feedstock because it is less expensive than coal.[1] However, the existing coal plants are continuing to produce liquid fuel in South Africa. The company estimates that the production of diesel fuel from natural gas now is almost competitive with diesel fuel from crude oil and the coal-to-liquid fuel process would be economical once the price of crude oil reaches about $30 per gallon.

The Fischer-Tropsch synthesis process is based on three steps. First, a synthetic gas containing mostly carbon monoxide and hydrogen is produced. If natural gas is the feedstock, it is reformed with steam or via partial oxidation with oxygen. If coal is the feedstock, it is gasified in the presence of oxygen and steam. In the second step, the synthesis gas is converted to liquid hydrocarbons by means of the Fischer-Tropsch reaction. The length of hydrocarbon chain and the type of fuel produced is determined by catalyst selectivity and reaction condition. In the third step, the waxy synthetic crude produced in step two is upgraded by means of hydrocracking and isomerization processes that are widely used in the conventional oil industry. The product is finally fractionated into middle distillated liquid fuels such as diesel or gasoline.[2]

In a Department of Energy supported test program, the National Renewable Energy Laboratory performed tests to assess the performance of Fischer-Tropsch diesel fuels in heavy-duty diesel-powered trucks. The trucks were found to perform adequately on neat synthetic diesel fuel, and emitted about 12 percent less $NO_x$, 18 percent less CO, and 24 percent less particulate matter. Total hydrocarbon emissions were reduced by an average of 40 percent compared to a California conventional diesel fuel. The test also demonstrated that the Fischer-Tropsch diesel fuel can be used in unmodified diesel engines. It should be noted that Shell Oil Company has built a commercial diesel fuel production facility in Malaysia. Exxon, Texaco, Phillips and Arco, among others, are developing their own pilot or commercial scale plants to produce synthetic fuels using the Fischer-Tropsch process.

On the basis of available engineering and economic data, it is concluded that gasoline and diesel fuel can be produced from domestic feedstocks such as coal, natural gas or municipal waste at lower costs than alternative fuels such as ethanol and methanol. Moreover, tests conducted by the National Renewable Energy Laboratory, although preliminary in nature, demonstrate that heavy trucks emit less pollution when fueled by Fischer-Tropsch synthetic diesel fuel, than when they are fueled by conventional California diesel fuel. According to information from Rentech—a company that specializes if the F-T process—similar reductions have been reported in pollution emitted by passenger vehicles fueled by synthetic diesel.[3]

# Appendix H. Intelligent Transportation System Technology

## Travel and Transportation Management

En-Route
Driver
Assistance

En-route driver information provides drivers with information pertaining to traffic conditions, incidents, construction, transit schedules, weather conditions, hazardous road conditions and recommended safe speeds while en-route. This information allows drivers to select the route that is best for them, or to change routes mid-travel. Information can be provided while en-route by variable message signs, commercial radio, highway advisory radio, personal communication devices (pagers, cellular telephones) or in-vehicle navigational systems.

Route
Guidance

Route guidance provides travelers with instructions about how to reach their destinations. It identifies a suggested route to reach a specified destination. Public transit route guidance could be determined from static information (e.g., bus schedules) or real-time information through automatic vehicle location systems that track the locations and progress of busses while en-route. Route guidance for motorists could be determined simply from roadway network models, or in a more advanced manner by using real-time information describing the current traffic conditions, incidents, closures, and so forth.

**Traveler Services Information**

Traveler services information includes the location, operating hours, and availability of food, parking, auto repair shops, hospitals and police facilities. In addition, information pertaining to various modes of transport available to the public could be provided. This information would be accessible from home, work, shopping centers, airports and other locations through a variety of ways, including the internet, kiosks, interactive telephone, television and other means.

**Traffic Control**

Traffic control provides for the integration and control of freeway and surface street systems to improve the flow of traffic, improve safety for vehicular and non motorized travelers, give preference to transit or other high occupancy vehicles, and minimize congestion while maximizing the movement of people and goods. A traffic control system consists of a series of linked technologies. Traffic control technologies include ramp metering, lane control systems and traffic signals. For systems with centralized control, the control strategy is accomplished at the Traffic management center. For local systems, local controllers set the control strategy.

**Incident Management**

The costs of nonrecurring congestion caused by traffic incidents are well-documented. Integrating ITS technologies into traffic surveillance systems promises to reduce these costs by improving transportation authorities' ability to detect and clear incidents. The resulting incident management programs consist of three major elements: detection and verification, clearance, and motorist information.

| Emissions Testing and Mitigation | Emissions testing and mitigation provides information for monitoring air quality and develops air quality improvement strategies. Advanced vehicle emissions testing systems are used to determine when the quality of air approaches critical levels. Some technologies provide for the remote sensing of vehicle emissions. The service then implements strategies to reroute traffic around sensitive air quality areas such as tunnels or limits access to these areas. |
| --- | --- |
| Demand Management and Operations | Travel demand management attempts to modify existing travel demand patterns through a variety of strategies promoting increased use of high occupancy vehicles and public transit. This user service must be supported by the development and regulation of policies. Recurring congestion, specifically during the morning and evening peak commute periods, could be smoothed through the adaptation of variable work hours, compressed work weeks and telecommuting. This service also identifies methods to persuade drivers to alter their mode of transportation and even travel behavior. Some examples include congestion pricing and parking fees and decreased public transit fares. |
| Pre-Trip Travel Information | One of the user services under the umbrella of advanced traveler information systems is the provision of pre-trip information about traffic and transit levels of service. Its objective is to inform potential travelers of current network conditions so they can best assess their travel options before they commit themselves to a particular route, mode, time of day, or decide whether to make the trip at all. |
| Ride Matching and Reservation | Ride matching and reservation make ridesharing more convenient by matching information and reservations, and providing the information to (potential) users. Users are able to access this information |

from the internet, home computers, office computers, interactive telephone and other means.

**Highway-Rail Intersection**  This user service deals with the interface of railway and roadway vehicles. Collisions are reduced by monitoring rail and vehicular movements and providing advance warning to drivers and by implementing improved crossing control and warning devices for at-grade crossing sites.

## Public Transportation Options

**Public Transportation Management**  Public transportation management collects and analyzes real-time (deviations from schedule) and facility (passenger loading, running times, mileage) information. This processed information is used to automate operations and to assist in the planning and management of public services.

**Personalized Public Transit**  Personalized public transit assists in providing on-demand routing to pick up passengers and deliver them to their destinations by implementing advanced technologies for dispatching and routing the vehicles. The vehicles used could include small buses, taxicabs or other small shared ride vehicles. This service is extremely useful for less-populated locations and neighborhoods where public transit is not an option.

**Public Travel Security**  Public travel security assists in creating a secure environment for public transportation patrons and operators. Public travel security can be achieved through monitoring of conditions at transit stations, bus stops and parking lots and on vehicles through the use of security cameras. In addition, devices can be installed to trigger automatic alarms and allow for a quick response to criminal activities.

## Electronic Payment

**Electronic Payment Services**

Electronic payment services allows travelers to pay for transportation services electronically. Smart cards or other technologies can be used to increase the efficiency of toll payments, public transit fares and parking services. This technology can operate on pre-payment or a post-billing basis.

## Commercial Vehicle Operations

**Commercial Vehicle Electronic Clearance**

Commercial vehicle electronic clearance allows commercial vehicles to pass inspection and weigh facilities at border crossings (or other check points) without delay, provided that their safety status, credentials and weight all are within acceptable limits. The above criteria may be measured automatically at mainline speeds on all trucks and buses which are equipped with a transponder or GPS.

**Automated Roadside Safety Inspection**

Automated roadside safety inspection provides real-time access to commercial vehicle safety performance records (including previously identified problems). This increases the accuracy and decreases the time required for roadside inspections. In addition, some aspects of the manual inspection process (e.g., brake performance ) may be automated through the use of sensors and diagnostics.

**On-Board Safety Monitoring**

On-board safety monitoring senses the safety status of a commercial vehicle (e.g., brakes, tires and driver alertness). This information is determined automatically at mainline speeds.

**Commercial Vehicle Administration Processes**

Commercial vehicle administrative processes include the automatic collection and recording of travel distance, fuel purchased, and trip and vehicle data by jurisdiction. This information is useful in preparing

fuel tax and registration reports for affected jurisdictions.

| | |
|---|---|
| **Hazardous Materials Incident Response** | In the event of an accident in involving a truck carrying hazardous materials, this user service would provide an immediate description of the hazardous material to the emergency responders. |

## Emergency Management

| | |
|---|---|
| **Emergency Notification and Personal Security** | This user service provides immediate notification of an incident and an immediate request for assistance. The notification might be initiated manually or automatically. Driver and personal security capabilities provide for user initiated distress signals for incidents such as mechanical breakdowns. When activated, automatic collision notification transmits information regarding the location, nature and sensitivity of the crash to emergency personnel. |
| **Emergency Vehicle Management** | The primary objective of this user service is to reduce the time it takes emergency vehicles to respond to an incident after its detection. This can be achieved in several ways, including fleet management, route guidance and signal priority. |

## Advanced Vehicle Control and Safety Systems

| | |
|---|---|
| **Longitudinal Collision Avoidance** | Collision avoidance systems (CAS) represent the first step toward achieving fully automated highways. However, the development and near-term implementation of CAS is driven by the system's role in preventing rear-end vehicle collisions. |
| **Lateral Collision Avoidance** | Lateral collision avoidance provides crash warning and controls for potential lateral collisions between two vehicles in adjacent lanes or between a vehicle and the roadway infrastructure (such as a concrete barrier). Lane changes, weaving sections and road |

departures and entrances are principal causes of lateral collisions.

**Intersection Collision Avoidance**

This user service warns a driver of imminent collisions when approaching or crossing an intersection that has some form of traffic control. This service also alerts the driver when proper right of way at the intersection is unclear or ambiguous.

**Vision Enhancement for Crash Avoidance**

Vision enhancement for crash avoidance uses an in-vehicle forward-looking collision warning system that warns drivers of potential upstream collisions with other vehicles or obstacles in the roadway that are not yet visible to the driver.

**Safety Readiness**

In-vehicle equipment unobtrusively monitors the driver's condition and provides a warning if he or she is becoming drowsy or otherwise impaired. This service also could internally monitor critical components of the automobile and alert the driver to impending malfunctions such as overheating, a flat tire or failing belts. This user service if similar to the on-board safety monitoring user service, except that it is for noncommercial vehicles.

**Pre-Crash Restraint Deployment**

Pre-crash restrain deployment uses sensors located on the vehicle to respond to a potential collision based on the velocity, mass and direction of the vehicles or objects involved and the number, location and major physical characteristics of any occupants. Responses include tightening lap and shoulder belts, arming and deploying air bags at the optimal pressure, and deploying roll bars.

**Automated Highway System**

Automated vehicle operations provide driving environments where vehicles are guided automatically using roadway and vehicle magnets, among other technologies. The anticipated benefits include in-

creased roadway capacity, enhanced safety, reduced
fuel consumption and reduced emissions.

**Source:** *LEAP-Learning from the Evaluation and Analysis of Performance of Intelligent Transportation Systems*, California PATH
(a joint venture between the University of California at Berkeley, California Department of Transportation and private industry), http://www.path.berkeley.edu/~leap, 1999.

# NOTES

## Chapter 1

1.   Stacy C. Davis, *Transportation Energy Data Book* (18th ed.) (Oak Ridge, Tenn.: U.S. Department of Transportation, Center for Transportation Analysis, 1998).

2.   U.S. Department of Energy, Energy Information Administration, *Annual Energy Outlook 1999*. URL=http://www.eia.doe.gov/oiaf/aeo99/results.html#tables; World Wide Web.

3.   Ibid., *supra*, no. 1.

4.   Texas Transportation Institute, *TTI Mobility Study* (February 1999).  URL=http://mobility.tamu.edu/; World Wide Web.

5.   U.S. Department of Transportation, Bureau of Transportation Statistics, *Transportation Statistics Annual Report 1997* (Washington, D.C.: U.S. DOT 1997).

6.   Barbara Goodman, Center for Transportation Technologies and Systems, personal communication, July 28, 1999.

## Chapter 2

1.   Frank Kreith, Paul Norton, and Dena Sue Potestio, "Electric Vehicles: Promise and Reality," *Current Municipal Problems* 22, no. 2 (1995).

## Chapter 3

1.  John O'Dell, "Electric Cars Lose Support," *Los Angeles Times*, April 30, 1998.

2.  John B. Rae, "The Electric Vehicle Company: A Monopoly that Missed," *Business History Review*, Massachusetts Institute of Technology, 1955.

3.  Ibid.

4.  David A. Kirsch, "The Electric Car and the Burden of History: Studies in Automotive Systems Rivalry in America, 1890-1996." *Business and Economic History* 26, no. 2, (Winter 1997).

5.  Douglas Drauch, Partnership for a New Generation of Vehicles, e-mail correspondence.

6.  U.S. Department of Energy, General Services Department/ Resource Management Division, City of Albuquerque, Energy Task Force of the Urban Consortium for Technology Initiatives, *Alternative Vehicle Fuels: A Demonstration Project* (DOE/IR/05106-T147, December 1988).

7.  Norma D. Gurovich and Stephan Ahearn, *Potential Uses of Zero Emission Vehicles in Arizona State Fleets* (Arizona Department of Commerce Energy Office, November 1991).

8.  Evelyn Matheson, *Are Electric Vehicles the Future in our Region?* (Bonneville Power Administration, August 9, 1992).

9.  U.S. Department of Energy, Office of Alternative Fuels, Office of Transportation Technologies, Conservation and Renewable Energy, Introduction to *Alternative Fuel Vehicles* (January 1993).

10. Energy Information Administration, *Alternatives to Traditional Transportation Fuels* (DOE/EIA-0585/O, June 1994).

11. Steve Revenaugh, "Electric Vehicle Charging Station Pricing Schedule As of 4/30/99," Personal Correspondence and Price Sheet, Sacramento Municipal Utility District (April 30, 1999).

## Chapter 4

1. John Eaton, "Prius: A Clean Driving Hybrid," *The Denver Post*, Oct. 28, 1998, sec. C, p. 1.

2. Victor E. Wouk, "Hybrid Electric Vehicles, They will reduce pollution and conserve petroleum. But will people buy them, even if the vehicles have astounding fuel efficiency?" *Scientific American*, (October 1997).

3. Janet B. Goehring et al., "Hybrid Electric Vehicles: Options for State Policymakers," *Transportation Series*, no. 4 (Denver: National Conference of State Legislatures, July 1996).

4. William Siegel and Charles Mendler, *The Technological Opportunities of Hybrid Electric Vehicles*, Prepared for the Symposium for the Promotion of Low Emission Vehicles (Tokyo, Japan, Jan. 11-12, 1996).

5. Michelle Perez, "New, Green Cars: Are They for Real?" *Update: Alliance to Save Energy* 9, no. 1 (Spring 1998).

6. "Chrysler Simulating Hybrid Options in Defining Next Generation Powertrain," *United States Council for Automotive Research* (December 1998). URL=http://www.uscar.org/techno/hyb_chry.htm; World Wide Web.

## Chapter 5

1. Fuel Commercialization Group, *What Is a Fuel Cell?* (Washington D.C., 1996).

2. Jeffrey Ball, "Auto Makers Are Racing To Market 'Green Cars' Powered by Fuel Cells—DaimlerChrysler Sets Deadline To Sell a

Version by 2004; Happy Times for Ballard—But 'Who Buys the First One?" *The Wall Street Journal* (March 15, 1999).

3.  Pandit G. Patil, *Fundamentals of Fuel Cells*, U.S. Department of Energy, November 1992. URL=http://afdc3.nrel.gov/pdfs/text/0040.txt; World Wide Web

4.  Weston, Kenneth C. *Energy Conversion*, West Publishing Company, 1992. p. 443. and *Fuel Cells 2000: Online Fuel Cell Information Center* (Breakthrough Technologies Institute, 1999). URL=http://www.fuelcells.org; World Wide Web.

5.  Gregory P. Nowell, *Looking Beyond the Internal Combustion Engine: The Promise of Methanol Fuel Cell Vehicles* (Washington D.C.: American Methanol Institute, 1998) p. 3-6 and 10-16.

6.  Ibid.

7.  Peter Lehman, "Fuel Cells: The Key to a Sustainable Energy Future?" *Positive Alternatives* (Winter 1998).

8.  Kathleen Koch, "DaimlerChrysler Introduces Car Powered by Fuel Cells," (CNN, March 17, 1999). URL=http://www.cnn.com.

9.  Peter Lehman, "Fuel Cells: The Key to a Sustainable Energy Future?" *Positive Alternatives*, Winter 1998.

10. Sean J. Kearns, "Humboldt State to Unveil America's First Street-Ready Fuel-Cell Car in Palm Desert," (Humboldt State University, Office of Public Affairs, April 21, 1998).

11. John Lang, "New Hydrogen-Powered Autos Both Emission-Free and Speedy," *Boulder Daily Camera*, 1999.

12. "Air Products Goes 'On the Road' with Hydrogen Fuel," *Air Products News*, URL=http://www.airproducts.com/corp/spring98/road.htm (web update, 1998).

13. Daniel Morgan and Fred Sissine, *Hydrogen: Technology and Policy* (Congressional Research Service, Report for Congress, April 28, 1995).

14. DaimlerChrysler, 1999, URL=http://www.mercedes.com/e/innovation/fmobil/necar3.htm.

15. Gregory P. Nowell, *Looking Beyond the Internal Combustion Engine: The Promise of Methanol Fuel Cell Vehicles* (Washington D.C.: American Methanol Institute, 1998).

## Chapter 6

1. Daniel Sperling, "A New Agenda," *Access* 11 (Fall 1997).

2. U.S. Department of Energy, *Transportation Energy Data Book* (Washington, D.C. 1998).

3. Ibid.

4. Don Stedman, personal correspondence, 1999.

## Chapter 7

1. U.S. Department of Energy, *Transportation Energy Data Book* (Washington, D.C. 1998).

2. Paul Norton, "Alternative Fuels for Motor Vehicles," in *The CRC Handbook of Mechanical Engineering*, edited by Frank Kreith (Boca Raton, Fla.: CRC Press, 1998), 10.5.

3. American Petroleum Institute, *New Transportation Fuels* (Washington, D.C. 1994).

4. Internal Revenue Service. IRS Tax Code Title 26, Subtitle A, Chapter 1, Subchapter A, Part IV, Subpart D, Section 40.

5. Patty Stulp, Ethanol Management Company, personal communication, 9/20/99.

6. Internal Revenue Service. IRS Tax Code Title 26, Subtitle D, Chapter 32, Subchapter A, Part III, Subpart A, Section 4081, and Internal Revenue Service. IRS Tax Code Title 26, Subtitle D, Chapter 31, Subchapter B, Part III, Section 4041.

7. Ibid.

8. *1998 Fuel Ethanol Fact Book: For the Record*, U.S. Fuel Ethanol Program, Clean Fuels Development Coalition, p. 19.

9. David Pimentel, "Energy Security, Economics, and the Environment," *Focus* 2, no.3 (1992).

10. Bardall, *Solar Today* (Sept./Oct. 1995).

11. Argonne National Laboratory, *Effects of Fuel Ethanol Use on Fuel-Cycle Energy and Greenhouse Gas Emissions* (Written for the United States Department of Energy, January 1999).

12. Mark Delucchi, Institute of Transportation Studies at the University of California, personal communication, 1999.

13. U.S. Department of Energy, *US Refueling Site Counts by State and Fuel Type* Alternative Fuels Data Center, February 1999) URL=http://www.afdc.nrel.gov/newrefuel/state_tot.cgi.

14. U.S. Department of Energy, *US Refueling Site Counts by State and Fuel Type* Alternative Fuels Data Center, February 1999) URL=http://www.afdc.nrel.gov/newrefuel/state_tot.cgi.

15. U.S. Department of Energy, Energy Information Administration, *Alternatives to Traditional Fuels 1994* Volume 2 (Greenhouse Gas Emissions). URL=http://www.eia.doe.gov/cneaf/pubs_html/attf94_v2/chap3.html.

16. Commission on Geosciences, Environment, and Resources (CGER), National Research Council, *Ozone-Forming Potential of Reformulated Gasoline* (Washington, D.C.: National Academy Press, 1999).

17. Committee on Tropospheric Ozone, National Academy of Science, *National Research Council, Rethinking the Ozone Problem in Urban and Regional Air Pollution* (National Academy Press, 1992).

18. Mr. Lu Ha, Engineer and Manager of Technical Support, Regional Transportation District, personal communication, March 17, 1999.

19. Kelley S. Coynes, "Charting a New Course for Transportation Research and Technology," *Transportation Review News* 199 (Nov.-Dec. 1998).

## Chapter 8

1.  J. Weyrich and F. Lind, "Conservatives and Mass Transit: Is It Time for A New Look?" (Washington, D.C.: Free Congress Foundation, 1996).

2.  J. Klein and M. Olson, *"Taken for a Ride (video),"* (Yellow Springs, Ohio: New Day Films 1996).

3.  Thomas Cooper, *Highway Financing*, Federal Highway Administration, U.S. Department of Transportation, *Public Roads* 61, No. 4 (March/April 1998).

4.  Stacy C. Davis, Center for Transportation Analysis, Oak Ridge National Laboratory, U.S. Department of Energy, *Transportation Energy Data Book*. Table 2.12, Edition 18, ORNL-6941, 1998.

5.  Ibid.

6.  American Public Transit Association (APTA), *Transit Fact Book* (Washington, D.C.: American Public Transit Association, February 1998).

7.  Office of Highway Information Management, Federal Highway Administration, U.S. Department of Transportation, *1996 Highway Statistics*, Section 4: Highway Finance, Table HF-10 (October, 1997).

8.  Ibid.

9.  American Public Transit Association (APTA), *Transit Fact Book* (Washington, D.C.: American Public Transit Association, February 1998).

10. Ibid.

11. Ibid.

12. Hugh K. Wilson, Janet B. Goehring, and James Reed, "High-Speed Trains for the United States?  History and Options," *Transportation Series,* no. 2 (Denver:  National Conference of State Legislatures, March 1996).

13. Ibid.

14. Ibid.

15. Ibid.

## Chapter 9

1.  Kitamura, Ryuichi, Mokhtarian, Pendyala, and Goulias, *An Evaluation of Telecommuting as a Trip Reduction Measure*, Institute of Transportation Studies (Davis:  University of California at Davis, 1991).

2.  "Telecommute America! In Tampa Bay," Center for Urban Transportation Research, University of South Florida, February 1999. URL=http://www.cutr.eng.usf.edu/ research/tdm/tele.htm.

3.  "Overview of Telework America 1999," International Telework Association and Council (February 1999).  URL=http://www.telecommute.org/twa_overview.htm/; World Wide Web.

4.  "Telecommute America: California Style!" Smart Valley Inc. (February, 1999). URL=http://smart2.svi.org/telework/.

5. Ibid.

6. "Overview of Telework America 1999," International Telework Association and Council (February 1999). URL=http://www.telecommute.org/twa_overview.htm/.

# Chapter 10

1. *LEAP-Learning from the Evaluation and Analysis of Performance of Intelligent Transportation Systems,* California PATH (a joint venture between the University of California at Berkeley, the California Department of Transportation and private industry, 1999). URL=http://www.path.berkeley.edu/~leap.

2. Ibid.

3. U.S. Department of Transportation, *ITS in Connecticut* (February 1999). URL=http://www.its.dot.gov/staterpt/ct.HTM.

4. U.S. Department of Transportation, *ITS in Kansas* (February 1999). URL=http://www.its.dot.gov/ staterpt/ks.HTM.

5. U.S. Department of Transportation, *ITS in Massachusetts* (February 1999). URL=http://www.its.dot.gov/staterpt/ma.HTM.

6. U.S. Department of Transportation, *ITS in Maryland* (February 1999). URL= http://www.its.dot.gov/ staterpt/md.HTM; World Wide Web.

7. U.S. Department of Transportation, *ITS in New Jersey* (February 1999). URL= http://www.its.dot.gov/ staterpt/NJ.HTM; World Wide Web.

8. U.S. Department of Transportation, *ITS in Illinois* (February 1999). URL= http://www.its.dot.gov/ staterpt/IL.HTM; World Wide Web.

## Appendix C

1. The Electric Vehicle Association of the Americas, *EV Charging Site Directory* (December 1998). URL= http://www.evaa.org/directory/ev_directory.html; World Wide Web.

## Appendix H

1. Lana Van Wyk, Sasol, personal correspondence, 1999.

2. M.E. Dry, *The Sasol Fischer-Tropsch Process*, Extract from Applied Industrial Catalysis 2, Chapter 5 (Academic Press, Inc., 1983).

3. Mark Bohn, Rentech, personal correspondence, 1999.

# GLOSSARY

**Acceleration power**—Pulse power obtainable from a battery that is used to accelerate an electric vehicle, measured in kilowatts. This is based on a constant current pulse for 30 seconds at no less than two-thirds of the maximum open-circuit-voltage, at 80 percent depth-of-discharge relative to the battery's rated capacity and at 20° Celsius ambient temperature.

**Additives**—Chemicals added to fuel in very small quantities to improve and maintain fuel quality. Examples of gasoline additives include detergents and corrosion inhibitors.

**Advanced technology vehicle (ATV)**—Any light duty vehicle or light-duty truck that is covered by a federal certificate of conformity or an executive order. An ATV is either 1) a duel fuel, flexible fuel, or dedicated alternatively fueled vehicle certified as a transitional low emissions vehicle (TLEV) or more stringent when operated on the alternative fuel; 2) an ultra low emission vehicle (ULEV) or inherently low emission vehicle (ILEV) either conventionally or alternatively fueled; or 3) a hybrid electric vehicle (HEV) or a zero emissions vehicle (ZEV).

**Air toxics**—Toxic air pollutants defined under Title II of the CAAA, including benzene, formaldehyde, acetaldehyde, 1-3 butadiene and polycyclic organic matter (POM). Benzene is a constituent of motor

---

This glossary was prepared by A. Fred Enisz and Kathleen Gatliffe, ASME interns at NCSL.

vehicle exhaust, evaporative and refueling emissions. The other compounds are exhaust pollutants from the tailpipe.

**Alcohol**—The family name of a group of organic chemical compounds; includes methanol and ethanol, which are composed of carbon, hydrogen and oxygen.

**Alternative fuel**—As defined pursuant to the EPACT; methanol, denatured ethanol and other alcohols, separately or in mixtures of 85 percent by volume or more (but not less than 70 percent as determined by U.S. Department of Energy rule) with gasoline or other fuels, CNG, LNG, LPG, hydrogen, "coal-derived liquid fuels," fuels "other than alcohols" derived from "biological materials," electricity or any other fuel determined to be "substantially not petroleum" and yielding "substantial energy security benefits and substantial environmental benefits."

**Alternative Fuels Data Center (AFDC)**—A program sponsored by the U.S. Department of Energy and managed by the National Renewable Energy Laboratory to collect emissions, operational and maintenance data on all types of AFVs nationwide. http://www.afdc.doe.gov/

**Alternative Fuels Utilization Program (AFUP)**—A program managed by the U.S. Department of Energy with the goals of improving national energy security by displacing imported oil, improving air quality by development and widespread use of alternative fuels for transportation, and increasing the production of AFVs.

**Alternative Motor Fuels Act of 1988 (AMFA)**—Public Law 100-494. Encourages the development, production and demonstration of alternative motor fuels and AFVs.

**Amtrak**—See Rail.

**Automobile size classifications**—Size classifications of automobiles are established by the U.S. Environmental Protection Agency as follows:

*Mini-compact*—Less than 85 cubic feet of passenger and luggage volume.

*Subcompact*—Between 85 to 100 cubic feet of passenger and luggage volume.

*Compact*—Between 100 to 110 cubic feet of passenger and luggage volume.

*Midsize*—Between 110 to 120 cubic feet of passenger and luggage volume.

*Large*—More than 120 cubic feet of passenger and luggage volume.

*Two-seater*—Automobiles designed primarily to seat only two adults.

*Station wagons* are included in the size class of the sedan of the same name.

**Barrel**—Unit of measure for petroleum; one barrel equals 42 gallons.

**Battery efficiency**—Measured in percentage. Net direct current (DC) energy delivered on discharge, as a percentage of the total DC energy required to restore the initial state-of-charge. The efficiency value must include energy losses resulting from self-discharge, cell equalization, thermal loss compensation, and all battery-specific auxiliary equipment.

**Bi-fuel vehicle**—A vehicle with two separate fuel systems designed to run on either an alternative fuel or conventional gasoline, using only one fuel at a time. These systems are advantageous for drivers who do not always have access to an alternative fuel refueling station, but sacrifice the potential for optimized combustion and very low evaporative emissions. Bi-fuel systems usually are used in passenger cars or trucks. These vehicles are referred to as "dual-fuel" in the CAAA and EPACT.

**Biochemical conversion**—The use of enzymes and catalysts to change biological substances chemically to produce energy products. For example, the digestion of organic wastes or sewage by microorganisms to produce methane is a biochemical conversion  process.

**Biodiesel**—A biodegradable transportation fuel for use in diesel engines that is produced through transesterification of organically derived oils or fats.  Biodiesel is used as a component of diesel fuel.  In the future it may replace diesel.

**Biomass**—Renewable organic matter such as agricultural crops, crop-waste residues, wood, animal and municipal wastes, aquatic plants, fungal growth, etc., that is used for the production of energy.

**Btu (British thermal unit)**—The amount of energy required to raise the temperature of 1 pound of water 1 degree Fahrenheit at or near 39.2 degrees Fahrenheit.  The average Btu content of a fuel is the thermal energy (or heat) obtained per unit quantity of fuel (e.g., gallon) as determined from tests of fuel samples.

**Bus**—A large motor vehicle capable of carrying a large number of passengers, generally along a fixed route.

**Butane**—An easily liquefied gas recovered from natural gas.  Used as a low-volatility component of motor gasoline, processed further for a high-octane gasoline component, used in LPG for domestic and industrial applications and used as a raw material for petrochemical synthesis.

**California Air Resource Board (CARB)**—A state agency that regulates the air quality in California.  Air quality regulations established by CARB often are stricter than those set by the federal government.

**California Low Emission Vehicle Program**—State requirement for automakers to produce vehicles with fewer emissions than current EPA standards.  The four categories of California Low Emission Vehicle Program standards from least to most stringent are TLEV, LEV, ULEV and ZEV.

**Carbon dioxide ($CO_2$)**—A colorless, odorless, nonpoisonous gas that is a normal part of the ambient air. Carbon dioxide is an inevitable product of fossil fuel combustion.  It does not impair human health but is a "greenhouse gas" that traps the earth's heat and contributes to the potential of global warming. Carbon dioxide is not an EPA criteria pollutant.

**Carbon monoxide (CO)**—A colorless, odorless, highly toxic gas that is a normal by-product of incomplete fossil fuel combustion. Carbon monoxide, one of the major air pollutants, can be harmful in small amounts if inhaled. It enters the bloodstream through the lungs and inhibits the blood's capacity to carry oxygen to organs and tissues. CO can impair exercise capacity, visual perception, manual dexterity and learning functions.

**Catalyst**—A substance, the presence of which changes the rate of chemical reaction without itself undergoing a permanent change in its composition. Catalysts may be accelerators that increase the rate of reaction, or retarders that decrease it. Most inorganic catalysts are powdered metals and metal oxides, chiefly used in petroleum, vehicles and heavy chemical industries.

**Clean Air Act Amendments of 1990 (CAAA)**—The original Clean Air Act (CAA) was signed in 1963. The law set emission standards for stationary sources. The CAA was amended several times, most recently in 1990 (P.L. 101-549). The amendments of 1970 introduced motor vehicle emission standards for criteria pollutants, i.e., lead, ozone, CO, $SO_2$, $NO_x$ and particulate mater, as well as air toxins. The CAAA include reformulated gasoline (RFG) and oxygenated gasoline provisions. The RFG provision requires the use of RFG all year in certain areas. The oxygenated gasoline provision requires the use of oxygenated gasoline during certain months when CO and ozone pollution are most serious. The regulations also require that certain fleet operators in 22 cities use "clean fuel vehicles."

**Clean fuel vehicle (CFV)**—Any vehicle that meets the clean fuel vehicle exhaust emissions standards with no restriction on fuel type. Any vehicle certified by EPA as meeting certain federal emissions standards. The four categories of federal CFV standards from least to most stringent are LEV, ULEV, ILEV and ZEV. CFVs are eligible for two federal programs, the California Pilot Program and the Clean-Fuel Fleet Program. CFV exhaust emissions standards for light-duty vehicles and light-duty trucks are numerically identical to those of

CARB's California Low Emission Vehicle Program, which also includes TLEV as a fifth standard.

**Compressed natural gas (CNG)**—Natural gas that has been compressed to high pressures, typically between 2,000 and 3,600 pounds per square inch (psi), in a container. The gas expands when released for use as a fuel.

**Compression ignition**—The form of ignition that initiates combustion in a diesel engine by compression of the fuel-air mixture.

**Constant dollars**—A series of figures where the effect of change in the purchasing power of the dollar has been removed. Usually the data are expressed in terms of dollars from a selected year or the average of a set of years.

**Converted vehicle**—A vehicle originally designed to operate on gasoline or diesel that has been modified or altered to run on an alternative fuel.

**Corporate average fuel economy (CAFE) standards**—CAFE standards originally were established by Congress for new automobiles, and later for light trucks, in Title V of the Motor Vehicle Information and Cost Savings Act (15 U.S.C.1901, et seq.) with subsequent amendments. Under CAFE, automobile manufacturers are required by law to produce vehicle fleets with a composite sales-weighted fuel economy that cannot be lower than the CAFE standards in a given year, or for every vehicle that does not meet the standard, a fine of $5 is paid for every .1 miles per gallon (mpg) below the standard.

**Criteria pollutants**—The EPA designed a clean air criteria regulating certain pollutants as part of the 1990 Clean Air Act. Cities must meet two standards—health (primary) and environment (secondary). These pollutants include carbon monoxide (CO), nitrous oxides ($NO_x$), sulfur dioxide ($SO_2$), carbon dioxide ($CO_2$), hydrocarbons, particulate matter (called PM-10; includes dust, smoke, and soot) and volatile organic compounds (VOC).

**Crude oil**—A mixture of hydrocarbons that exists in the liquid phase in natural underground reservoirs and remains liquid at atmospheric pressure after passing through surface separating facilities.

**Crude oil imports**—The volume of crude oil imported into the 50 states and the District Of Columbia, including imports from U.S. territories, but excluding imports of crude oil into the Hawaiian Foreign Trade Zone.

**Cryogenic storage**—Extreme low-temperature storage.

**Dedicated ethanol vehicle**—Any ethanol-fueled motor vehicle that is engineered and designed to be operated solely on ethanol.

**Dedicated methanol vehicle**—Any methanol-fueled motor vehicle that is engineered and designed to be operated solely on methanol.

**Diesel engine**—Any engine powered with diesel fuel, gaseous fuel or alcohol fuel for which diesel engine speed/torque characteristics and vehicle applications are retained.

**Dual-fuel vehicle**—A vehicle with two separate fuel tanks from which both fuels are injected into the combustion chamber simultaneously. Typically, a dual-fuel system is used in heavy-duty or diesel engines.

> *EPACT definition*—Vehicle designed to operate on a combination of an alternative fuel and a conventional fuel. This includes: a) vehicles using a mixture of gasoline or diesel and an alternative fuel in one fuel tank, commonly called flexible-fueled vehicles; and b) vehicles capable of operating either on an alternative fuel, a conventional fuel or both, using two fuel systems.

> *CAAA definition*—Vehicle with two separate fuel systems designed to run on either an alternative fuel, a conventional fuel or both, using two fuel systems.

**E10 (Gasohol)**—Ethanol/gasoline mixture containing 10 percent denatured ethanol and 90 percent gasoline by volume.

**E85**—Ethanol/gasoline mixture containing 85 percent denatured ethanol and 15 percent gasoline by volume.

**Electric utilities sector**—Consists of privately and publicly owned establishments that generate electricity for resale.

**Electric vehicle**—Any vehicle that operates solely by use of a battery or battery pack, including vehicles powered mainly through the use of an electric battery or battery pack but which uses a flywheel that stores energy produced by the electric motor or through regenerative braking to assist in vehicle operation.

**Emission standards**—Standards for the levels of pollutants emitted from automobiles and trucks.

**Energy capacity**—The energy delivered by the battery, measured in kilowatt hours.

**Energy efficiency**—In reference to transportation, the inverse of energy intensity: the ratio of energy outputs from a process to the energy inputs.

**Energy intensity**—In reference to transportation, the ratio of energy or fuel input to a process to the useful output from that process; for example, gallons of fuel per passenger-mile or Btu per ton-mile.

**Ethanol**—Any fuel for motor vehicles and motor vehicle engines that is composed of either commercially available or chemically pure ethanol ($CH_3CH_2OH$) and gasoline. The required fuel blend is based on the type of ethanol-fueled vehicle being certified and the particular aspect of the certification procedure being conducted.

**Ethanol vehicle**—Any motor vehicle that is engineered and designed to be operated using ethanol as fuel.

**Feedstock**—A material that is converted to fuel.

**Fischer Tropsch**—A technology for converting natural gas, coal and other carbon-bearing feedstocks into high-value, clean-burning, liquid fuels by rearranging the chemical makeup of the carbon and hydrogen present in the substance.

**Fleet vehicles**—Vehicles that are operated in mass by a corporation or institution, operated under unified control, and used for non-personal activities. Some companies make a distinction between cars that were bought in bulk rather than singularly, or whether they are operated in bulk, as well as the minimum number of vehicles that constitute a fleet (i.e. four or 10).

**Flexible-fuel vehicles**—Passenger cars designed to run on blends of unleaded gasoline with either ethanol or methanol.

**Fuel cell**—An electrochemical engine with no moving parts that converts the chemical energy of a fuel directly into electricity. The fuel is not burned, but is oxidized electrochemically.

> *Proton exchange membrane (PEM)*—A fuel cell that converts hydrogen into water by using a membrane coated with a catalyst (platinum). Water and a moderate amount of heat are the only by-products.

**Fuel Cell Conversion Efficiency**—the efficiency in which the fuel cell converts its fuel (hydrogen or another hydrocarbon rich fuel) into electricity.

**Gas-guzzler tax**—A tax, paid by the purchaser, on new car acquisitions that have a combined city/highway fuel economy rating that is below the standard for that year. For model years 1986 and later, the standard is 22.5 mpg. This tax originates from the 1978 Energy Tax Act (Public Law 95-618).

**Gaseous fuels**—Liquefied petroleum gas, compressed natural gas and liquefied natural gas fuels for use in motor vehicles.

**Gasohol**—In the United States, gasohol refers to gasoline that contains 10 percent ethanol by volume. This term was used in the late 1970s and early 1980s but has been replaced by terms such as E10, super unleaded plus ethanol or unleaded plus.

**Gasoline**—A mixture of volatile hydrocarbons that is suitable for operation of an internal combustion engine. Its major components are hydrocarbons with boiling points ranging from 78 to 217 degrees centigrade (172° to 423° Fahrenheit). The major source is distillation of petroleum and cracking, polymerization and other chemical reactions by which the naturally occurring petroleum hydrocarbons are converted into those that have superior fuel properties.

**Global warming**—The escalation of global temperatures caused by the increase of greenhouse gases in the lower atmosphere.

**Greenhouse effect**—A warming of the earth and its atmosphere as a result of trapping incoming solar radiation by $CO_2$, water vapor, methane, nitrous oxide, chlorofluorocarbons and other gases, both natural and manmade.

**Gridlock**—A traffic condition experienced on intersecting streets (hence the term "grid") when congestion is so severe that little or no vehicular movement is possible.

**Gross national product (GNP)**—A measure of monetary value of the goods and services available to the nation from economic activity. The calculation includes the total value at market prices of all goods and services produced by the nation's economy. Calculated quarterly by the U.S. Department of Commerce, GNP is the broadest available measure of the level of economic activity.

**Heating Value**—The amount of thermal energy per unit mass or volume.

**Hybrid electric vehicle (HEV)**—Any vehicle that is included in the definition of a "series hybrid electric vehicle," a "parallel hybrid electric vehicle," or a "battery assisted combustion engine vehicle."

**Hydrocarbon (HC)**—A compound that contains only hydrogen and carbon. The simplest and lightest forms of hydrocarbon are gaseous. With greater molecular weights they are liquid; the heaviest are solids.

**Light-duty vehicles**—Automobiles and light trucks.

**Light truck**—Unless otherwise noted, light trucks are defined in this publication as two-axle, four-tire trucks. The U.S. Bureau of Census classifies as light trucks all trucks with a gross vehicle weight of less than 10,000 pounds (see *truck size classifications*).

**Liquefied petroleum gas (LPG)**—Commonly called propane, $C_3H_8$—a colorless, hydrocarbon gas—usually is derived from natural gas or from crude oil. In locations where there is no natural gas and the gasoline consumption is low, naphtha is converted to LPG by catalytic reforming. Of the propane used in the United States, 90 percent is domestically produced.

**Liquefied natural gas (LNG)**—Natural gas that has been condensed to a liquid, typically by cryogenically cooling the gas.

**M85**—A motor fuel used in AFVs that is 85 percent methanol and 15 percent unleaded gasoline by volume.

**Methane ($CH_4$)**—The simplest of the hydrocarbons and the principal constituent of natural gas. Pure methane has a heating value of 1,012 Btu per standard cubic foot.

**Methanol**—Any fuel for motor vehicles and motor vehicle engines that is composed of either commercially available or chemically pure methanol ($CH_3OH$) and gasoline. The required fuel blend is based on the type of methanol-fueled vehicle being certified and the particular aspect of the certification procedure being conducted.

**Methanol vehicle**—Any motor vehicle that is engineered and designed to be operated using methanol as fuel.

**National Ambient Air Quality Standards (NAAQS)**—Ambient standards for air pollutants specifically regulated under the CAA. These pollutants include ozone, CO, $NO_2$, lead, particulate matter and SO.

**Nationwide Personal Transportation Study (NPTS)**—A nationwide home interview survey of households that provides information about the characteristics and personal travel patterns of the U.S. population. Surveys were conducted in 1969, 1977, 1983 and 1990 by the U.S. Bureau of Census for the U.S. Department of Transportation.

**Natural gas**—A mixture of hydrocarbon compounds and small quantities of various non- hydrocarbons existing in the gaseous phase or in solution with crude oil in natural underground reservoirs. It is used principally as a fuel and a feedstock for chemicals.

**Natural gas vehicle**—Any motor vehicle that is engineered and designed to be operated using either compressed natural gas or liquefied natural gas.

**Natural gas plant liquids**—Products obtained from processing natural gas at natural gas processing plants, including natural gasoline plants, cycling plants and fractionators. Products obtained include ethane, liquefied petroleum gases, (propane, butane, propane-butane mixtures and ethane-propane mixtures), isopentane, natural gasoline, unfractionated streams, plant condensate and other minor quantities of finished products, such as gasoline, special naphthas, jet fuel, kerosene and distillate fuel oil.

**Nitrogen oxides ($NO_x$)**—A product of the combustion of fossil fuels. $NO_x$ production increases with the temperature of the process. It can become an air pollutant if concentrations are excessive.

**Nonattainment area**—A region, determined by population density in accordance with the U.S. Census Bureau, that exceeds minimum acceptable NAAQS for one or more "criteria pollutants." Such areas are required to seek modifications to their state implementation plans (SIPs), setting forth a reasonable timetable using EPA-approved means to achieve the CAA requirements. If a nonattainment area fails to attain NAAQS, EPA may superimpose a federal implementation plan (FIP) with stricter requirements or impose fines, construction bans, cut off federal grant revenues, etc., until the area achieves the acceptable NAAQS.

**Oil reserves**—Crude oil stocks that have been discovered but not yet recovered.

**Oil stocks**—Oil stocks include crude oil (including strategic reserves), unfinished oils, natural gas plant liquids and refined petroleum products.

**Operating cost**—The various charges incurred when using a vehicle.

*Fixed operating cost*—In reference to a passenger car, refers to those expenditures that are independent of the amount of use of the car, such as insurance costs, fees for license and registration, depreciation and finance charges.

*Variable operating cost*—In reference to passenger car, refers to expenditures that are dependent on the amount of use of the car, such as the cost of gas and oil, tires and other maintenance.

**Organization for Economic Cooperation and Development (OECD)**—Consists of Australia, Austria, Belgium, Canada, the Czech Republic, Denmark, Finland, France, Germany, Greece, Hungary, Iceland, Ireland, Italy, Japan, Luxembourg, Mexico, the Netherlands, New Zealand, Norway, Poland, Portugal, South Korea, Spain, Sweden, Switzerland, Turkey, the United Kingdom, and United States. OECD also includes the U.S. territories. Total OECD figures exclude data for the Czech Republic, Hungary, Mexico, Poland and South Korea, which are not yet available.

*OECD Europe*—Consists of Austria, Belgium, the Czech Republic, Denmark, Finland, France, Germany, Greece, Hungary, Iceland, Ireland, Italy, Luxembourg, the Netherlands, Norway, Poland, Portugal, Spain, Sweden, Switzerland, Turkey, and the United Kingdom. OECD Europe figures exclude data for the Czech Republic, Hungary and Poland, which are not yet available.

*OECD Pacific*—Consists of Australia, Japan and New Zealand.

**Organization for Petroleum Exporting Countries (OPEC)**—Includes Saudi Arabia, Iran, Venezuela, Libya, Indonesia, the United Arab Emirates, Algeria, Nigeria, Ecuador, Gabon, Iraq, Kuwait and Qatar.

Data for Saudi Arabia and Kuwait include their shares from the Partitioned Zone (formerly the Neutral Zone).

*Arab OPEC*—Consists of Algeria, Iraq, Kuwait, Libya, Qatar, Saudi Arabia and the United Arab Emirates.

**Oxides of nitrogen ($NO_x$)**—Regulated air pollutants, primarily NO and $NO_2$, but including other substances in minute concentrations. Under the high pressure and temperature conditions in an engine, nitrogen and oxygen atoms in the air react to form $NO_x$. Like hydrocarbons, $NO_x$ are precursors to the formation of smog. They also contribute to the formation of acid rain.

**Oxygenate**—A term used in the petroleum industry to denote fuel additives containing hydrogen, carbon and oxygen in their molecular structure. Included are ethers such as MTBE and ETBE, and alcohols such as ethanol and methanol.

**Oxygenated gasoline**—Gasoline containing an oxygenate such as ethanol or MTBE. The goal of increased oxygen content is to promote more complete combustion, thereby reducing tailpipe emissions of CO. Recent studies have raised questions about the effectiveness of oxygenates.

**Ozone**—Tropospheric ozone (smog) is formed when volatile organic compounds (VOCs) oxygen and $NO_x$ react in the presence of sunlight (not to be confused with stratospheric ozone, which is found in the upper atmosphere and protects the earth from the sun's ultraviolet rays). Although beneficial in the upper atmosphere, at ground level ozone is a respiratory irritant and is considered a pollutant.

**Parallel hybrid electric vehicle**—Any vehicle that allows power to be delivered to the driven wheels by either a combustion engine and/or by a battery powered electric motor.

**Particulates/particulate matter (PM)**—Carbon particles formed by partial oxidation and reduction of hydrocarbon fuel that form smoke or soot and stick to lung tissue when inhaled. Also included are trace quantities of metal oxides and nitrides originating from engine wear, component degradation, and inorganic fuel additives.

**Passenger-miles traveled (PMT)**—One PMT is defined as a single person traveling one mile.

**Persian Gulf countries**—Consists of Bahrain, Iran, Iraq, Kuwait, Qatar, Saudi Arabia and the United Arab Emirates.

**Petroleum**—A generic term applied to oil and oil products in all forms, such as crude oil, lease condensate, unfinished oil, refined petroleum products, natural gas plant liquids, and non-hydrocarbon compounds blended into finished petroleum products.

**Petroleum consumption**—A calculated demand for petroleum products obtained by summing domestic production, imports of crude petroleum and natural gas liquids, imports of petroleum products, and the primary stocks at the beginning of the period and then subtracting the exports and the primary stocks at the end of the period. Petroleum imports—All imports of crude petroleum, natural gas liquids and petroleum products from foreign countries and receipts from Guam, Puerto Rico, the Virgin Islands and the Hawaiian Trade Zone. The commodities included are crude oil, unfinished oils, plant condensate and refined petroleum products.

**Petroleum inventories**—The amounts of crude oil, unfinished oil, petroleum products and natural gas liquids held at refineries, at natural gas processing plants, in pipelines, at bulk terminals operated by refining and pipeline companies, and at independent bulk terminals. Crude oil held in storage on leases also is included; these stocks are known as primary stocks. Secondary stocks—those held by wholesalers, dealers, service station operators and consumers—are excluded. Before 1975, stock held at independent bulk terminals were classified as secondary stocks.

**Propane**—See *Liquefied petroleum gas (LPG)*.

**Proved reserves of crude oil**—The estimated quantities of all liquids defined as crude oil, which geological and engineering data demonstrate with reasonable certainty to be recoverable in future years from known reservoirs under existing economic and operating conditions.

**Quad**—Quadrillion, $10^{15}$. In this publication, a quad refers to quadrillion Btu.

**Rail (Transit railroad)**—Urban railway transportation, including "heavy" and "light" transit rail. Heavy transit rail, characterized by exclusive rights-of-way, multi-car trains, high-speed rapid acceleration, sophisticated signaling and high platform loading, also is known as subway, elevated railway or metropolitan railway (metro). Features of light transit rail may include exclusive or shared rights-of-way, high or low platform loading, multi-car trains or single cars, and automated or manual operation. In generic usage, light rail includes streetcars, trolley cars and tramways.

**Reformulated gasoline**—Gasoline that has had its composition or characteristics altered to reduce vehicular emissions of pollutants, particularly pursuant to EPA regulations under the CAA.

**Series hybrid electric vehicle**—Any vehicle that allows power to be delivered to the driven wheels solely by a battery powered electric motor, but that also incorporates the use of a combustion engine to provide power to the battery and/or electric motor.

**Smog**—A petrochemical haze caused primarily by the reaction of hydrocarbons and $NO_x$ with sunlight.

**Spark ignition engine**—An internal combustion engine in which the charge is ignited electrically (e.g. via spark plug).

**Specific energy**—The rated energy capacity of a battery divided by the total battery system weight measured in watt-hours per kilogram (Wh/kg).

**Tax incentives**—In general, a means of employing the U.S. federal and/or state tax codes to stimulate investment in or development of a socially desirable economic objective without direct expenditure from the budget of a given unit of government. Such incentives can take the form of tax exemptions or credits.

**Total Efficiency** (of an Internal Combustion Engine)—The efficiency of an engine that includes both the mechanical efficiency of the engine as well as the efficiency with which the engine converts the energy value of the fuel (through combustion) into useful work (e.g. to propel the vehicle).

**Toxic emission**—Any pollutant emitted from a source that can negatively affect human health or the environment.

**Transitional low emission vehicle**—Any vehicle certified to the transitional low emission vehicle standards specified in 40 CFR part 86. Transportation control measures (TCM)—Restrictions imposed by state or local governments to limit use or access by vehicles during certain times or subject to specific operating requirements, e.g., high-occupancy vehicle (HOV) lanes.

**Ultra-low emission vehicle (ULEV)**—Any vehicle certified to the ultra-low emission vehicle standards specified in 40 CFR part 86.

**U.S. Department of Energy (DOE)**—A department of the federal government established by the Carter administration in 1977 to consolidate energy-oriented programs and agencies. The DOE mission includes the coordination and management of energy conservation, supply, information dissemination, regulation, research, development and demonstration. The department includes the Office of Transportation Technologies, within which the Office of Technology Utilization's Clean Cities program operates.

**U.S. Environmental Protection Agency (EPA)**—A government agency established in 1970 that is responsible for the protection of the environment and public health. EPA seeks to reduce air, water and land pollution and pollution from solid waste, radiation, pesticides and toxic substances. EPA also controls fuels, fuel additives and motor vehicle emissions.

**Vehicle classifications:**

*Alternative fuel vehicles (AFV)*—A vehicle that uses a fuel other than gasoline or diesel.

*Electric vehicle (EV)*—A vehicle powered by electricity, generally provided by storage batteries but also provided by photovoltaic cells or a fuel cell.

*Hybrid electric vehicle (HEV)*—A vehicle that is powered by two or more energy sources, one of which is electricity. HEVs combine the engine and fuel tank of a conventional vehicle with the battery and electric motor of an electric vehicle in a single drive train.

*Fuel cell vehicle*—A vehicle driven by electricity produced by an electrochemical engine with no moving parts that converts the chemical energy of a fuel directly into electricity.

**Vehicle emission classifications**—These vehicles meet the following standards.

*Low emission vehicles (LEV)*—A vehicle that meets either EPA's clean fuel vehicle LEV standards or CARB's California Low Emission Vehicle Program standards. LEVs produce fewer emissions than TLEVs.

*Transitional low emission vehicles (TLEV)*—A vehicle that meets either EPA's CFV TLEV standards or CARB's California Low Emission Vehicle Program standards. TLEV's produce fewer emissions than federal tier 1 vehicles. TLEV's are eligible for the federal California Pilot Program, but not for the Clean-Fuel Fleet Program.

*Ultra-low emission vehicles (ULEV)*—A vehicle that meets either EPA's CFV ULEV standards or CARB's California Low Emission Vehicle Program standards. ULEVs produce fewer emissions than LEVs. Fleets that purchase CFV ULEVs may earn credits under the Clean-Fuel Fleet Vehicle Program. Manufacturers that sell CFV ULEVs may earn credits under the federal California Pilot Program.

*Zero emission vehicles (ZEV)*—Any vehicle that is certified to produce zero emissions of any criteria pollutants under any and all possible operational modes and conditions. Incorporation of a fuel-fired heater shall not preclude a vehicle from being certified as a ZEV, provided the fuel-fired heater cannot be operated at ambient temperatures above 40 degrees Fahrenheit and the heater is demonstrated to have zero evaporative emissions under any and all possible operational modes and conditions. A vehicle that meets either EPA's CFV ZEV standards or CARB's California Low Emission Vehicle Program ZEV standards, usually met with electric vehicles, require zero vehicle (not power plant) source emissions. ZEVs earn more Clean-Fuel Fleet Vehicle credits than ULEVs. ZEVs also may meet ILEV standards if evaporative emissions are near zero.

*Zero emission vehicle mandate*—Any state regulation or other law that imposes (or purports to impose) obligations on auto manufacturers to produce, deliver for sale, or sell a certain number or percentage of ZEVs.

Inherently low emission vehicle (ILEV)—Federal only. Describes a vehicle that meets EPA's CFV ILEV standards. Tailpipe standards may be LEV, ULEV or ZEV, but include the requirement that evaporative emissions be 2 grams per test over the full test procedure and 5 grams per test without the use of any auxiliary emission control devices. ILEVs will be dedicated AFVs, in most cases. Dual-fuel vehicles will be considered ILEVs only if both fuels meet the standard. (Very low-volatility gasoline also may meet the standard.) ILEVs are exempt from certain transportation control measures, including high occupancy vehicle lane restrictions.

**Volatile organic compound (VOC)**—Hydrocarbon gases released during combustion or evaporation of fuel and regulated by EPA. VOCs combine with $NO_x$ in the presence of sunlight to form ozone.

# BIBLIOGRAPHY

*Air Products Goes 'On the Road' with Hydrogen Fuel,* Air Products News, 1998. URL= http://www.airproducts.com/corp/spring98/road.htm; World Wide Web

American Public Transit Association (APTA). *Transit Fact Book.* Washington, D.C.: APTA, February, 1998.

*Annual Energy Outlook 1998,* Washington, D.C.: United States Department of Energy, Energy Information Administration December, 1997. URL= http://ftp.eia.doe.gov/pub/pdf/multi.fuel/038398.pdf, World Wide Web.

Ball, Jeffrey. "Auto Makers Are Racing To Market 'Green Cars' Powered by Fuel Cells—DaimlerChrysler Sets Deadline To Sell a Version by 2004; Happy Times for Ballard—But 'Who Buys the First One?'," *The Wall Street Journal,* March 15, 1999.

Bardall, *Solar Today,* Sept./Oct. 1995.

Breakthrough Technologies Institute. *Fuel Cells 2000: Online Fuel Cell Information Center.* 1999. URL= http://www.fuelcells.org, 1999; World Wide Web.

California PATH. *LEAP-Learning from the Evaluation and Analysis of Performance of Intelligent Transportation Systems.* 1999. URL= http://www.path.berkeley.edu/~leap; World Wide Web.

Center for Urban Transportation Research, University of South Florida. *Telecommute America! In Tampa Bay.* February 1999. URL= http://www.cutr.eng.usf.edu/ research/tdm/tele.htm ; World Wide Web

Cooper, Thomas. "Highway Financing." *Public Roads*, Volume 61, no. 4 (March/April 1998).

Davis, Stacy C. *Transportation Energy Data Book*, 18th ed. Oak Ridge, Tenn.: United States Department of Transportation, Center for Transportation Analysis, 1998.

Department of Energy, Office of Alternative Fuels, Office of Transportation Technologies, Conservation and Renewable Energy, *Introduction to Alternative Fuel Vehicles*, Washington, D.C: January 1993.

Dry, M.E. *The Sasol Fischer-Tropsch Process.* Extract from Applied Industrial Catalysis 2, Chapter 5, Academic Press, Inc., 1983.

Eaton, John. "Prius: A Clean Driving Hybrid," *The Denver Post*, October 28, 1998, p. 1C.

*Effects of Fuel Ethanol Use on Fuel-Cycle Energy and Greenhouse Gas Emissions*, Argonne National Laboratory: United States Department of Energy, January 1999.

Energy Information Administration, *Alternatives to Traditional Transportation Fuels*, Washington, D.C.: DOE/EIA-0585/O, June 1994.

Electric Vehicle Association of the Americas. *EV Charging Site Directory.* December 1998. Obtained from URL= http://www.evaa.org/directory/ev_directory.html; World Wide Web.

Electric Vehicle Association of the Americas. *EVs Coming to Market.* 1997.

Fuel Commercialization Group. *What is a Fuel Cell?* Washington D.C.: 1996.

Goehring, Janet B., et al. *Hybrid Electric Vehicles: Options for State Policymakers.* Denver: National Conference of State Legislatures, *Transportation Series*, no. 4., July 1996.

Gurovich, Norma D. and Stephan Ahearn. *Potential Uses of Zero Emission Vehicles in Arizona State Fleets.* Phoenix: Arizona Department of Commerce Energy Office, November, 1991.

Internal Revenue Service. IRS tax code Title 26, Subtitle A, Chapter 1, Subchapter A, part VI subpart D, section 40.

International Telework Association and Council. *Overview of Telework America 1999*, February 1999. URL= http://www.telecommute.org/twa_overview.htm/; World Wide Web.

Kearns, Sean J. "Humboldt State to Unveil America's First Street-Ready Fuel-Cell Car in Palm Desert," Humboldt State University, Office of Public Affairs, April 21, 1998.

Kirsch, David A. "The Electric Car and the Burden of History: Studies in Automotive Systems Rivalry in America, 1890-1996," *Business and Economic History* 26. no. 2, (Winter 1997).

Kitamura; Ryuichi; Mokhtarian; Pendyala; and Goulias. *An Evaluation of Telecommuting as a Trip Reduction Measure.* Davis: Institute of Transportation Studies, University of California at Davis, 1991.

Klein, J., and M. Olson. *"Taken for a Ride (video),"* New Day Films, Yellow Springs, Ohio, 55 minutes, 1996.

Koch, Kathleen. "DaimlerChrysler Introduces Car Powered by Fuel Cells," CNN, March 17, 1999. URL= http://www.cnn.com; World Wide Web.

Kreith, Frank; Paul Norton; and Dena Sue Potestio. "Electric Vehicles: Promise and Reality," *Current Municipal Problems* 22, Number 2 (1995).

Kreith, Frank and Ron E. West, editors. *Economics of Solar Energy and Conservation Systems* 1. CRC Press, 1980.

Lehman, Peter. "Fuel Cells: The Key to a Sustainable Energy Future?," *Positive Alternatives*, Winter, 1998.

Matheson, Evelyn. *Are Electric Vehicles the Future in our Region?* Bonneville Power Administration, August 9, 1992.

Morgan, Daniel and Fred Sissine. *Hydrogen: Technology and Policy.* Congressional Research Service, Report for Congress, April 28, 1995.

National Academy of Science, Committee on Tropospheric Ozone. *National Research Council, Rethinking the Ozone Problem in Urban and Regional Air Pollution.* National Academy Press, 1992.

Norton, Paul. *Alternative Fuels for Motor Vehicles.* Boca Raton: *CRC Handbook of Mechanical Engineering*, ed. Frank Kreith, CRC Press, 1998.

Nowell, Gregory P. *Looking Beyond the Internal Combustion Engine: The Promise of Methanol Fuel Cell Vehicles.* Washington D.C.: American Methanol Institute, 1998.

Office of Highway Information Management, Federal Highway Administration, United States Department of Transportation, *1996 Highway Statistics, Section 4, Highway Finance, Table HF- 10*, Washington, D.C., October, 1997.

Ogden, A. J. and R.H. Williams. *Solar Hydrogen Moving Beyond Fossils Fuels.* Washington, D.C.: World Resources Institute, October 1989.

Patil, Pandit G. *Fundamentals of Fuel Cells.* Washington, D.C.: United States Department of Energy, November, 1992. URL=http://afdc3.nrel.gov/pdfs/text/0040.txt; World Wide Web.

Perez, Michelle. "New, Green Cars: Are They for Real?," *Update: Alliance to Save Energy* 9, no. 1, (Spring 1998)

Pimentel, David. "Energy Security, Economics, and the Environment." *Focus* 2, no. 3 (1992).

"Quick Payback. That's Exactly What El Paso's Sun Metro Has Gotten From Its Natural Gas Buses." *Natural Gas Fuels*, (September 1998).

Rae, John B. "The Electric Vehicle Company: A Monopoly that Missed." *Massachusetts Institute of Technology Business History Review*, 1955.

Revenaugh, Steve. "Electric Vehicle Charging Station Pricing Schedule As of 4/30/99," personal correspondence and Price Sheet, Sacramento Municipal Utility District (SMUD), April 30, 1999.

Siegel, William; and Charles Mendler. "The Technological Opportunities of Hybrid Electric Vehicles." Prepared for the Symposium for the Promotion of Low Emission Vehicles, Tokyo, Japan, January 11-12, 1996.

Smart Valley, Inc. *Telecommute America: California Style!* February, 1999. URL= http://smart2.svi.org/telework/; World Wide Web.

Texas Transportation Institute, *TTI Mobility Study*, February 1999. URL=http://mobility.tamu.edu//; World Wide Web.

"Traffic Congestion Quadruples in Smaller Cities; LA is Worst." *Metro Magazine*, January/February 1999, p. 74.

United States Council for Automotive Research. *Chrysler Simulating Hybrid Options in Defining Next Generation Powertrain.* December 1998. URL= http://www.uscar.org/ techno/ hyb_chry.htm; World Wide Web.

United States Department of Energy, Center for Transportation Analysis. *Transportation Energy Data Book.* Oak Ridge: 1998.

United States Department of Energy, Energy Information Administration, *Annual Energy Outlook 1999.* URL= http:// www.eia.doe.gov/oiaf/aeo99/results.html#tables; World Wide Web.

United States Department of Energy, General Services Department/ Resource Management Division, City of Albuquerque, Energy Task Force of the Urban Consortium for Technology Initiatives. *Alternative Vehicle Fuels: A Demonstration Project.* DOE/IR/ 05106-T147. December, 1988.

United States Department of Transportation, Bureau of Transportation Statistics. *Transportation Statistics Annual Report 1997.* Washington, D.C., 1997.

United States Department of Transportation. "ITS in Your State." February 1999. URL= http://www.its.dot.gov/staterpt/state.htm; World Wide Web.

Weston, Kenneth C. *Energy Conversion.* St. Paul: West Publishing Company, 1992. p. 443.

Weyrich, J., and F. Lind. *Conservatives and Mass Transit: Is It Time for A New Look?* Washington, D.C.: Free Congress Foundation, 1996.

Wilson, Hugh K.; Janet B. Goehring; and James Reed. *High-Speed Trains for the United States? History and Options.* Denver: National Conference of State Legislatures, *Transportation Series, Number 2*, March, 1996.

Wouk, Victor E. "Hybrid Electric Vehicles, They will reduce pollution and conserve petroleum. But will people buy them, even if the vehicles have astounding fuel efficiency?" *Scientific American*, October, 1997.

"It's hard to connect with your child without first understanding where they are. As counselors and speakers at parenting events across the country, we spend a great deal of time teaching parents about development. To know *where* your child is—not just physically, but emotionally, socially, and spiritually, helps you to truly know and understand *who* your child is. And that understanding is the key to connecting. The Phase Guides give you the tools to do just that. Our wise friends Reggie and Kristen have put together an insightful, hopeful, practical, and literal year-by-year guide that will help you to understand and connect with your child at every age."

**SISSY GOFF**
*M.ED., LPC-MHSP, DIRECTOR OF CHILD & ADOLESCENT COUNSELING AT DAYSTAR COUNSELING MINISTRIES IN NASHVILLE, TENNESSEE, SPEAKER AND AUTHOR OF ARE MY KIDS ON TRACK?*

"These resources for parents are fantastically empowering, absolute in their simplicity, and completely doable in every way. The hard work that has gone into the Phase Project will echo through the next generation of children in powerful ways."

**JENNIFER WALKER**
*RN BSN, AUTHOR AND FOUNDER OF MOMS ON CALL*

"We all know where we want to end up in our parenting, but how to get there can seem like an unsolved mystery. Through the Phase Project series, Reggie Joiner and Kristen Ivy team up to help us out. The result is a resource that guides us through the different seasons of raising children, and provides a road map to parenting in such a way that we finish up with very few regrets."

**SANDRA STANLEY**
*FOSTER CARE ADVOCATE, BLOGGER, WIFE TO ANDY STANLEY, MOTHER OF THREE*

"Not only are the Phase Guides the most creative and well-thought-out guides to parenting I have ever encountered, these books are ESSENTIAL to my daily parenting. With a 13-year-old, 11-year-old, and 9-year-old at home, I am swimming in their wake of daily drama and delicacy. These books are a reminder to enjoy every second. Because it's just a phase."

**CARLOS WHITTAKER**
*AUTHOR, SPEAKER, FATHER OF THREE*

"As the founder of Minnie's Food Pantry, I see thousands of people each month with children who will benefit from the advice, guidance, and nuggets of information on how to celebrate and understand the phases of their child's life. Too often we feel like we're losing our mind when sweet little Johnny starts to change his behavior into a person we do not know. I can't wait to start implementing the principles of these books with my clients to remind them . . . it's just a phase."

**CHERYL JACKSON**
*FOUNDER OF MINNIE'S FOOD PANTRY, AWARD-WINNING PHILANTHROPIST, AND GRANDMOTHER*

"I began exploring this resource with my counselor hat on, thinking how valuable this will be for the many parents I spend time with in my office. I ended up taking my counselor hat off and putting on my parent hat. Then I kept thinking about friends who are teachers, coaches, youth pastors, and children's ministers, who would want this in their hands. What a valuable resource the Orange team has given us to better understand and care for the kids and adolescents we love. I look forward to sharing it broadly."

**DAVID THOMAS**
*LMSW, DIRECTOR OF FAMILY COUNSELING, DAYSTAR COUNSELING MINISTRIES, SPEAKER AND AUTHOR OF* ARE MY KIDS ON TRACK? *AND* WILD THINGS: THE ART OF NURTURING BOYS

"I have always wished someone would hand me a manual for parenting. Well, the Phase Guides are more than what I wished for. They guide, inspire, and challenge me as a parent—while giving me incredible insight into my children at each age and phase. Our family will be using these every year!"

**COURTNEY DEFEO**
*AUTHOR OF* IN THIS HOUSE, WE WILL GIGGLE, *MOTHER OF TWO*

"As I speak to high school students and their parents, I always wonder to myself: What would it have been like if they had better seen what was coming next? What if they had a guide that would tell them what to expect and how to be ready? What if they could anticipate what is predictable about the high school years before they actually hit? These Phase Guides give a parent that kind of preparation so they can have a plan when they need it most."

**JOSH SHIPP**
*AUTHOR, TEEN EXPERT, AND YOUTH SPEAKER*

"The Phase Guides are incredibly creative, well researched, and filled with inspirational actions for everyday life. Each age-specific guide is catalytic for equipping parents to lead and love their kids as they grow up. I'm blown away and deeply encouraged by the content and by its creators. I highly recommend Phase resources for all parents, teachers, and influencers of children. This is the stuff that challenges us and changes our world. Get them. Read them. And use them!"

**DANIELLE STRICKLAND**
*OFFICER WITH THE SALVATION ARMY, AUTHOR, SPEAKER, MOTHER OF TWO*

"It's true that parenting is one of life's greatest joys but it is not without its challenges. If we're honest, parenting can sometimes feel like trying to choreograph a dance to an ever-changing beat. It can be clumsy and riddled with well-meaning missteps. If parenting is a dance, this Parenting Guide is a skilled instructor refining your technique and helping you move gracefully to a steady beat. For those of us who love to plan ahead, this guide will help you anticipate what's to come so you can be poised and ready to embrace the moments you want to enjoy."

**TINA NAIDOO**
*MSSW, LCSW EXECUTIVE DIRECTOR, THE POTTER'S HOUSE OF DALLAS, INC.*

# PARENTING YOUR ELEVENTH GRADER

## A GUIDE TO MAKING THE MOST OF THE "JUST TRUST ME" PHASE

KRISTEN IVY AND REGGIE JOINER

# PARENTING YOUR ELEVENTH GRADER
## A GUIDE TO MAKING THE MOST OF THE
## "JUST TRUST ME" PHASE

Published by Orange, a division of The reThink Group, Inc.,
5870 Charlotte Lane, Suite 300,
Cumming, GA 30040 U.S.A.

All Scripture quotations, unless otherwise indicated, are taken from the Holy
Bible, New International Version®, NIV®. Copyright ©1973, 1978, 1984, 2011 by
Biblica, Inc.™ Used by permission of Zondervan. All rights reserved worldwide.
www.zondervan.com The "NIV" and "New International Version" are trademarks
registered in the United States Patent and Trademark Office by Biblica, Inc.™

©2017 Kristen Ivy and Reggie Joiner
Authors: Kristen Ivy and Reggie Joiner
Lead Editor: Karen Wilson
Editing Team: Melanie Williams, Hannah Crosby, Sherry Surratt

Art Direction: Ryan Boon and Hannah Crosby
Book Design: FiveStone and Sharon van Rossum

Printed in the United States of America
First Edition 2017
1 2 3 4 5 6 7 8 9 10

*Special thanks to:*

*Jim Burns, Ph.D for guidance and consultation on having conversations about sexual integrity*

*Jon Acuff for guidance and consultation on having conversations about technological responsibility*

*Jean Sumner, MD for guidance and consultation on having conversations about healthy habits*

*Every educator, counselor, community leader, and researcher who invested in the Phase Project*

# TABLE OF CONTENTS

# HOW TO USE THIS ~~BOOK~~ ~~JOURNAL~~ GUIDE

The guide you hold in your hand doesn't have very many words, but it does have a lot of ideas. Some of these ideas come from thousands of hours of research. Others come from parents, educators, and volunteers who spend every day with kids the same age as yours. This guide won't tell you everything about your kid, but it will tell you a few things about kids at this age.

The best way to use this guide is to take what these pages tell you about eleventh graders and combine it with what you know is true about *your* eleventh grader.

Let's sum it up:

**THINGS ABOUT ELEVENTH GRADERS +**
**THOUGHTS ABOUT *YOUR* ELEVENTH GRADER =**
**YOUR GUIDE TO THE NEXT 52 WEEKS OF PARENTING**

After each idea in this guide, there are pages with a few questions designed to prompt you to think about your kid, your family, and yourself as a parent. The only guarantee we give to parents who use this guide is this: You will mess up some things as a parent this year. Actually, that's a guarantee to every parent, regardless. But you, you picked up this book! You want to be a better parent. And that's what we hope this guide will do: help you parent your eleventh grader just a little better, simply because you paused to consider a few ideas that can help you make the most of this phase.

# THE ELEVENTH GRADE PHASE

I absolutely love this phase.

Sure, junior year can be exhausting. Most high school educators will tell you this is the most academically challenging year. Most athletic coaches expect their juniors to be at peak performance. And most juniors begin to feel as if they carry increasingly more adult responsibilities.

Teenagers in this phase feel pressure to make more significant choices. Whether those choices are about school, work, or their social life, you have to admit your kid is making more choices than they did in years past. As the father of three teenagers, and a volunteer high school coach for the last six years, I can say with absolute confidence that teenagers today are faced with ten billion times more choices than my friends and I did when we rocked mullets, drove Camaros, and blasted Van Halen.

Ironically, *choice* is the hallmark of freedom (the very thing every teenager wants above all else). And yet, *choice* can also be the very thing that causes someone to get stuck. If you've ever wondered why your teenager may seem apathetic at times, it may be that they simply don't know how to choose.

Imagine a busy city intersection. The more one-way streets you can picture, all moving in different directions, the better it will resemble your teenager's mind. Imagine now that you are one car in the middle of traffic. You have somewhere to be. How should you move? Where will you turn?

That picture describes the gridlock that happens in the mind of an eleventh grader—an emotional, relational, sexual, theological, spiritual gridlock. The stress many juniors feel has a lot to do with these three words: "I don't know."

I don't know . . . what to do now that I've been benched.
I don't know . . . what to do to bring up my math grade.
I don't know . . . if I should go.
I don't know . . . what to do now that I went.
I don't know . . . if I love him.
I don't know . . . if she loves me back.
I don't know . . . what I believe.
I don't know . . .

Now, you're probably thinking, *Didn't you say you love this phase?* Yes. I absolutely love this phase. Here's why: An unquestioned conviction is a weak conviction. "I don't know" means, "I have questions." That's the gift of junior year. Your kid has questions, and you get to be there to help them navigate their uncertainties.

I can honestly say some of my wife's and my greatest moments as parents have been when—through tears, frustration, legitimate idiocy, and apathy—we were able to come alongside our teenagers to facilitate their decisions. They may not always choose what we would have chosen. But, if you stay present in the process, you may have more influence than you ever imagined possible.

Enjoy the gridlock!

**- STUART HALL**
*COMMUNICATOR, AUTHOR, & FATHER OF THREE TEENAGERS*

# 52 WEEKS

## —

# TO PARENT YOUR ELEVENTH GRADER

WHEN YOU SEE
HOW MUCH

*Time*

YOU HAVE LEFT

—

YOU TEND TO DO

*More*

WITH THE TIME
YOU HAVE NOW.

**THERE ARE APPROXIMATELY**

# 936 WEEKS

**FROM THE TIME A BABY IS BORN
UNTIL THEY GROW UP AND MOVE TO
WHATEVER IS NEXT.**

On the day your kid starts eleventh grade, you have 104 weeks remaining. Your eleventh grader may tell you your job as a parent is already over., but you still have 104 weeks to go. What happens in eleventh grade can influence the opportunities they have available in their future.

That's why every week counts. Of course, each week might not feel significant. There may be weeks when all you feel like you accomplished was trying to figure out where your eleventh grader is.

Take a deep breath.
You don't have to get everything done this week.

But what happens in your teenager's life week after week, for the next two years, adds up. So, it might be a good idea to put a number to your weeks.

## MEASURE IT OUT.

Write down the number of weeks you have left with your eleventh grader before they potentially graduate high school.

**HINT:** If you want a little help counting it out, you can download the free Parent Cue app on all mobile platforms.

_____

_____

_____

_____

## CREATE A VISUAL COUNTDOWN.

Find a jar and fill it with one marble for each week you have remaining with your eleventh grader. Then remove one marble every week as a reminder to make the most of your time.

Where can you place your visual countdown so you will see it frequently?

_____

_____

_____

_____

_____

**Which day of the week is best for you to remove a marble?**

_____

_____

_____


**Is there anything you want to do each week as you remove a marble?** *(Examples: say a prayer, send an encouraging text, retell one favorite memory from this past week)*

_____

_____

_____

_____

_____

_____

_____

_____

_____

_____

_____

_____

EVERY PHASE IS A
TIMEFRAME
IN A KID'S LIFE
WHEN YOU CAN
LEVERAGE
DISTINCTIVE
OPPORTUNITIES
TO INFLUENCE
THEIR

*future.*

## YOU ONLY HAVE
# 52 WEEKS
## WITH YOUR ELEVENTH GRADER

*while they are still in eleventh grade.*

Then they will be a senior,

*and you will never know them as an eleventh grader again.*

---

Or, to say it another way:

Before you know it, your teenager will . . .

vote in an election.

open a personal bank account.

get a tattoo (or know someone who did).

That's not to stress you out.

It's to remind you of the potential of this phase.

---

Before eleventh grade is finished, there are some distinctive opportunities you don't want to miss. So, as you count down the next 52 weeks with your junior, pay attention to what makes these weeks uniquely different from the time you've already spent together and the weeks you will have when they move to the next phase.

Time travel for a minute. Remember what it was like to be a junior in high school. What are the best things your parents did for you during that phase of your life? What do you want to try to do differently than your parents?

_____

_____

_____

_____

_____

_____

_____

_____

_____

_____

_____

_____

_____

_____

_____

_____

_____

_____

**What do you think is going to be different about your eleventh grader's junior year than *your* junior year?**

_____

_____

_____

_____

_____

_____

_____

_____

_____

_____

_____

_____

_____

_____

_____

_____

_____

_____

_____

_____

_____

**What are some things you have noticed about your eleventh grader in this phase that you really enjoy?**

**What is something new you're learning as a parent during this phase?**

_____

_____

_____

_____

_____

_____

_____

_____

_____

_____

_____

_____

_____

_____

_____

_____

_____

_____

_____

_____

# ELEVENTH GRADE

—

THE PHASE WHEN THERE'S LESS DRAMA, MORE STRESS, AND YOUR VERY BUSY TEENAGER ANSWERS ALL YOUR QUESTIONS WITH,

*"Just trust me."*

## YOUR JUNIOR MAY IMPRESS YOU.

The rapid influx of hormones has regulated, the fight for peer acceptance has subsided, and the intensity of conflict over independence . . . well, they've worn you down. You may begin to see glimpses of rationality as your junior finds their voice, fills their calendar, and accomplishes surprising things.

## "ACCOMPLISH" IS THE WORD FOR THIS PHASE.

Juniors often take on AP courses, volunteer activities, leadership roles, SAT prep, or an internship. Whether your teen is caught up in the race to win, or simply trying to survive, junior year is filled with pressure. Navigating all of this pressure is your junior's major accomplishment.

## IT CAN BE HARD TO KEEP UP.

Actually, they don't expect you to keep up. What they really want is for you to trust them. After all, they will be out of the house soon, and you will have to trust them anyway. Let this be a practice year for both of you. Help them prove the ways they can be trusted, choose your battles wisely, and parent them in the areas that seem to be most challenging for them personally.

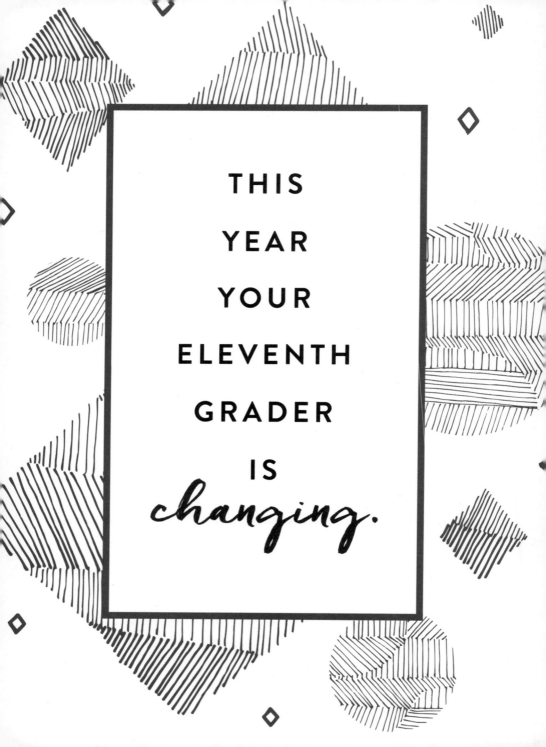

THIS
YEAR
YOUR
ELEVENTH
GRADER
IS
*changing.*

## PHYSICALLY

- Has difficulty falling asleep before 11pm (it's biological)

- Needs nine hours of sleep and one hour of exercise per day

- Girls have likely reached adult height and body development

- Guys may continue to grow in height, and develop muscle mass, body and facial hair

## SOCIALLY

- Dating relationships may become more "committed"

- Increased interest in sexual expression (54% of eleventh graders report being sexually active.)

- Cares deeply about issues like control, responsibility, and freedom (both personally and globally)

- Tends to be self-focused, busy, and unavailable

## MENTALLY

- Can be insightful and incisive about complex issues

- Wired for risk-taking and sensational experiences

- Tends to be opportunistic and idealistic

- Struggles with long-term thinking

- Expanding mental capabilities to grasp paradox, hyperbole, innuendo, and satire

## EMOTIONALLY

- Values humor as a positive point of connection

- Becoming more at ease with who they are; may become more honest than in previous phases

- Often takes on more than they can handle

- May struggle with regulating emotions and social control

What are some changes you are noticing in your eleventh grader?

_____

_____

_____

_____

_____

_____

_____

You may disagree with some of the characteristics we've shared
about eleventh graders. That's because every eleventh grader
is unique. What makes your eleventh grader different from
eleventh graders in general?

_____

_____

_____

_____

_____

_____

_____

_____

## What impresses you about your eleventh grader?

Mark this page. Some weeks it may be easy to focus only on what your eleventh grader does wrong, so try to catch them doing something right. Write it down here. If you want to be really thorough, there are about 52 blank lines.

_____

_____

_____

_____

_____

_____

_____

_____

_____

_____

_____

_____

_____

_____

_____

_____

_____

_____

_____

_____

# SIX
# THINGS

—

## EVERY KID
## NEEDS

YOUR KID
NEEDS 6 THINGS
OVER TIME

LOVE

WORDS WORK STORIES

PEOPLE

FUN

# OVER THE NEXT 104 WEEKS, YOUR ELEVENTH GRADER WILL NEED MANY THINGS:

Some of the things your teenager needs will change over the next 104 weeks, but there are six things every kid needs at every phase. In fact, these things may be the most important things you give your high schooler (even more important than money—but they will probably ask you for money more often).

**EVERY KID, AT EVERY PHASE, NEEDS...**

♡ **LOVE**
to give them a sense of WORTH.

📖 **STORIES**
to give them a bigger PERSPECTIVE.

🏋 **WORK**
to give them PURPOSE.

♟ **FUN**
to give them CONNECTION.

👥 **PEOPLE**
to give them BELONGING.

💬 **WORDS**
to give them DIRECTION.

The next few pages are designed to help you think about how you will give your teenager these six things, right now—while they are in eleventh grade.

EVERY KID

NEEDS

*love*

OVER TIME

—

TO GIVE THEM

A SENSE OF

*worth.*

# ONE QUESTION YOUR ELEVENTH GRADER IS ASKING

Your eleventh grader is ready to live the life they feel they were born to live—and they don't want to wait to get started. Two years is too long! Actually, next semester feels like forever in the future. Your junior is ready to do something, right now.

Your eleventh grader is asking one major question:

## "HOW CAN I MATTER?"

Your junior gravitates toward experiences that will enrich their life story. Guide and encourage their self-expression by helping them find positive experiences. But you may also want to monitor their level of stress and activity. You love your eleventh grader best when you do one thing:

## MOBILIZE their potential.

Your eleventh grader will feel most loved when they feel like they have the trust and respect of someone who values their present circumstances. If you want to mobilize their potential, look for opportunities to communicate, "I trust you, I am for you, and I love you no matter what."

Mobilizing your junior's potential requires paying attention to what they like. What does your eleventh grader seem to enjoy most right now? *(If you don't know, it's okay to ask them.)*

_____

_____

_____

_____

_____

_____

_____

_____

_____

_____

_____

_____

_____

_____

_____

_____

_____

_____

**What experiences are enriching your eleventh grader's interests and giving them something significant to do?**

_____

_____

_____

_____

_____

_____

_____

_____

_____

_____

_____

_____

_____

_____

_____

_____

_____

_____

_____

Mobilizing your eleventh grader toward future freedom also requires boundaries. What are the most important boundaries for your eleventh grader? *(Consider deciding on rules and consequences together. Talk about ways they can earn future freedom as they build trust.)*

_____

_____

_____

_____

_____

_____

_____

_____

_____

_____

_____

_____

_____

_____

_____

_____

_____

As you know, parenting a teenager can be tough. It's impossible to love your eleventh grader well if you are running on empty. What can you do to refuel each week so you are able to give your eleventh grader the love they need?

_____

_____

_____

_____

_____

_____

_____

_____

_____

_____

_____

_____

_____

_____

_____

_____

_____

EVERY KID

NEEDS

*stories*

OVER TIME

—

TO GIVE THEM

A BIGGER

*perspective.*

# BOOKS YOUR ELEVENTH GRADER MIGHT BE READING

**UNCLE TOM'S CABIN**
by Harriet Beecher Stowe

**GIRL WITH A PEARL EARRING**
by Tracy Chevalier

**HEART OF DARKNESS**
by Joseph Conrad

**NARRATIVE OF THE LIFE OF FREDERICK DOUGLASS**
by Frederick Douglass

**INVISIBLE MAN**
by Ralph Ellison

**THE GREAT GATSBY**
by F. Scott Fitzgerald

**GRENDEL**
by John Gardner

**A RAISIN IN THE SUN**
by Lorrainne Hansberry

**THE SCARLET LETTER**
by Nathaniel Hawthorne

**A FAREWELL TO ARMS**
by Ernest Hemingway

**THE KITE RUNNER**
by Khaled Hosseini

**A PRAYER FOR OWEN MEANY**
by John Irving

**THE SCREWTAPE LETTERS**
by C.S. Lewis

**THE LIFE OF PI**
by Yann Martel

**THE CRUCIBLE**
by Arthur Miller

**THE LOVELY BONES**
by Alice Sebold

**THE ART OF RACING IN THE RAIN**
by Garth Stein

**THE LORD OF THE RINGS TRILOGY**
by J.R.R. Tolkien

**THE ADVENTURES OF HUCKLEBERRY FINN**
by Mark Twain

**THE COLOR PURPLE**
by Alice Walker

Share a story. Whether it's a book, play, TV series, or movie, what are some stories that engage your eleventh grader?

_____

_____

_____

_____

_____

_____

_____

_____

_____

_____

_____

_____

_____

_____

_____

_____

_____

_____

_____

_____

_____

_____

**What might happen to your relationship when you watch or read the same story together?**

_____

_____

_____

_____

_____

_____

_____

_____

_____

_____

_____

_____

_____

_____

_____

_____

_____

_____

_____

_____

Tell a story. As you watch your eleventh grader live out their story, how can you act like a narrator to help them interpret who they are and what's happening? *(Example: "You have a way of knowing exactly what someone needs to hear.")*

_____

_____

_____

_____

_____

_____

_____

_____

_____

_____

_____

_____

_____

_____

_____

_____

_____

_____

_____

**Live a story.** When an eleventh grader serves others, they broaden their perspective by learning about someone else's story. Is there somewhere your junior would enjoy serving on a regular basis?

# WORK YOUR ELEVENTH GRADER CAN DO

**DO HOMEWORK**

**MANAGE A PERSONAL CALENDAR**

**PREPARE A MEAL PLAN, GROCERY LIST, AND HELP COOK FAMILY MEALS**

**SORT, WASH, FOLD, AND PUT AWAY LAUNDRY**

**RUN FAMILY ERRANDS**
("Can you grab some milk at the store before you come home?")

**MAKE APPOINTMENTS**
(doctor, hair cut, dentist, etc.)

**CHANGE A FLAT TIRE**

**GET A PART-TIME JOB OR INTERNSHIP**

**MANAGE A BUDGET**

**OPEN A CHECKING ACCOUNT**

**RESEARCH POST-HIGH SCHOOL OPTIONS**

**REFINE A SKILL: ART, MUSICAL, TECHNICAL, MECHANICAL, OR ATHLETIC**

What are some ways your eleventh grader already shows responsibility at home, at school, and in-between?

_____

_____

_____

_____

_____

_____

_____

_____

_____

_____

_____

_____

_____

_____

_____

_____

_____

_____

_____

How can you collaborate with your eleventh grader to agree on which of their responsibilities matter most for your family and their future?

_____

_____

_____

_____

_____

_____

_____

_____

_____

_____

_____

_____

_____

_____

_____

_____

_____

_____

**Some days might be easier than others to motivate your eleventh grader. What are some strategies you could employ to keep your eleventh grader motivated?**

_____

_____

_____

_____

_____

_____

_____

_____

_____

_____

_____

_____

_____

_____

_____

_____

_____

_____

What are things you (and your eleventh grader) hope they will be able to do independently next year? How are you helping them develop those skills now?

_____

_____

_____

_____

_____

_____

_____

_____

_____

_____

_____

_____

_____

_____

_____

_____

_____

_____

# WAYS TO HAVE FUN
# WITH YOUR ELEVENTH GRADER

WATCH A MOVIE

ATTEND A SPORTING EVENT

GO TO A CONCERT

WORK OUT TOGETHER

PLAY MUSIC TOGETHER

BUILD SOMETHING

COOK SOMETHING

GO ON A RUN

GO ON A HIKE

GO SHOPPING

SHOOT SOME HOOPS

WORK ON CAR REPAIRS

GET A MANICURE

WATCH A TV SERIES

GO TO A PLAY

GO FISHING

GO BOWLING

PLAY LASER TAG

HAVE A RESTAURANT THAT'S "YOURS"

TRY A NEW RESTAURANT OR FOOD TRUCK

PLANT A GARDEN

PLAY A BOARD GAME

PLAY A VIDEO GAME

PLAY CARDS

PLAY A GAME ON A PHONE APP

LAUNCH MODEL ROCKETS

LEARN TO DANCE

GO TO THE LAKE

RIDE A ROLLER COASTER

GO OUT FOR COFFEE

GO OUT FOR ICE CREAM

GO SEE A COMEDIAN

Whatever you do together for fun, try to offer suggestions based on what they enjoy—even at the expense of what you might enjoy a little more.

**What are some activities your eleventh grader enjoys that you could do as a family** *(and maybe sometimes include their friends)?*

_____

_____

_____

_____

_____

_____

_____

_____

_____

_____

_____

_____

_____

_____

_____

_____

_____

_____

_____

What are some activities your eleventh grader enjoys that you could occasionally do together, one-on-one?

_____

_____

_____

_____

_____

_____

_____

_____

When are the best times of the day, or week, for you to set aside to just have fun with your eleventh grader?

_____

_____

_____

_____

_____

_____

_____

Some days are *extra* fun days. What are some ways you want to celebrate the special days coming up this year?

## NEXT BIRTHDAY

_____

_____

_____

_____

_____

_____

_____

_____

_____

_____

_____

_____

_____

_____

_____

_____

_____

## HOLIDAYS

Consider celebrating a few random holidays: the first/last day of school, a driver's license, SAT testing, prom.

ADULTS WHO MIGHT INFLUENCE YOUR ELEVENTH GRADER

**PARENTS**

**COMMUNITY LEADERS**

**CHURCH LEADERS**

**GRANDPARENTS**

**FRIENDS' PARENTS**

**COACHES**

**CLUB SPONSORS**

**HIGH SCHOOL TEACHERS**

**BOSS OR CO-WORKERS**
(at an afterschool job)

As great as you are *(and you're clearly an awesome parent)* you aren't the only adult influence your eleventh grader needs. List at least five adults who have the potential to positively influence your eleventh grader.

_____

_____

_____

_____

_____

_____

_____

_____

_____

_____

_____

_____

_____

_____

_____

_____

_____

_____

**What would be good information for these people to know if they want to help or support your eleventh grader this year?**

_____

_____

_____

_____

_____

_____

_____

_____

_____

_____

_____

_____

_____

_____

_____

_____

_____

_____

_____

_____

What are some upcoming events in your eleventh grader's life that you could invite one or more of these adults to attend?

_____

_____

_____

_____

_____

_____

_____

_____

_____

_____

_____

_____

_____

_____

_____

_____

_____

_____

_____

_____

What are a few ways you could show these adults appreciation for the significant role they play in your kid's life?

_____

_____

_____

_____

_____

_____

_____

_____

_____

_____

_____

_____

_____

_____

_____

_____

_____

_____

_____

EVERY KID

NEEDS

*words*

OVER TIME

—

TO GIVE

THEM

*direction.*

# WORDS YOUR ELEVENTH GRADER NEEDS TO HEAR

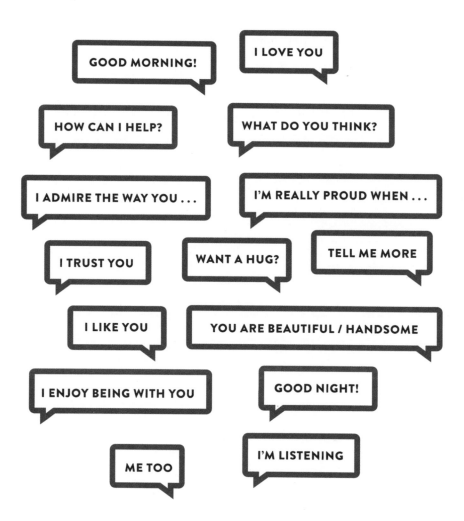

**What are some ways you can share personal and specific encouragement with your eleventh grader?**

Hint: You might start with the things that impress you about your eleventh grader from page 29.

_____

_____

_____

_____

_____

_____

_____

_____

_____

_____

_____

_____

_____

_____

_____

_____

_____

You might be impressed by the words that inspire your junior. How might you encourage your eleventh grader to share a quote, song lyric, Scripture, or thought that inspired them?

_____

_____

_____

_____

_____

_____

_____

_____

_____

_____

_____

_____

_____

_____

_____

_____

_____

_____

What are some quotes, lyrics, Scriptures, or inspirational thoughts you want to share with your eleventh grader? Make it a habit to regularly text or send encouraging thoughts their way.

_____

_____

_____

_____

_____

_____

_____

_____

_____

_____

_____

_____

_____

_____

_____

_____

_____

_____

_____

_____

# FOUR CONVERSATIONS

—

## TO HAVE IN THIS PHASE

WHEN YOU KNOW
WHERE YOU WANT
TO GO,

AND YOU KNOW
WHERE YOU ARE
NOW,

YOU CAN ALWAYS
DO SOMETHING

TO MOVE IN A
BETTER DIRECTION.

# OVER THE NEXT 104 WEEKS, IT MAY BE HARD TO FIND TIME FOR CONVERSATIONS. WHEN YOU *DO* GET A FEW MINUTES TO TALK, IT CAN BE HARD TO KNOW WHAT TO SAY FIRST.

You want to ask if they can pick up milk at the store.
They want to ask if they can stay over at a friend's house.

But, in the middle of everything that's urgent, don't forget to have a few important conversations along the way as well.

**WHAT YOU SAY ABOUT . . .**
Health
Sex
Technology
or Faith

**MAY IMPACT YOUR ELEVENTH GRADER'S FUTURE EVEN MORE THAN WHO PICKS UP THE GROCERIES.**

The next pages are about the conversations that matter most. On the left page is a destination—what you might want to be true in your kid's life 104 weeks from now. On the right page is a goal for conversations with your eleventh grader this year, and a few suggestions about what you might want to say.

# Healthy habits

---

LEARNING TO
STRENGTHEN
MY BODY THROUGH
EXERCISE, NUTRITION,
AND SELF-ADVOCACY

## THIS YEAR YOU WILL
# ENCOURAGE A HEALTHY LIFESTYLE
## SO THEY WILL SHARPEN THEIR PERSONAL AWARENESS AND BALANCE DIET AND EXERCISE.

Maintain a good relationship with your pediatrician, and schedule a physical at least once per year. You can also encourage your eleventh grader to develop healthy habits with a few simple words.

## SAY THINGS LIKE . . .

**"I BOUGHT MORE TRAIL MIX AND THERE'S SOME YOGURT IN THE FRIDGE."**
(Stock the kitchen with healthy options.)

**"CAN I MAKE YOU SOME EGGS BEFORE YOU HEAD OUT?"**
(Encourage breakfast.)

**"WHEN CAN WE HAVE DINNER TOGETHER THIS WEEK?"**
(Eat meals together—whenever possible.)

**IT MIGHT BE GOOD TO TAKE A STUDY BREAK AND GO ON A WALK.**
(Coach healthy stress-management.)

**"I'M NOT SURE FAST WEIGHT LOSS IS REALLY HEALTHY."**

**"IT MIGHT BE GOOD TO TAKE A STUDY BREAK AND GO ON A WALK."**
(Coach healthy stress-management.)

What are some activities you can do with your eleventh grader that require a little bit of exercise?

_____

_____

_____

_____

_____

_____

_____

_____

_____

_____

_____

_____

_____

_____

_____

_____

_____

_____

_____

_____

_____

_____

Junior year can be stressful, and mismanaged stress can lead to unhealthy habits. How do you handle stress in your own life? How does your junior manage stress?

_____

_____

_____

_____

_____

_____

_____

_____

_____

_____

_____

_____

_____

_____

_____

_____

_____

Do you have any specific concerns when it comes to your eleventh grader's physical or mental health? Who will help you monitor and improve their health this year?

**What are your own health goals for this year? How can you improve the habits in your own life?**

_____

_____

_____

_____

_____

_____

_____

_____

_____

_____

_____

_____

_____

_____

_____

_____

_____

_____

_____

_____

*Sexual integrity*

—

GUARDING MY

POTENTIAL FOR

INTIMACY THROUGH

APPROPRIATE

BOUNDARIES

AND MUTUAL

RESPECT

**THIS YEAR YOU WILL**

# COACH THEM TOWARD HEALTHY RELATIONSHIPS

**SO THEY WILL ESTABLISH PERSONAL BOUNDARIES AND PRACTICE MUTUAL RESPECT.**

Whether your eleventh grader dates casually (someone new every few weeks), isn't dating, or they've found the one true love of their life, romance is part of the upper-classman scene. Stay aware and curious not only about your own kid, but also about your kid's friends and peers. Talk about sex and dating.

**SAY THINGS LIKE . . .**

**THANK YOU FOR TELLING ME.**

**I'M SO GLAD YOU ASKED ME.**

**"THANK YOU FOR TALKING ABOUT THIS. CAN WE TALK ABOUT IT AGAIN ANOTHER TIME?"**
(Always finish the conversation with room to pick it back up again later.)

**"WHAT ARE YOUR FAVORITE THINGS ABOUT HIM/HER?"**
(If your eleventh grader is dating, ask questions to help them think objectively about the relationship.)

**"ARE YOU OKAY? DO YOU WANT TO TALK ABOUT IT?"**

**"DO YOU THINK HE IS GOOD FOR HER?"**
(Let your eleventh grader talk with you about their friends' relationships—you might learn a lot.)

**"IF YOU EVER FEEL PRESSURED TO DO SOMETHING YOU DON'T WANT TO DO, YOU COULD ALWAYS SAY . . . "**
(Help them script responses to difficult situations.)

83

What guardrails do you have in place to help protect your junior when it comes to dating and sexuality?

_____

_____

_____

_____

_____

_____

_____

_____

_____

_____

_____

_____

_____

_____

_____

_____

_____

_____

_____

_____

_____

**Who, besides you, is influencing your junior's values about dating and sexuality?**

_____

_____

_____

_____

_____

_____

_____

_____

_____

_____

_____

_____

_____

_____

_____

_____

_____

_____

_____

_____

_____

If your eleventh grader is dating, it's best to talk about how their relationships impact them right now. How would you say their relationships influence their immediate circumstances?

_____

_____

_____

_____

_____

_____

_____

_____

_____

_____

_____

_____

_____

_____

_____

_____

_____

_____

At least 27% of high schoolers are not dating. If your eleventh grader isn't interested in dating, what are a few ways you can help them develop and deepen healthy friendships?

_____

_____

_____

_____

_____

_____

_____

If your eleventh grader wants to date, but isn't yet, how can you affirm them now, and discuss their thoughts about the future?

_____

_____

_____

_____

_____

_____

_____

# Technological responsibility

—

LEVERAGING THE
POTENTIAL OF ONLINE
EXPERIENCES TO
ENHANCE MY OFFLINE
COMMUNITY
AND SUCCESS

**THIS YEAR YOU WILL**

# EXPAND THEIR POTENTIAL

**SO THEY WILL ESTABLISH PERSONAL BOUNDARIES AND LEVERAGE ONLINE OPPORTUNITIES.**

Technology is best used when it helps us connect. Or, stated another way: every digital device is a platform that can improve the way we respect ourselves and love others. That's what makes technology especially wonderful in this phase—your eleventh grader is ready to do something that matters, right now. So encourage them to use technology for good.

**SAY THINGS LIKE . . .**

**"WHAT DO YOU THINK ABOUT ONLINE CLASSES?"**

**"IT WOULD HELP ME TO SHARE OUR CALENDARS SO WE CAN COORDINATE MEALS."**

**"DID YOU KNOW WE COULD WRITE LETTERS TO OUR COMPASSION CHILD ONLINE?"**
(Find ways to use technology to connect to a global mission.)

**CAN YOU HELP ME SET UP A CARING BRIDGE FOR MRS. MARGARET?**
(Leverage technology to serve and care for friends, neighbors, and family.)

**"CAN I SEE WHAT YOU'VE BEEN CREATING LATELY?"**
(Show interest in everything from art to engineering to design to fan websites.)

What are some ways you've seen your eleventh grader use technology to do something good?

_____

_____

_____

_____

_____

_____

_____

_____

_____

_____

_____

_____

_____

_____

_____

_____

_____

_____

_____

_____

What are your concerns about your eleventh grader's engagement with digital devices? How are you guarding their engagement and helping them create self-regulated boundaries?

_____

_____

_____

_____

_____

_____

_____

_____

_____

_____

_____

_____

_____

_____

_____

_____

_____

_____

_____

When you aren't sure what to do about an issue related to parenting and technology, who can you go to for advice?

_____

_____

_____

_____

_____

_____

_____

_____

_____

_____

_____

_____

_____

_____

_____

_____

_____

_____

What are your own personal values and disciplines when it comes to leveraging technology? Are there ways you want to improve your own savvy, skill, or responsibility in this area?

_____

_____

_____

_____

_____

_____

_____

_____

_____

_____

_____

_____

_____

_____

_____

_____

_____

_____

# Authentic faith

—

TRUSTING JESUS
IN A WAY THAT
TRANSFORMS HOW
I LOVE GOD,
MYSELF,
AND THE REST
OF THE WORLD

**THIS YEAR YOU WILL**

# FUEL PASSION

**SO THEY WILL KEEP PURSUING AUTHENTIC FAITH
AND DISCOVER A PERSONAL MISSION.**

In this phase, your eleventh grader is asking, "How can I matter?"
A faith community can help them find significance by giving them
opportunities to give, serve, and love others. Your eleventh grader will
never get over seeing how God can work through them in meaningful
ways. Encourage their personal faith journey by having conversations
at home.

**SAY THINGS LIKE . . .**

> **THERE'S NOTHING YOU WILL
> EVER DO THAT COULD MAKE
> GOD STOP LOVING YOU.**

**"HOW CAN I PRAY FOR YOU TODAY /
THIS WEEK?"**

**"WHEN DO YOU FEEL CLOSE TO GOD?"**

**"LATELY I'M FINDING I CONNECT BEST
WITH GOD WHEN I'M . . . "**

**"I DON'T KNOW."**

**"WHEN YOU TOLD ME ABOUT . . .
IT MADE ME THINK OF A VERSE
IN PROVERBS."**
(Share Bible verses that relate to
their present circumstances.)

**"WHAT DO YOU THINK ABOUT
CHURCH / YOUTH GROUP?"**

**"THAT'S A GOOD QUESTION. I'M NOT
SURE I WILL EVER KNOW THE FULL
ANSWER, BUT I BELIEVE . . . "**
(Let them know it's okay to ask
hard questions.)

**"ARE THERE WAYS YOU WOULD
WANT TO SERVE IN OUR CHURCH
OR COMMUNITY?"**

What are some ways you can help deepen your eleventh grader's connection with friends and adult leaders who follow Jesus?

If your eleventh grader isn't connecting well at church, what other adult believer might they connect with? Are there other adult mentors who could influence your eleventh grader?

_____

_____

_____

_____

_____

_____

_____

_____

_____

_____

_____

_____

_____

_____

_____

_____

_____

_____

_____

What are some retreats, youth camps, or mission trip opportunities provided by your church or a local youth ministry? Which ones seem most appealing to your eleventh grader?

_____

_____

_____

_____

_____

_____

_____

_____

_____

_____

_____

_____

_____

_____

_____

_____

_____

_____

**What service opportunities are available for high schoolers at your church? What would it take for you to help your eleventh grader participate?**

_____

_____

_____

_____

_____

_____

_____

_____

_____

_____

_____

_____

_____

_____

_____

_____

_____

_____

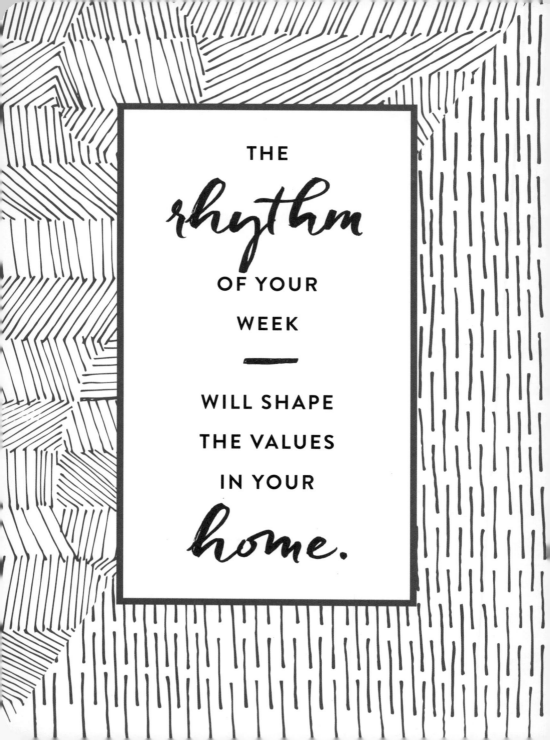

THE

*rhythm*

OF YOUR

WEEK

—

WILL SHAPE

THE VALUES

IN YOUR

*home.*

# NOW THAT YOU HAVE FILLED THIS BOOK WITH IDEAS, IT MAY SEEM AS IF YOU WILL NEVER HAVE TIME TO GET IT ALL DONE.

Actually, you still have *104 weeks.*

And every week has potential.

The secret to making the most of this phase is to find time to spend together—even if it's only an hour each week. You may have less quality time together, but look for opportunities during three consistent times (and one that's less predictable).

Instill purpose by starting the day with encouraging words.

Connect regularly by scheduling time to eat together (even if it's once a week).

Interpret life when they occasionally open up at the end of the day (stay consistently available—just in case).

Strengthen your relationship by adjusting your plans to show up whenever they need you.

101

**How are you adjusting to a new rhythm in this phase?**

**What are some of your favorite traditions with your eleventh grader?**

_____

_____

_____

_____

_____

_____

_____

_____

_____

_____

_____

_____

_____

_____

_____

_____

_____

_____

**Write down any other thoughts or questions about parenting your eleventh grader.**

YOU HAVE

APPROXIMATELY

104 WEEKS.

# EVERY KID $\longrightarrow$ MADE IN THE IMAGE OF GOD

---

**Incite**
*wonder* $\longrightarrow$ SO THEY WILL . . .
KNOW GOD'S LOVE
& MEET GOD'S FAMILY

---

**BEGINNING**
(Baby dedication)

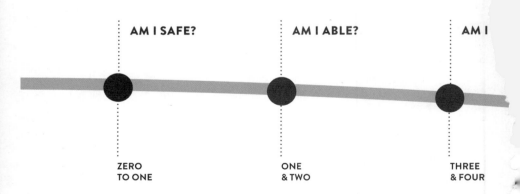

AM I SAFE?            AM I ABLE?            AM I

ZERO            ONE            THREE
TO ONE          & TWO          & FOUR

EMBRACE *their physical needs*

E  TO # LOVE GOD

---

## Provoke
*discovery*

$\longrightarrow$

SO THEY WILL . . .
**TRUST GOD'S CHARACTER
& EXPERIENCE GOD'S FAMILY**

---

 **WISDOM**
(First day of school)

 **FAITH**
(Trust Jesus)

?

**DO I HAVE YOUR
ATTENTION?**

**DO I HAVE WHAT
IT TAKES?**

**DO I HAVE
FRIENDS?**

K &
FIRST

SECOND
& THIRD

FOURTH
& FIFTH

ENGAGE **their interests**

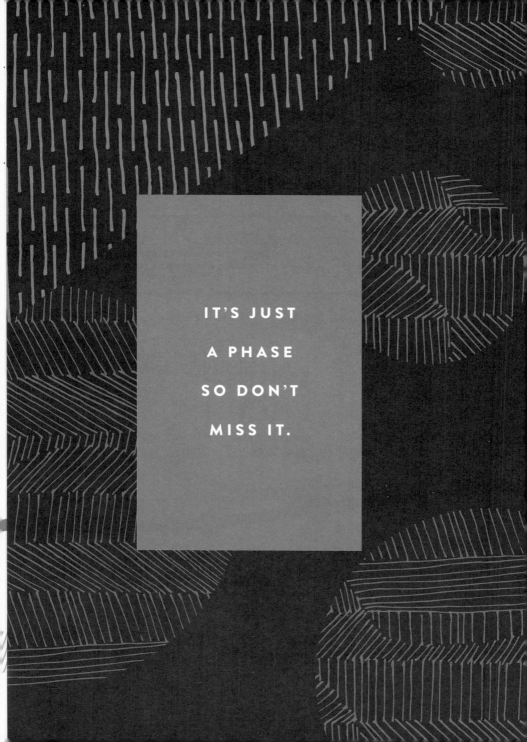

IT'S JUST
A PHASE
SO DON'T
MISS IT.

## ABOUT THE AUTHORS

**KRISTEN IVY** @kristen_ivy

Kristen Ivy is executive director of the Phase Project. She and her husband, Matt, are in the preschool and elementary phases with three kids: Sawyer, Hensley, and Raleigh.

Kristen earned her Bachelors of Education from Baylor University in 2004 and received a Master of Divinity from Mercer University in 2009. She worked in the public school system as a high school biology and English teacher, where she learned firsthand the importance of influencing the next generation.

Kristen is also the President at Orange and has played an integral role in the development of the elementary, middle school, and high school curriculum and has shared her experiences at speaking events across the country. She is the co-author of *Playing for Keeps*, *Creating a Lead Small Culture*, *It's Just a Phase*, and *Don't Miss It*.

**REGGIE JOINER** @reggiejoiner

Reggie Joiner is founder and CEO of the reThink Group and co-founder of the Phase Project. He and his wife, Debbie, have reared four kids into adulthood. They now also have two grandchildren.

The reThink Group (also known as Orange) is a non-profit organization whose purpose is to influence those who influence the next generation. Orange provides resources and training for churches and organizations that create environments for parents, kids, and teenagers.

Before starting the reThink Group in 2006, Reggie was one of the founders of North Point Community Church. During his 11 years with Andy Stanley, Reggie was the executive director of family ministry, where he developed a new concept for relevant ministry to children, teenagers, and married adults. Reggie has authored and co-authored more than 10 books including: *Think Orange, Seven Practices of Effective Ministry, Parenting Beyond Your Capacity, Playing for Keeps, Lead Small, Creating a Lead Small Culture,* and his latest, *A New Kind of Leader* and *Don't Miss It.*

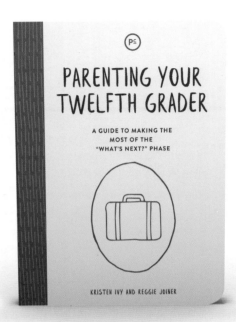

# MAKE THE MOST OF EVERY PHASE IN YOUR CHILD'S LIFE

**The guide in your hand is one of an eighteen-part series.**

So, unless you've figured out a way to freeze time and keep your eleventh grader from turning into a twelfth grader, you might want to check out the next guide in this set.

Designed in partnership with Parent Cue, each guide will help you rediscover . . .

what's changing about your kid,
the 6 things your kid needs most,
and 4 conversations to have each year.

# WANT TO GIFT A FRIEND WITH ALL 18 GUIDES
## OR HAVE ALL THE GUIDES ON HAND FOR YOURSELF?

# ORDER THE ENTIRE SERIES
# OF PHASE GUIDES TODAY.

ORDER NOW AT:   WWW.PHASEGUIDES.COM